Women Pioneers in Texas Medicine

NUMBER SEVENTY:

*The Centennial Series of the Association of Former Students,
Texas A&M University*

WOMEN PIONEERS
in Texas Medicine

Elizabeth Silverthorne & Geneva Fulgham

Texas A&M University Press
College Station

frontispiece: Dr. Claudia Potter with her fellow doctors at Scott and White Hospital.
Courtesy Scott and White Hospital Archives, Temple, Texas

Library of Congress Cataloging-in-Publication Date

Silverthorne, Elizabeth.
    Women pioneers in Texas medicine / Elizabeth
Silverthorne and Geneva Fulgham.
        p.   cm. — (The Centennial series of the Association of
Former Students, Texas A&M University ; no. 70)
    Includes bibliographical references and index.
    ISBN 0-89096-789-X
    1. Women in medicine—Texas—History.   I. Fulgham,
Geneva. II. Title.   III. Series.
R692.S586   1997   97-18885
610'.9764—dc21   CIP

To a pioneer
in Texas medicine,
our grandmother
Emily Smith Fletcher

Every woman is born a doctor.
Men have to study to become one.
—DR. ELLA FLAGG YOUNG

I will be home soon, for I know you have
lost your mind if you have employed a woman doctor.
—DR. RALEIGH WHITE TO HIS PARTNER,
DR. A. C. SCOTT, JUNE, 1906

CONTENTS

ILLUSTRATIONS

PREFACE

PIONEER:

(noun) *One who goes before, as into the wilderness,*
preparing the way for others to follow.
(verb) *To discover or explore in advance of others; to open*
up a way for others to follow; to clear the way.
(adjective) *First of its kind.*

—Webster

Our interest in women pioneers in Texas medicine began early in our lives in the heart of our own family. England in the 1890s was suffering from a depression brought on by the American Civil War and the subsequent loss of raw cotton for the English textile industry. Emily Smith Fletcher, our grandmother, and her siblings, all of whom beat the odds and lived to adulthood, found that the Smith family resources were not sufficient to provide for all twelve of them. Consequently, Emily; her husband, Edwin Fletcher; their three-year-old daughter, Ivy; and five more Smiths emigrated to America during the late 1890s.

The Fletchers joined a little group of English settlers who found their way into Brazoria County and eventually to Angleton, formerly known as English Crossing. Since Edwin's ability as a violinist (he had played in the Crystal Palace in London) was not useful for earning a living on the Texas frontier, he and Emily set out to apply other skills to support themselves. Edwin set up shop as a barber for awhile, farmed, and directed the two or three church choirs in town. Emily, drawing on her years of experience nursing her mother during a long illness and caring for younger siblings, began a career of practical nursing and midwifing. She usually attended cases along with Dr. S. B. Maxey, who depended on her services in many nursing situations. He would leave her with pregnant women or with seriously ill patients for several days at a time. Even after Emily outlived her ability to go out nursing, she continued to receive cards and letters at Christmas and on her birthday from grateful former patients—many of whom she had brought into the world.

We have tried in this book to illuminate by examples the roles a great many valiant and determined women have played throughout the history of medicine, particularly in Texas. Each time we explained to medical professionals (both male and female) that our project was to celebrate the contribution of women to Texas medicine, the response was strongly enthusiastic—usually with some such addendum as, "It's about time!"

Women entering medical practice in the early days overcame many of the same difficulties encountered by men, such as lack of funds and personal health problems. In addition, however, the women encountered much opposition simply because of gender bias. Our medical women, in most cases, do not seem to have paid much attention to such prejudice, shrugging it off as to be expected. Seeking the source of their spiritual strength and determination, we found again and again not a vague, general desire for world improvement but instead a focused, imperative will to heal. From Jewel Babb in her tumbledown tie house on the Mexican border to Janet Butel taking technological "baby steps" toward new discoveries in virology, these women were and are deeply imbued with a passion for healing.

In this book, we have used *pioneer* in all three of Mr. Webster's meanings. Many of our exemplary medical women have been "first" in some way. Being first in the chronological sense is important; so is being first to break new ground in science, in social acceptance, and in the advancement of human well-being. In some cases, we decided that overcoming obstacles of gender and race or personal handicaps such as poverty, physical disabilities, or ill health amounted to pioneering in the sense of preparing the way for others to follow.

Some of our featured women in medicine are native Texans, but a sizable number were brought here as children from other states or other countries. Some came as young adults or young married people just at the beginning of their careers. Others, like Dr. Katharine Hsu of China, were invited to the Lone Star State to fill a particular need. In two cases, each of the women was sixty before she began her Texas career. Dr. Lena Edwards, the "Missionary to the Migrants" in the Texas panhandle, came of her own volition after retirement from a northern medical career because she had always dreamed of giving her services to the needy in such a place.

Dr. Hilde Bruch fled Germany in time to escape the Holocaust. After a brief stay in England, she established herself as an independent-minded psychoanalyst in the New York area. Although she was sixty when she accepted an invitation to practice in Texas, her influence on the ideas and practices of Dr. Mabel Wilkin had predated her arrival by twelve years. And Dr. Bruch herself put in a full twenty years of teaching and practicing in our state. Four of her five books were published during her Texas years, and her penetrating challenge to psychiatric assumptions still reverberates in the hearts and procedures of her many Texas students. We are convinced that the contributions made by these women who arrived in Texas late in their lives richly merit inclusion in our discussion of women pioneers in Texas medicine.

Some of our major difficulties have been the necessity of paring reports of fascinating lives and having to omit entirely many deserving medical pioneers. There is no way to balance exactly the content of such a book as this. Everyone will know of other wonderful women who are not cited here. It is our hope that readers will take this to be a sampling, an effort to illustrate the kinds of women who contributed so much—medically and socially—to the elevation of their sisters in the modern consciousness.

Our method of organization is partially chronological because that is the way women's increasing role in medicine evolved. For the most part, it seemed natural to group our individual profiles according to the areas of need in which these women served. Much latitude was needed in this plan since the earlier physicians, for a variety of reasons, often began with one kind of practice in mind and then changed to another.

Looking back, we recognize our grandmother as one of a small, courageous band of women pioneers who learned to cope with medical problems through necessity and practical experience. Their care and nurturing made possible the survival and success of the early adventurers and settlers whose families they tended. It is our belief that their stouthearted determination and well-applied energy merit recognition and appreciation, as do the efforts of the more formally trained women who entered the practice of medicine and won approval and acceptance in more civilized circumstances. This book is our salute to all of them.

Our book exists because of the kind assistance and encouragement of many generous people, some of them relatives, some of them close friends, and some brand-new acquaintances. Frequently, in the case of an earlier medical woman practitioner, although the contribution was large, there were scanty records to help us assess her achievements. Testimony of colleagues, friends, relatives, and patients is a valuable ingredient in our material. We are grateful to those among our later women medical pioneers who took precious time to record and to discuss with us the speculations, discoveries, and conclusions they encountered during their working years. We hope the bibliography provided will prove useful to readers who want to follow one or another individual's trail further.

For interviews, including responses by telephone and mail, we are indebted to Miss Frances Marion Allen, Dr. Hal Anderson, Dr. Virginia Blocker, Dr. G. V. Brindley, Jr., Dr. E. O. Bradfield, Dr. Janet S. Butel, Dr. Dorothy Annette Cato, Dr. Louis Daily, Mrs. Elizabeth Hanson Duerr, Mrs. Marian Fleming, Ms. Suzanne Gallo, Dr. and Mrs. Charles H. Gillespie, Mr. Elmer Grape, Dr. Katharine H. K. Hsu, Dr. Daniel Jenkins, Dr. Francine Jensen, Mrs. Lucy Cox Latham, Mrs. Dean Little, Dr. B. J. McConnell, Dr. Joseph Melnick, Dr. Marion Primomo, Miss Mildred Robertson, Dr. J. G. Rodarte, Mrs. Brooksie Nell Wolf, and Dr. Huda Y. Zoghbi.

Gracious gifts of time and materials and valuable leads came from Dr. Chester R. Burns, Institute for the Medical Humanities at the University of Texas Medical Branch at Galveston; Dr. Inci A. Bowman, Curator Truman G. Blocker, Jr., History of Medicine Collection, UTMB; Ms. Diane Coonrod, UTMB Alumni Association; Mrs. Alice Bonnette, UTMB Moody Medical Library; Ms. Elizabeth Borst White, Archivist, Houston Academy of Medicine-Texas Medical Center Library; Ms. Margaret A. Irin, Special Collections Librarian, HAM-TMC Library; Ms. Michelle Mears, Archivist, Scott and White, Temple; Mr. Casey Edward Greene, Assistant Archivist, Rosenberg Library, Galveston; Ms. Terri Mote, Reference Librarian, City of Bellaire Library; Ms. Claire R. Kuehn, Archivist/Librarian, Panhandle-Plains Historical Museum, Canyon, Texas; Ms. Linda Wood, Librarian, Brazoria County Central Library, Angleton, Texas; Ms. Dawn Letson, Head of Special Collections, Texas Woman's University, Denton; Ms. Georgia Donatis, Library Assistant, Texas Woman's University; Mr. Michael Toon, Librarian, The Texas Collection, Baylor University,

Waco; Ms. Annie Brown, Deaf Smith County Library, Hereford, Texas; Ms. Terri Hugo, Librarian, Waco-McLennan County Library; Ms. C. Jane Dees, Research Librarian, Museum of Science and History, Fort Worth; Ms. Debbie Adams, Publicity Assistant, Tarrant County Medical Society, Fort Worth; Ms. Shelagh Yospur, Publications Director, Baylor College of Medicine; Col. James A. Crehan USAF (ret.), Assistant to the President, Strake Jesuit College Preparatory School; Ms. Lesley Brunet, Archivist, Hermann Hospital; Mr. Mike Hallaway, AV Department, Memorial Hospital Southwest; and from the staff of the psychiatric library in Houston's Medical Center.

We appreciate deeply the extra efforts made to assist us by Ms. Patricia Kay Benoit, Mr. Paul E. Berndt III, Dr. David Braden, Dr. Robert W. Dibrell, Mayor Robert Appel, Jr., of Brenham, Mr. Wallace Giddings, Mr. Ernest Beerstecher, Dr. Susan Murphey, Dr. P. Woodbury Smith, Dr. J. Rudy Kasel, Dr. Maurice Meynier, Mr. Kevin Ladd, Dr. Mabel A. Wandelt, Ms. Barbara Dent, Mr. Tom Shelton, Mrs. H. H. Sharpe, Dr. Robert Merrill, and Mrs. Martha Harper.

INTRODUCTION

The progress of women in medicine has not been orderly. Not like a rising tide but more like the tides that ebb and flow, they have survived in the field through waves of acceptance and through long periods of subsidence. From time immemorial there were goddesses of healing and their earthly representatives who were sought out for medical advice and honored for their skills as obstetricians and bone setters and for their knowledge of medicinal herbs.

EARLIEST TIMES: WIDE ACCEPTANCE

In the Stone and Bronze Ages there were women surgeons in Sumeria, Egypt, and Greece. And records show that Chinese and Siamese women were not only midwives and herbalists but also surgeons before 1000 B.C.[1]

In Egypt, where Isis was worshiped as the great goddess of healing, the queens of Egypt from Mentuhetep (c. 2300 B.C.) through Cleopatra (69–30 B.C.) were students of medicine. The medicine chest of Queen Mentuhetep along with her jars for tinctures and ointments, mixing dish, and dried herbs are in the Berlin Museum. Heliopolis (city of the sun), on the Nile delta about six miles below Cairo, was famous for its schools, including the women's medical school at the Temple of Sais. Apparently women were the professors, as an inscription found at the location reads: "I have come from the school of medicine at Heliopolis, and have studied at the woman's school at Sais where the divine mothers have taught me how to cure diseases."[2] Moses and his wife, Zipporah, were said to have trained at Heliopolis, and a biblical reference indicates that she was accustomed to performing circumcisions: "She took a sharp stone and cut off the foreskin of her son" (Exodus 4:25).

In Greece the names of two mythical women healers have survived in medical terminology. The ancient Hippocratic oath begins, "I swear by Apollo physician and Asclepius and Hygieia and Panaceia, and all the gods and goddesses . . ." Asclepius, the god of medicine, may have had his origins in a real man by that name who was supposed to have performed miraculous cures. The daughters of the god Asclepius, Hygieia and Panaceia, were worshiped as healers in their own right: Hygieia, whose name survives in "hygiene," was the Greek goddess of health; and Panaceia, whose name endures in "panacea," personified the healing power of herbs.

Homer has given us the legend that Helen of Troy studied medicine and used the famous drug nepenthe to soothe pain and anger by bringing about forgetfulness. He also praises Agamede, daughter of King Augeas (in Greek mythology, the owner of the famous stables), for her use of herbs in healing:

> *Agamede, with the golden hair,*
> *A leech was she,*
> *And well she knew*
> *All herbs on ground that grew.*
> *(Iliad XI, 739–45)*

THE ROMANS: SURVIVING CHRISTIANITY

In the waning days of the Roman Empire, women practitioners of medicine were on an equal footing with men, and the legal description was *medicus, sive masculus, sive foemina*. But as Christianity rose, the status of women fell, and the early church considered women inferior and not worth educating. Nevertheless the names of a few determined women who found ways to advance the practice of medicine have come down to us. For example, Saint Fabiola (d.c. 399), a Roman noblewoman who was converted to Christianity, is credited with founding (in Rome) the first public hospital in western Europe.[3]

THE MIDDLE AGES

A millennium after the birth of Christ, medical women began to appear more often in historical records. One of the most famous women practitioners of the Middle Ages was Trotula (eleventh century). Several historians of the time called her a "wise woman" and noted that she was given the title *magistra medicinae* at the medical school at Salerno where she was on the faculty. Trotula wrote works on obstetrics and gynecology that were in use for centuries after her death. And she was such an excellent diagnostician that men as well as women consulted her. With her husband and son John, who were also on the faculty of the medical school, Trotula compiled a medical encyclopedia, *Practica brevis.*[4]

As religious retreats proliferated in Europe, monks and abbesses acquired and passed along medical skills. The Abbess Heloise (1101–64), who was trained by her lover, Abelard, was the most learned medical woman in France during her time. About the same time, in Germany, another abbess, Hildegard (1098–1179), was writing medical and psychological treatises on a number of subjects including the use of herbs, plants, and minerals in treating diseases.

QUACKERY AND LEGAL CONTROLS

In general, however, the miasma of ignorance and superstition that shrouded life in the Middle Ages extended to medicine. Magic and science were so intertwined that all kinds of quackery prevailed. Women who used herbal medicines effectively were called "old wives," and some, who had a natural talent for healing and used natural substances, were dubbed "wise women." But those who depended on charms and spells and invoked supernatural beings to aid their healing were considered to be witches.

In England, the increase in the number of both men and women declaring themselves healers without any kind of training finally resulted in laws to regulate the profession. A petition was sent to Parliament by a group of English physicians requesting that men be required to have "a degree in physic from a university" before they could practice medicine and stipulating that "no woman be permitted to practice under any circumstance." Royal midwives could win fame and substantial rewards for successfully attending their illustrious patients, but midwives attending the lower classes sometimes resorted to barbaric methods. Accordingly, laws were finally passed in England in the seventeenth century prohibiting midwives from using pothooks, pack needles, thatcher's hooks, and knives as instruments in difficult births.[5]

MOTHER HUTTON AND THE DISCOVERY OF DIGITALIS

In the eighteenth century, a Mrs. Hutton, who was a botanist, pharmacist, and general practitioner of medicine in Shropshire, England, made a valuable contribution to medicine for which she is seldom given credit. Through experimentation she had discovered that foxglove (digitalis) was useful in treating "heart disease, kidney troubles and dropsy."

News of her ability to cure seemingly hopeless cases spread, and many well-known patients came to Mother Hutton from all over England to be treated with her secret remedy. In 1785, Dr. William Withering, a resident of Shropshire, persuaded her to sell him her prescription. Recognizing foxglove as the important ingredient in her mixture of herbs, he began to study its use in treating the edema of congestive heart failure. In 1785 he published a paper that became a classic in medical literature: *An Account of the Foxglove and Some of Its Medical Uses.* The discovery of digitalis has ever since been associated with his name instead of hers.[6]

COLONIAL MEDICINE IN AMERICA: UNEQUAL OPPORTUNITIES

From the earliest days of colonization in New England, women as well as men practiced medicine without licenses. Although there were no medical schools, young men became doctors by apprenticing themselves to practicing physicians. Few such opportunities existed for women, who had to learn medical skills through practical experience and self-teaching.

When medical schools were established in the United States, they followed the European practice of barring women. Among the women who practiced medicine without a diploma was Harriot Hunt. Through her skill as a physician she had earned an excellent reputation and was addressed as "doctor" by her numerous patients in Boston. But she wanted to earn a degree. Her application to Harvard Medical School was sponsored by Oliver Wendell Holmes, poet and physician, who was dean of the school. The faculty reluctantly concluded that there was nothing in the statutes that allowed them to deny a woman the right to attend lectures, but they would not go so far as to say that she might earn a degree. Learning of the impending female invasion, the male students passed angry resolutions objecting to "having the company of any female forced upon us, who is disposed to unsex herself, and to sacrifice her modesty by appearing with men in the lecture room."[7] In the face of such hostility, Harriot Hunt withdrew her application.

Women Doctors and Formal Education

ELIZABETH BLACKWELL (1821–1910)

The first female to gain an M.D. degree from a medical school in the United States, Elizabeth Blackwell was a trailblazer who opened the way for other women pioneers in medicine by founding several institutions for their education. The Blackwell family emigrated from England to New York in 1832, and after the death of her father in 1838, Elizabeth began reading medical books and studying privately with the intention of becoming a physician in order to help support her family. Her applications to medical schools were consistently rejected until Geneva (N.Y.) Medical School (forerunner of Hobart College) finally accepted her. In 1849 she became the first woman to earn a degree from an American medical school. Graduating at the head of her class, she accepted the degree and the responsibility she felt as she promised, "By the help of the Most High it shall be the effort of my life to shed honour on my diploma."[8]

After graduate study in London she returned to the United States to practice medicine. In the meantime her sister, Emily Blackwell, graduated from Cleveland Medical College, and together with Dr. Marie Zakrzewska they opened the New York Infirmary for Women and Children in May, 1857. In addition to caring for the sick, the women doctors undertook the training of nurses and bedside instruction for female medical students. This clinical instruction was essential for the young doctors-to-be because most of their formal instruction was theoretical. Also, in the nineteenth century it was much easier for women to gain admittance to sectarian schools of the eclectic or homeopathic persuasion than it was to enter orthodox medical schools. And the training in some of the former schools was justifiably considered to be inferior.

Consequently, in 1868, when the Blackwell sisters finally realized their dream of opening a medical college for women, they set high standards for the school and attracted excellent instructors and outstanding students. Although the Woman's Medical College of the New York Infirmary was only intended to fill the need for adequate and equal education for women students until the day when medical schools would be truly coeducational, the school continued in operation for over thirty years and graduated 364 women doctors. When Elizabeth Blackwell returned to England to help establish the London School of Medicine for Women, Emily Blackwell remained in New York as the guiding genius of both the infirmary and the medical school. Speaking of Emily in an article in the *Journal of the American Medical Women's Association* (3:201, 1948), Dr. Frederick Waite remarked, "Dr. Elizabeth Blackwell is more widely known because of priority in graduation, but the younger sister was better educated, did most of the administrative work in the New York institutions, and was the first woman physician to engage extensively in major surgery."

LYDIA FOLGER FOWLER

About the same time Harriot Hunt was trying to get into Harvard Medical School, Lydia Folger Fowler (1822–79) was attempting to persuade New York medical schools to admit her. The Folger family of Nantucket included several illustrious members. One of her ancestors was Benjamin Franklin, to whom Lydia bore a striking physical resemblance. Another was her cousin Lucretia Mott, noted Quaker preacher and woman suffrage leader, who strongly supported the idea that women should be admitted to medical schools. Lydia Folger married Lorenzo Niles Fowler, an ardent phrenologist, and became interested in phrenology and also in anatomy, physiology, and hygiene. She lectured successfully to large groups of women on these subjects and decided to become a physician. Consequently, when Central Medical College of New York opened with a coeducational policy, Lydia Folger was waiting at the door to enter the first class. In 1850, she became the first woman born in the United States to receive a doctor of medicine degree from a medical school in the United States.

The sectarian college promoted eclecticism, which at its best involved selecting features of competing medical systems and stressed the use of plant remedies. Although its practices were not generally accepted by regular doctors, it was popular with many patients who preferred its kinder and gentler treatments to the harsh blood-letting, purging, and other heroic methods practiced by most physicians in the nineteenth century.

Dr. Fowler achieved other firsts when she joined the faculty of Rochester Eclectic Medical College and became the first woman to hold a professorship in a legally authorized American medical school. She also addressed the New York State Eclectic Medical Society, the first time any woman had appeared before an organized society of medical men. She practiced in New York City for eleven years and was highly regarded as a doctor, lecturer, and medical-social writer.[9]

FIRST WOMEN'S MEDICAL SCHOOL

The Female Medical College of Pennsylvania, the first chartered medical school for women in the world, opened in Philadelphia in October of 1850. Similar institutions in Boston, New York, Chicago, Cleveland, and other cities came and went over the next century, but the Philadelphia school persevered. With only a slight name change—to Woman's Medical School of Pennsylvania—the institution celebrated its centennial in 1950. By 1995 the school had become the Medical College of Pennsylvania, a coeducational institution with 328 female medical students out of a total enrollment of 617.

The going had not been easy. At the first commencement ceremony held on December 30, 1851, Lucretia Mott, Dr. Lydia Fowler's cousin, sat on the platform and watched as the eight candidates received their medical diplomas. She probably nodded in agreement when Dr. Joseph Longshore told the graduates: "We have all been engaged in a new but momentous enterprise. We have met alike the frowns and prejudices of the community and labored hand in hand to sustain our institution against powerful opposing influences."[10] Dr. Longshore was one of a group of liberal Quaker physicians and businessmen who founded the college for Quaker women who wanted to study medicine but could not gain admittance to existing medical schools.

The opposition was far from ended. In 1858 the board of censors of the Philadelphia County Medical Society passed a resolution recommending that "members of the regular profession" refrain from consulting or holding "professional intercourse" with the professors or graduates of female medical colleges. Compensation for professors depended on donations from friends of the college. Medical journals would not publish the school's advertisements. Hospitals were extremely reluctant to admit the students for clinical studies.

An unlikely warrior led the fight for equality. Quaker Ann Preston, one of the first graduates of the school, was appointed dean in 1866. With relentless persistence she proved that faith with works can move mountains of prejudice and obstruction. When passive resistance failed, she used her pen and her quiet, firm voice of reason to fight injustice, telling her sister physicians, "Women must subdue opposition by showing the world that it is unjust."[11]

THE WOMAN QUESTION

Subtle or overt, prejudice against women doctors was widespread. When the Minnesota State Medical Society refused to grant Dr. Will Mayo's request to admit a female colleague at the Mayo Clinic to membership, many men *and* women agreed with a member of the society who stated: "Women who have stepped aside from the usual course of obtaining a living adopted by their sex are strong-minded women with whom it is desirable to have nothing to do."[12]

In the late nineteenth century, articles about "the woman question" appeared frequently in both scholarly and popular periodicals; these often contained passionate discussions about the nature of women and their place in society. Suffrage and the danger to the family if women became emancipated and were allowed to enter "men's" fields were hotly debated issues in taverns, over tea tables, and from pulpits. Inevitably, some of the best fiction writers of the day explored the subject of women in the medical profession, and three of the most popular writers arrived at different solutions for the dilemma of their protagonists.

In William Dean Howell's *Doctor Breen's Practice,* Dr. Breen opts to marry and give up her career. In Elizabeth Stuart Phelp's *Doctor Zay,* Dr. Zay marries on the condition that she can continue her career. But in Sarah Orne Jewett's *A Country Doctor,* Dr. Nan Prince refuses to marry the man she loves in order to devote herself to her career. If polls had been taken at that time, the majority of readers would probably have considered Dr. Prince's choice a willful abandonment of her chance to be a happy wife and mother and would have maintained that Dr. Breen's choice was the proper one for a young lady. Undoubtedly Dr. Zay's option would have been ranked as the most unrealistic of the three.

In real life, Harriot Hunt said that she considered herself married to medicine and celebrated her silver anniversary in 1860 after twenty-five years of practice. Elizabeth Blackwell, in her autobiography, admitted that medicine kept her "permanently distracted" from the temptation to marry. Some women, like the fictional Dr. Breen, gave up medicine entirely when they married. Others, however, like Mary Putnam Jacobi, a contemporary of Elizabeth Blackwell, managed to combine career and marriage successfully. A graduate of Woman's Medical College in Philadelphia and the École de Médicine in Paris, Mary Putnam was better educated than most male physicians of her time. In 1873 she married Dr. Abraham Jacobi, a distinguished physician who has been called the father of modern pediatrics. Although the relationship of these two brilliant scientists was sometimes stormy, it was a relationship of equals in which each respected the abilities of the other—and it was an enduring one.[13]

WOMEN'S MEDICAL COLLEGES: RISE AND DECLINE

In response to the exclusionary policies of established medical schools, a number of sectarian and orthodox women's medical colleges were founded by female pioneers between 1850 and 1900. Five of the orthodox colleges achieved outstanding success in training competent women doctors despite such overwhelming difficulties as financial problems, persistent prejudice, and outright hostility. In addition to the Woman's Medical School of Pennsylvania (1850 to present) and the Woman's Medical College of the New York Infirmary (1868–99) discussed above, the other most successful schools were New England Female Medical College (1856–73) in Boston; Woman's Hospital Medical College of Chicago (1870) which merged with Northwestern University in 1892 and continued until 1902; and Woman's Medical College of Baltimore (1882–1909).

Although there were obvious advantages in separate women's medical schools such as a nurturing atmosphere and women professors as role models, most women, including many founders of the schools, continued to believe that coeducation was preferable. Consequently, the fight to gain admittance to male institutions continued. A turning point came in 1893 when Johns Hopkins Medical School opened, due to aggressive fundraising by a committee of determined women led by Mary Elizabeth Garrett, daughter of the president of the Baltimore and Ohio Railroad. Before they turned the money over, the committee stipulated that women were to be admitted to the medical school on equal terms with men.

Gradually other medical schools followed suit, and women's medical institutions began to close until only the Woman's Medical School of Pennsylvania remained. In 1971, when six men entered the freshman class and the school became the Medical College of Pennsylvania, the last woman's medical institution ceased to exist.

TEXAS: OPPOSITION DIES HARD

In Texas, women were never officially denied admission to the Medical Branch of the University of Texas because of their sex. There were many, however, including Dr. Leslie Waggener, the president of the university, who did not approve of this policy. In his last public address, delivered in Austin in May, 1896, before the Texas Woman's Press Association, Dr. Waggener said: "I understand that many young women are looking forward to studying medicine as a profession and that already there is hardly a large city, even in the South, in which there are not one or two 'female doctors.' Against these personally I have not a word to say. But I deplore the effect of the example they set. The work of a doctor or surgeon is not work for a woman."[14] Dr. Waggener died later that year and did not live to see Marie Delalondre Dietzel become the first woman to graduate in medicine from the university the following year. At the meeting of the Board of Regents on May 15, 1897, the dean of the Medical Branch, Dr. J. F. Y. Paine, reported:

> While women have been admitted on equal terms with men to all the lectures and other exercises of both schools, medicine and pharmacy, since the organization of the medical department, it is worthy of mention that this is the first occasion on which they have been recommended for degrees. It is a source of gratification that the young lady made notable in the history of this college by being the first lady of her sex to secure a degree in medicine is a modest and gentle lady, yet brave and independent.[15]

In 1947 Dr. Dietzel received her fifty-year award pin from the University of Texas Medical Branch. She had met the challenge and fulfilled the promise made by Ann Preston to the class of 1855–56 at the first women's medical college in the United States. And so have all the other women in this book who have honored Preston's covenant with her aspiring young female medical students: "Our day will come; we will work in faith and bide our time."[16]

Women Pioneers in Texas Medicine

chapter 1

EARLY HEALERS

Through all the millennia of our developing civilization, healing hands have reached out to help the ailing and the feeble in every human community. This age-old tradition came to Texas with its earliest inhabitants, the various tribes of Native Americans who first settled the area.

It is important to distinguish from pseudomedical opportunists the dedicated early settlers who sometimes became doctors by necessity without the benefit of official licenses they had had no opportunity to earn. Also important to remember is that the state of Texas did not begin regulating the practice of medicine until it adopted its present constitution in 1875.

Beginning its historical life as a province in Spain's colony of Mexico, Texas evolved into a Mexican province when our southern neighbor broke its ties with Europe. Many and deep are the Hispanic cultural imprints in Texas. One of these is the widespread use of *curanderismo* by our Hispanic population. Although the semi-legendary founder and developer of this kind of medical practice was a male, since his time and still today many such practitioners are *curanderas*—females. A closer look at four early healers—Jewel Babb, Annie Buchanan, Ada Elliott, and Elizabeth Boyle Smith—offers an insight into the wide-ranging and eclectic scope of this kind of folk medicine.

Texas always had unique varieties of folk and faith healers who were not in the Hispanic tradition. Readers will find a great deal of overlapping in their treatment methods and the accompanying spiritual practices. Some, like Jewel Babb, allowed their healing work to grow and change into new forms as the spirit moved them or visionary experiences advised them.

In 1837, a year after Texas won its independence from Mexico, the Republic of Texas set up a board of medical censors. However, that and other laws of the republic were revoked by a general repealing law passed by the new state legislature in 1847, soon after Texas became part of the United States.[1]

During the twenty-six years that included the Mexican War, the Civil War, and some of the Reconstruction era, Texas legislators made no regulatory laws concerning medical practice. In 1873, the Texas Legislature produced a law that established a board of examiners in each county and required a practitioner of medicine to have either a degree from a reputable medical school or a certificate from a board of medical examiners.[2]

In 1875, state control over medical practitioners was strengthened by adoption of the new constitution, which enabled the state to pass laws requiring medical qualifications and to punish malpractice. A year later, Texas legislators repealed the 1873 statute concerning boards of county examiners and passed a substitute law that required each district court to appoint three licensed doctors as a board of examiners. Later amendments added a heavy fine for unauthorized practice or the "offer and attempt to practice."[3]

Very likely, Mrs. Mary Jane Whittet was entirely unconscious of any legal prohibitions in the late 1880s when she began her unlicensed medical career in Anchorage, Atascosa County, by riding horseback to the aid of a badly burned Latin-American woman. Mary Jane's daughter, Louise Whittet, recalled, "Mother didn't know anything about medicine then, but she had a lot of common sense. She used home remedies and the patient recovered."[4] There was no doctor in her community, so Mrs. Whittet kept answering increasingly frequent calls for "the Madama's" medical aid. Eventually she became known as the community doctor. In 1905, having learned that Texas law required medical licensing, Mrs. Whittet "got some medical books" and passed the state board examination, thus becoming in law what she had been in fact for many years.[5]

The Texas Legislature in 1901 wiped the slate clean of all former laws regarding medicine and forged a three-branch division of medical practice with a separate board of examiners for each. There was a board of medical examiners, a board of eclectic examiners, and a board of homeopathic medical examiners.[6] Once again, practical application had outrun legal acceptance. Dr. Mary B. Ray, who graduated from Cleveland Homeopathic Hospital College in 1886, was practicing in the Galveston and Beaumont areas around 1900.[7]

In 1907, the Texas Medical Practice Act was voted in. This act remained in force in the late 1990s, though it became a patchwork of amendments passed to meet changing times and rapidly increasing scientific and technological advances. Regulation of advertising practices and such modern problems as honesty in labeling and packaging have inspired many of these amendments.[8]

Folk and Faith Healers

Long before white men arrived in Texas, Native Americans had developed methods of caring for their sick and wounded. Certain old women in most of the tribes were designated as midwives, who understood the importance of the rituals connected with childbirth as well as practical ways to assist the mother and ensure that the child was properly cared for.

Researchers have distinguished various classes of shamans among the Texas tribes. These medicine men traditionally included ritualistic magic in their cures and sometimes used sleight-of-hand tricks in producing objects that supposedly caused the illness. Much less respected, but probably much more efficient in producing cures, were the shaman herbalists—often women—who, like Sacajawea, knew the specific properties of different plants and understood how to collect and prepare herbs, roots, bark, and berries to treat various ailments.[9]

According to Wichita Indian belief, the Earth Mother was a terrestrial goddess who gave birth to everything. In her desire to nourish and preserve mankind, she provided plants for food and also roots and tubers that were useful in curing illnesses.[10] For countless years her knowledge was handed down orally from the older women to the younger ones; eventually, through encounters with Native Americans, some of it was assimilated by the white settlers in Texas.

A variety of folk healers, faith healers, and menders of mind and body have established themselves in the rich tapestry of Texas history. A strong religious element is usually present in the techniques of unorthodox healers, perhaps dating back to the days when physical afflictions were generally assumed to be signs of a deity's displeasure. Usually working alone and more often than not among poor patients, these practitioners developed their skills haphazardly. As the healer's reputation and rate of successes increased, he or she was free to change treatments and techniques.

Certain circumstances have shaped nearly all the lives of the curanderas, midwives, and folk and faith healers examined here. Poverty and lives of abrupt changes and hardship seem to have been the rule for them. Perhaps because of their own hard lives, most of them gave inexpensive treatments and prescribed only the cheapest drugs or such teas and medicines as the patients could make for themselves. Often they charged no fees or accepted payment in kind.

Almost always a curandera or other folk healer would demonstrate a vigorous belief in divine intervention and would often prescribe prayers or religious rituals as vital to the patient's recovery. In many cases, the healer also demanded the patient's faith in his or her personal powers; sometimes, people who admitted doubts were turned away untreated.

Instead of the "hero worship" or romantic fantasy often felt by women patients for their male doctors, a bonding with the midwife or curandera or folk healer more closely resembled a parent-child relationship. Patients in the cases cited would not fear to ask any questions of their healers, for they would not be ridiculed, ignored, or taken to task for any ignorance displayed. Instead, they received a sympathetic answer, even if it was just, "I don't know."

Only in the case of Ada Elliott is hypnotism identified as a healer's tool, yet one can look at other examples and wonder if hypnosis, perhaps unknown to the user, figured in the successes of people like Jewel Babb, Annie Buchanan, and Mother Lane.

JEWEL BABB: A HEALER'S LIFE

Jewel Babb was always falling off her horse. That was because she refused to stay at home and do "women's work" when her husband, Walter, and the other cowboys were riding herd. From the way she narrated her childhood and young adult experiences, she seems to have been as low in dexterity and physical skills as she was high in courage and perseverance throughout most of her life. That makes it all the more remarkable that Jewel achieved local fame and a steadfast following during the last part of her life as a "mind healer."[11] Her father and grandfather

Jewel Babb. Photograph by Ann Savino, El Paso, Texas

were professional water-well drillers, so Jewel's earliest memories were of nomadic wanderings around west Texas wherever their services were wanted. Although Jewel and her siblings had no toys because of the constant traveling, they found delight in nature and all the plant and animal life around them.[12]

Walter and Jewel Babb tried to earn their living in a variety of ways: trapping, milking cows, and running a tourist court. Walter, a natural loner, spent a good deal of time trapping animals in Texas and Mexico. The Babbs had four children: Dixie, Irvin, Azalea, and Wayne. After eight years of struggle to make the tourist court pay, Jewel gave up the financial battle and went to live at Indian Hot Springs on land her son

Dixie had bought some years before. Walter Babb, trapping lions in Mexico, died of a heart attack at about that time.[13]

At first, Mrs. Babb considered the hotel and the row of cabins at Indian Hot Springs just another home. She rented the cabins to people who came to use the springs, but she knew nothing then of how or why the waters were beneficial. Her discovery that she could enhance the benefits received by people visiting the springs and her pressing need to earn a living coincided to encourage her to study the different waters, muds, and mosses that made up the hot springs complex. Jewel Babb not only became convinced of the springs' benefits herself but also encouraged many others to believe in them and contributed her growing powers of healing in an attempt to make their lives better.[14]

Her hotel at Indian Hot Springs was so close to the border that she could look across the Rio Grande to the little town of Ojos Calientes in Mexico. Jewel got along well then and later with her neighbors south of the border and received many visits from Mexicans needing treatment. They usually brought small gifts of food and other useful items, especially welcome when she was feeling deserted by most of her Anglo fellow citizens.[15]

When Mrs. Babb eventually lost the hot springs property for nonpayment of back taxes, she moved into a little house built of railroad ties by her son Dixie. Visions of bright lights, spirit animals, and tiny human healers began to come to Jewel Babb during her years of healing others. From time to time she had inexplicable physical sensations, too; all these experiences seemed to be connected with her increasing ability to heal by mental effort. When Babb's biographer, Pat Ellis Taylor, and her husband, Chuck Taylor, visited her in the tie house, they saw and felt her skills first hand. Mrs. Taylor experienced a most pleasurable and relaxing foot massage. Her husband felt his pain and discomfort being dispelled when Mrs. Babb sat close to him and simply talked quietly to him. She related to the Taylors various examples of occasions when she had been able to stop pain and other symptoms in patients without any physical contact at all.[16]

Mrs. Babb knew and used many different cacti for medicinal purposes. In addition, two of her favorite items for treatment were kerosene oil and the aloe vera plant. She told of stopping a workman's dangerous bleeding by saturating the wounded leg with kerosene.[17]

Her last move, to Valentine, Texas, came about when Jewel eventually needed more protection from the weather and hard desert living than she could find in the tie house among her goats and chickens. With her came a barrel containing notes and letters of gratitude and praise from the many people she had treated over the years. In Valentine she remained, a source of healing and reassurance for a trickle of faithful friends and visitors.[18]

In an afterword to Mrs. Babb's narrated autobiography, Pat Ellis Taylor analyzed her life and career compared with those of the curanderas who have lived and worked along the Texas-Mexican border for decades. The evidence seems clear that her similarities to the practitioners of *curanderismo* greatly exceeded her differences from them. Most likely, however, Jewel Babb remained too engaged in her useful, busy life to worry about being clearly defined.[19]

ANNIE BUCHANAN: CORSICANA'S "SEER"

"I built seven churches and a college for my colored people, but I ain't never went to school a day in my life," said Annie Buchanan of her career as a clairvoyant and faith healer. She was reportedly born about 1896 with a full set of teeth; the doctor told her mother she would become a clairvoyant. Because her mother didn't want such an unusual child, Annie recalled, she was "raised mostly by white folks."[20]

Much of the advice Annie gave was nonmedical. She tried to persuade her brother-in-law to hold onto some of his land because she believed it had oil under it. However, he retorted that there was "no such thing as oil under arth." He sold the land on which the first well at Mexia was later brought in.[21]

People of all races and from distant states would travel to Corsicana to consult Miss Annie on every sort of issue. One came to get relief for his wife's aches and pains; another had a sick daughter; still another came to buy medicine he could have gotten elsewhere because, he explained, the pills "seemed to do better" when he got them from Miss Annie.[22]

Miss Annie built quite a reputation for knowing where oil could be found. She also located lost and stolen animals and property. She described her fortune-telling ability this way: "Yo' life is in yo' palm, circling in yo' blood. I read by blood circling—yo' blood circling. It's not in yo' lines, it's yo' blood carried to the palms of yo' hands. I reads hands."[23]

Annie conducted church services in a church built next to the house that oilman Col. A. E. Humphreys provided for her. A visitor in search of historical materials about Texas's oil development described the hypnotic, moving quality of her highly original mixture of sermon, song, and worship.[24]

ADA ELLIOTT: ACTRESS, ACTIVIST, HYPNOTIST

When she was eighty-four years old in 1976, Ada Elliott could look back on a life as full of patterns as a patchwork quilt. In 1905 she traveled in a vaudeville act with a sister who later became a soloist with the Paul Whiteman orchestra. Ada herself became an actress and appeared in several Broadway productions.[25] She traveled by horse and buggy, giving lectures around Texas in 1919 promoting woman suffrage. Many years later, she remarked, "I hear the same silly arguments against the ERA that I heard against the vote—it is going to destroy the home; it will take away from femininity."[26]

Another career of Ada's was keeping a boardinghouse in Dallas, which she did for twenty-five years. She wrote a book about her experiences as a landlady entitled *801—Beans, Potatoes, and Apple Pie*. On one very interesting evening when she was in Mexico, she found herself at a gambling table next to Pancho Villa. When the Mexican folk hero offered his personal printed money to bet and the croupier objected, Villa summoned armed soldiers to stand by while he continued to gamble. Everyone else at the table was using gold.[27]

Elliott became interested in psychology and medical hypnosis. She used the latter technique successfully on her sister when the singer developed a severe neuritis that doctors were unable to alleviate. When she visited a young woman who was dying of cancer, Ada was able to calm her enough so that the patient could embrace her religion and face her death. Ada gave to a woman who was terrified of flying a strong suggestion that relieved her anxiety for the whole next trip.[28] A believer in hypnoanalysis, Ada pointed out that psychoanalysts earning hourly fees might naturally be slow to adopt such a technique.[29]

ELIZABETH BOYLE SMITH: MORE THAN A NEIGHBOR

It was lucky that Elizabeth Boyle Smith brought medicines along with her when she moved to Crosby County in 1877. She was the only medically experienced person in the area for the next ten years. Her nearest neighbor in the early days was a hundred miles away. Mrs. Smith had practiced nursing at Fort Griffin, Texas, and was able to meet the medical challenges of her new home. She and a neighbor "delivered each other's babies" as occasions arose.[30]

As long as poor people continue to have children and to develop diseases or illnesses of all kinds, there will continue to be curanderas, undocumented midwives, and other healers of all kinds to treat and comfort them.

Las Curanderas

A cult of *curanderismo* flourished in south and west Texas a hundred or more years before Anglos appeared on that mesquite-and-cactus-dotted scene. Some investigators report that advances in modern medicine and loss of faith among Spanish-speaking believers are diminishing the practice of *curanderismo;* even today, however, folk medicine healers are alive and prospering in areas of the Southwest. Around San Antonio and along the Texas-Mexican border there are still *curanderos* successfully functioning. (The masculine noun, *curanderos,* is used when only male practitioners are concerned and also when the practitioners are of both sexes. *Curanderas* is used to mean female practitioners only.) Perhaps because of its natural tie-in with midwifery, female practitioners of *curanderismo* seem always to have been as acceptable to believers as the male ones.

An article in the January, 1996, *Southwestern Historical Quarterly* identifies six types of curanderas. One who is called simply *curandera total* is like a general practitioner. The *yerbera* is a specialist in herbal medicine. A curandera or a *yerbera* may also be a *partera,* or midwife. The *señora* is one who predicts the future by reading cards. A curandera who works as a spiritual medium is an *espiritista.* A *sobadora* specializes in massage therapy.[31]

The range of treatments undertaken by curanderos and curanderas varies with the individual healer. Each in time becomes a specialist, and each learns *recetar:* to prescribe treatments invented to meet the needs of the individual client. Stock items for a curandero or curandera include original *recetas:* herbal teas of many kinds; special baths; applications of dried plants, which may be heated or powdered and applied directly to the sufferer's body; massage; and ritual behavior such as praying, lighting candles, or jumping over flames. Often a raw egg will be used to "draw" the harmful essence from the patient. Passed over the patient, then cracked into a dish and placed under the sickbed, the next morning the egg may be found "cooked" by evils it has consumed.

The beginning of a curandera's ministry is usually marked by a life-threatening affliction or crisis. Seeking a cure, the future healer often enters into a long period of unconsciousness, during which God, a heavenly messenger, or some deceased relatives inform the "sleeper" of her destiny as a curandera.

Don Pedro (or Pedrito) Jaramillo, who became *el mero jefe* (the real chief) of curanderos, was born in the mid-1800s of Turascan Indian parents near Guadalajara, Jalisco, Mexico. He once treated himself for severe nasal pain by covering his face in mud near a pool. Cured after three days, he slept and heard a voice saying that he had received a gift of healing from God. He came to Los Olmos, a small Brooks County settlement, as a young man and devoted his life to healing. After he died in 1907, worshipers covered his grave in a cemetery near Falfurrias with a small adobe hut. The hut has become a shrine filled with abandoned crutches, myriads of candles, and hand-drawn messages of thanks. Some considered Don Pedro an incarnation of God; today many believe him a saint not yet canonized.[32]

An altar is standard equipment for a curandera. On the altars of those trained by Don Pedro Jaramillo are sure to be found pictures of the Virgin—and of Don Pedro. (*Don* and *Doña*, titles formerly used in Spain to indicate nobility, are now bestowed by the faithful on their healers.)

Some illnesses commonly brought to curanderas include digestive upsets such as stomach cramps or diarrhea, *sustos* (frights), and *mal de ojo* (evil eye). The usual pathology of this affliction seems to be that a strong-willed person "eyes" a weaker character—either favorably or unfavorably, but without touching—and thereby causes the victim to develop *mal de ojo*, known by its symptoms of fever and vomiting. The cure: "sweep" the person with an unbroken egg, which is then placed under the bed.[33]

People who believe that beneficial magical powers reside in objects and words will also logically believe in the reverse: it is possible to put hexes on people, ill-wishing them into sickness or even death. Folks convinced that they are suffering from such malign influences often seek the curandera to cancel out the bad effects of someone's malice or jealousy.

Curanderismo does not lack psychological weapons. A recourse frequently used is putting clients in touch with their dead loved ones. Prayers are key parts of many *recetas*. Some curanderas win influence over their customers by revealing advance knowledge of their problems and needs. The healer's ability to predict future events and outcomes also impresses his or her patients.

Four curanderas were pursuing successful careers in southwest Texas as recently as the middle of this century. Doña María Chaney, Doña María Perez, Doña Graciela, and Mother Lane had to rise above handicaps of extreme poverty, the opposition of more conventional medical authorities, and personal afflictions to establish themselves. Each was supported in her struggle for recognition by a powerful faith in her religion and in her call to cure.

DOÑA MARÍA CHANEY

Although she was married to a ranch hand named Felix Valadez, Doña María Chaney practiced under the name of her Anglo first husband, Jim Chaney. A wan, fragile figure at mid-century, she would sit in a small room crowded with religious objects and paper streamers. Candles burned in colored glass containers. Visitors might leave donations of money beside these candles to honor their deceased relatives.[34]

Doña María never knew her parents. Her own origins were explained to her by a maid from their home in Vera Cruz, where María was born, probably in 1903. The maid informed María that her parents had been killed in a raid on Vera Cruz by a rebel group during the revolution. At fifteen, Doña María was taken to San Antonio by an aunt. There the aunt became ill and died at Santa Rosa Hospital. Finding herself a friendless orphan, Doña María became terribly *asustada* (afraid). Her left hand became twisted and deformed, but the hospital doctors could not discover a cause. She was beset with fevers that they could not cure.

A Mexican woman working in the hospital took Doña María to a "house of spirits" to consult a curandero. The man knew María's name, and he impressed her by producing "holy water," although he was not a priest. Apparently realizing that Doña María had never known her parents, he asked if there was any sign by which she would be able to recognize them. She could think of none.

When the curandero placed his hands on her forehead, Doña María felt a chill. She was still awake, but she began to dream that her mother and father appeared to her and asked why she was suffering. They said it was not necessary to suffer; she should come with them. Then her mother told María that she could join them after she had stayed on earth awhile to help others in pain. The girl finally came to herself, feeling exhausted but certain she had not been asleep.

The curandero then told her she would be cured within three days, but only after he put her to "sleep with her parents" for awhile. After María drank some tea he had prepared, she immediately fell into a deep sleep. When she woke, she found her hand was cured, and she was filled with a desire to cure others. Her first two patients, a German and a Cuban, were suffering from "colic"—*la tripa torcida* (twisted entrails). She and another woman treated the German with an *ayuda* (possibly an enema) and had him soak for two hours in a very hot bath of orange leaf tea. At the end of this time he was cured. The Cuban, on whom the doctors had given up, she also cured, according to Doña María's account.

Doña María heard that doctors had begun to take an interest in her as the number of her cures increased; her patients and their relatives, however, refused to give out her name for fear the established medical authorities would harm her. When Jim Chaney was dying, Doña María claimed, Christ appeared and touched her. Since then, she said, she had cured many people. She prescribed patent medicines such as SSS, 666, and Hadacol, along with some herbal teas. She also used a concentrated form of prayer by which a patient could achieve a sort of autohypnosis.[35]

DOÑA MARÍA PEREZ

A curandera practicing in Sinton, Texas, in the 1950s, Doña María Perez was born about 1882 near Delfina, a small Texas community close to Brownsville. In her thirties she worked as a midwife serving Mexican women in her area. One day she fell down a deep staircase. Knocked unconscious, she remained mentally abstracted "for many days." According to Doña María, she realized that fear was her problem, but like a person in a dream, she could not wake up enough to conquer her fear.

When her parents took her to the great Don Pedro Jaramillo, he treated her with herbs and told her not to be afraid. Since that visit, she said, she had never been afraid. As María recovered from the experience, she felt the need to cure others. She chose to practice under her maiden name, Perez. A portrait of Don Pedro with a long white beard hung on the wall behind her chair.[36]

Doña María Perez specialized in curing *sustos* (frights). In one case she treated a girl who had been declared crazy. Doña María decided the girl was only in an advanced state of fright. She prescribed several doses of oil derived from a seed and a bath in tea made from a combination of herbs. After one treatment the girl was better; after three days she was cured. Doña María's cure for simple headaches was peeled cactus leaves applied to the forehead. She explained that the cactus juice was the vital force in the treatment.

Like other curanderas, Doña María was restricted mainly to the use of patent medicines. She commented that people no longer wanted to take the trouble to make up the old herbal prescriptions. They were also too afraid of snakes to venture into the woods and gather the materials. In the old days, María said, she used to prescribe such herbs as *laurel cimarron* and *canela del monte*. Brownie McNeil suggested that her flashing black eyes might have been enough to scare the frights out of some of her patients.[37]

DOÑA GRACIELA

A more sophisticated curandera practicing in San Antonio as recently as the mid-1950s was Doña Graciela. She concentrated her efforts on fortune-telling, initiating a long process of revelation that was supposed to guide her clients in finding hidden treasures. The alluring prospect of finding a fortune in their backyard made her customers easy to convince. Of course, they had to keep coming back for the next part of the instructions.

Doña Graciela also helped people pass their driver's license tests. She chose a certain day on which they must go to take their test. Giving them a strong suggestion that they would surely pass, she would promise, "Don't be afraid. I will be near to protect you." Satisfied clients who had gained enough confidence to pass their tests were happy to recommend her services.

Mercedes Peña Lane was both an *espiritista* and a *sobadora*, or massage therapist. Details of how she became a faith healer are lacking; how she acquired the title of Mother Lane is not known. She was one of twelve children born to a Mexican grocer who moved his family in 1898 to Laredo, Texas. There Mercedes learned to speak and write English. She married Jesse B. Lane sometime between 1913 and 1919, when their son, Weldon, was born. Although she may have begun a career in *curanderismo* earlier, she was practicing in the 1930s in Kingsville, near the southern tip of Texas. Mercedes used a building in the Mexican part of town, where one patient at a time would be ushered in, wrapped in a sheet. The sufferer would then spread a second sheet on a plain wooden table. Mother Lane, in a simple white dress, would rub Vick's salve, alcohol, or olive oil on the patient's body.

She was credited with painlessly rubbing out pus, appendixes, tonsils, and gallstones, discarding the tissue into a bucket. She treated patients for gallstones, asthma, tonsillitis, rheumatism, infantile paralysis, goiter, appendicitis, arthritis, and other ailments.[38]

Because Mother Lane believed "heavy vibrations" from the growing moon deflected her healing powers, she practiced massaging only at each new moon and for the next two weeks. Her ardent admirers became known as "New Mooners." A cousin, Antero García, blamed opposition from Kingsville's medical community when in April, 1935, Mother Lane was arrested for practicing medicine without a license. Charges were dropped months later at the request of the county attorney. Moving her practice six miles north, Mother Lane continued to live in Kingsville (Kleberg County) and commuted to Bishop (Nueces County), where another cousin, Frank García, built a house for her professional use. He also constructed a tourist court because the little town's one hotel could not accommodate the *sobadora*'s many patients.

A most surprising aspect of this curandera's work was that a large majority of her clients were Anglos. Patients came from all over the United States and Canada seeking her treatments. For ten days at a time she would treat 100 to 250 sufferers, many of them rich enough to drive big cars and to come back repeatedly for more ten-day sessions. Although she followed *curanderismo* custom and did not charge for her services, Mother Lane placed a cigar box close to the entrance for the convenience of anyone wishing to make a donation. She prospered enough to build a new eight-room house in Kingsville, to take trips wherever she liked, and to send her son, Weldon, to college. (Jesse Lane seems to have drifted in and out of her life until his death in 1947.)

As a trance medium, Mother Lane could serve up to one hundred people at a time. She claimed that five different spirits would enter her in her trance state; among them was Don Pedrito Jaramillo. People attending the session asked questions, and the spirits would answer through Mother Lane. Health and personal advice were the topics usually discussed.

Organized medical opposition led to Mother Lane's arrest in March, 1938, on five counts of unlawful practice of medicine. Although all the criticism of her practices came from Anglo sources, Anglo patients were her most ardent defenders. After several continuances, the case was dismissed on the motion of the county attorney for lack of evidence. After this, Mother Lane moved her practice to Corpus Christi, where she kept a lower profile. At seventy, she told a cousin that her powers seemed to be failing. She died of congestive heart failure in 1959, at the age of seventy-five. Funeral services were held at Sacred Heart Catholic Church.

How did this most unusual curandera manage to break through the barriers of culture and communication that usually restricted the practitioner to a Mexican clientele? Word of mouth and newspaper stories were the only advertising she ever had, yet as late as the 1970s visitors still occasionally arrived from as far away as Missouri or Illinois to seek her help. This question and many others about *curanderismo* will remain unanswered until much more is known about individual curanderos.

McNeil speculated that some of the curanderos' remedies and practices "may be traced to the Gypsies of the Middle Ages . . . descended by oral tradition to the present." Others, he noted, come from a large fund of Indian folklore concerning herbs that have curative powers.[39]

An article on folk medicine published in the 1970s mentioned a line of popular curatives known as "Grandma's Remedies." Among these homely helps was "Grandma's Tea," a favorite *receta* of *curanderismo* practitioners. Also, it was noted that herbs long used by the Indians as contraceptives have proved effective in modern laboratory tests.[40]

A student of *curanderismo* as it is practiced in his native south Texas today pointed out that "many *curanderos* have a lot of plain common sense. The remedies they offer often are obvious things the person needs to do."[41] Observers who have noted the hero-like aspects of stories about the making of curanderos, their reliance on well-known substances wherever possible, their practical approach to problems, and their appeal to clients' religious feelings may well decide that *curanderismo* will remain a factor in Texas culture for a long time to come.

It should be understood that not every practitioner of faith or psychic healing along the Texas-Mexican border is Hispanic, and of course not all of them are referred to as curanderas. Nevertheless, practices of most folk and faith healers in the area seem to have much in common with those of the curanderas. Certainly their use of well-known remedies, including aloe vera and herbal teas, is in keeping with traditions of *curanderismo*.

Midwifery: A Very Old Profession

More than in past centuries, controversy swirls nowadays around the two life experiences common to all: birth and death. Perhaps that is only natural, since modern technological advances have brought us closer than ever to achieving the power to change the course of nature at both extremes of life. One aspect of the birth process that seems most resistant to change, however, is the reliance of many women on midwives.

Midwives have lived and worked all over the world for all of human existence. The motif of one woman helping another to give birth is repeated over and over in literature and in history. Shakespeare used midwife imagery frequently. Today, the reasons prompting a woman to call for a midwife instead of a doctor to deliver her baby range from cultural to economic.

As a practical matter, early American settlers could not have done without female medical practitioners. Colonial conditions made necessary the existence of numerous practicing "doctresses." In a collection of oral histories of women doctors, Regina Markell Morantz makes the point that "seventeenth-century ignorance of anatomy, physiology, and surgery put physicians, surgeons, and midwives on an equal plane in the management of parturition." In the 1800s, male doctors began to assert control over childbirth. As the physicians gained more technical skills and information, they shifted public attitudes toward childbearing from the traditional view that it was a normal life process to a new perspective: parturition was a "disease" best handled by trained experts. This change gradually shunted midwives into secondary roles, if they were still tolerated at all.[42]

During this state of affairs, there emerged a curious book written by Rev. D. L. Saunders, who was also a physician. Reverend Saunders's advice to midwives was published in 1858 with the title *Woman's Own Book; or, A Plain and Familiar Treatise on All Complaints and Diseases Peculiar to Females.—also—A Full System of Midwifery, Well Adapted to the Use of Common Readers. For the Ladies Themselves.* There are twenty-one sections in part 5, which is entitled "Labor: Instructions to the Midwife." Apparently the reverend doctor expected the entire birth process to be in the care of a midwife. Did he also expect the midwife to be able to read English? The good doctor's syntax and vocabulary do not seem at all restrained by the consideration that simplicity of statement might be needed by his readers.[43]

In a section called "Mother's Marks," Reverend Saunders explained that a sudden fright suffered by the mother can result in such anomalies as "snake-heads, lizzards, and the like" being "indellibly graven" on the child. Longings—or cravings—could also cause marking, according to Saunders. He encouraged pregnant women to express any strong desires in order to avoid marking the babies and advised them to avoid indulging in anger or grief. The reverend told of a case where the baby was born with flesh "like a dead person" and in fact died shortly after delivery. When the doctor inquired, he was informed that the mother had "lifted a corpse" shortly before delivery.[44]

For awhile, growing male dominance over the management of childbirth represented a distinct step backward for women practitioners in the eastern states. But on the distant frontiers of the young country there never ceased to be a need for midwives' services. Native American women, the very first women known to have inhabited Texas, sometimes used midwives: the Wichita and Lipan women were assisted by experienced midwives, although the Coahuiltecan, Tonkawa, and Caddo women are said to have given birth alone.

Describing a rural community in Texas, a writer on Texan cultures painted a picture of two black midwives of the old school. They reportedly "waited on" everyone—whites, blacks, and browns alike—in order to "catch" the baby. Many times they were paid for their services by assistance with their own deliveries or in goods instead of with money. These two women lived quite a distance apart, so each midwife had her own community to serve. Besides their services in delivering babies, they were expected to advise the troubled and medicate the sick. Their stocks consisted mainly of herb teas and homemade remedies, including salves. One of the women was Baptist, the other Methodist. They were fond of each other and proud of their friendship since childhood. Often one of them would hug some adult friend and say, "I brought you into the world—by the help of God and your mamma."[45]

The lives of midwives on the frontier could be incredibly adventurous and difficult. In the following sketches, some of the hardships and rewards of such lives are illustrated.

AUNT PAL WILSON (1859–1944)

"Babies come in different ways," remarked Mrs. Palestine Wilson, wife of a cotton and corn farmer who lived in the Bandera area. She said that whenever a birth was imminent in her area, they sent for her "whether or not they send for a doctor." She often went on calls with her mentor, a Dr. Johnson, with whom she had studied, "and [I] studied my doctor book, too." If anything unusual happened when she was handling a case by herself, Mrs. Wilson would go to Dr. Johnson, who "always told me what to do in such cases and how to do in others." She was proud of the fact that only two mothers under her care had died. Her standard equipment for a delivery included a bottle of ergot, which she always carried with her. Ergot is a fungus on grain that can be dried and used as a drug to inhibit bleeding and induce contractions.[46]

Most of the time Aunt Pal went to her patients riding a horse—sidesaddle. She recalled one bitter cold night when she was roused from her warm bed to ride ten miles to a patient. She put on all the clothes she could wear and still ride. They had to gallop most of the way. When they reached a river, she and her guide slid down the riverbank and crossed, with icy water splashing up and freezing on her feet and ankles. When they arrived, Aunt Pal had to be lifted off her horse, carried in, and walked back and forth until she thawed out enough to attend her patient.[47]

MATILDA BOOZIE RANDON (1847–1947)

For the twenty-five years from 1875 to 1900, Matilda Boozie Randon delivered most of the babies, black and white, born in Washington County. Matilda had seen her parents and siblings sold off in slavery to other slave owners during her young years with the Boozie family. She had been brought by the family from their South Carolina home to Mount Pleasant, Texas. After the Civil War, when Matilda was married, she and her husband, a minister, were given fifteen hundred acres of land by the Boozies.[48]

Matilda sold butter and eggs, but her chief source of income was midwifing. In an oral history, her granddaughter, Annie Mae Hunt, recalled, "She was woke up many a night and stayed right there with that woman until she got up." Her grandmother kept a black bag like a doctor's bag, Annie Mae said, but her children and grandchildren weren't allowed to touch it or to "even look at it too hard." Matilda carried scissors and spools of number eight thread to cut and tie the natal cord. She was paid sometimes with canned goods, hogs, chickens, eggs, quilts, or other objects of barter.[49]

CONSTANTINA ADAMIETZ (1846–1931)

Polish settlers who came to Texas in the mid-1800s had to create their own medical care. Every Polish housewife once had to know how to set fractured limbs, dress wounds, make poultices, and relieve suffering.[50]

The future Grandma Adamietz was born Constantina Pyka in Poland. When she was nine, her parents emigrated to Bandera, Texas, in search of a home. While peasants in Poland, they had heard that in America immigrants would have a chance to acquire land of their own. The Pykas settled down to improve their lot by their industry. Constantina married John Adamietz, with whom she had eleven children. As the eldest daughter in her own family, she was familiar with the duties of taking care of youngsters. She also "plowed, picked cotton, and did all kinds of farm work." She remembered being shown by an American neighbor how to eat corn on the cob—a practice unknown in Poland.[51]

For sixty years, Constantina Adamietz was a recognized midwife in the Bandera community, becoming affectionately known as Grandma Adamietz. Since there was no doctor nearer than Castroville or San

Antonio, Constantina often "filled this sphere of usefulness to the entire satisfaction of all concerned." She had learned midwifery from her mother, who was a licensed midwife. On her last trip to attend a delivery, Grandma Adamietz had to cross a swinging bridge over a flood-swollen river. Her son and a friend, who were carrying her across, accidentally dropped her, breaking several of her ribs. She arrived at her destination in time to assist in the birth.[52]

MARY ISABELLA "BELLE" STARRETT (1907–19??)

Having a dozen children of her own did not keep Belle Starrett from attending the births of friends and neighbors. She took a course provided by the Crosby County Health Department doctor and became a licensed midwife. One needed only to ring a long and a short on the old telephone to start Belle on her way (sidesaddle, of course) to attend a birthing or a sickbed. Her twelfth child, Lena Starrett Givens, told of her own birth: Belle had sent for the doctor, but when he did not arrive in time, she, helped by two neighbor women, coped with her own delivery, separating the baby from herself by cutting the cord with a knife from the kitchen.[53]

Having married her teacher, Samuel Franklin Starrett, Belle maintained a lifelong interest in learning of all kinds. She took sewing lessons by mail and earned a certificate for health hygiene to complement her license as a midwife. Lena Starrett Givens remembered that if a child of Belle's wanted to say he was sick and stay home from school, he could do that. The price was a dose of castor oil. Her children's teachers knew they would receive full cooperation from the Starretts in any matter concerning schoolwork. Belle herself found time to read while she did such chores as churning the butter.

Belle sold eggs, butter, and hens to help the family finances. An inventory of livestock she made in 1930 showed that the family owned 200 animals, including 169 chickens. One hopes the dozen Starrett children shared some of the care of this menagerie. When Belle Starrett died, a local newspaper referred to her as "Mother of the East Plains."

MAGGIE SMITH (1894–1965)

Texas-born Maggie English moved with her family to a ranch near Sierra Blanca when she was young. The ranch was near the Rio Grande, and the story is told that Pancho Villa came riding up with a group of followers one day and asked for water for his horses. Maggie's father told her to feed all of them. Pancho Villa is said to have given Maggie a pair of spurs in exchange for the hospitality.[54]

On a cattle-buying expedition into Mexico during the Mexican Revolution, Maggie and her father were warned that the revolutionaries were coming. The villagers asked Mr. English to take the silver church bells with them so they wouldn't be confiscated, and he agreed. Later, when the Englishes noticed a dust cloud behind them, they realized they were being followed. The two quickly stopped and buried the bells, taking time to cover their tracks to look as if they had not left the trail. Supposedly, years later, Maggie furnished a map by means of which the bells were returned to their village.

With her second husband, H. Baylor Smith, Maggie undertook the management of the Hot Springs, Texas, health resort at Big Bend. When Mr. Smith died three years later, Maggie was alone with five children to rear in a rugged country. She chose to stay. Soon she became the one that people on both sides of the Rio Grande looked to as doctor, midwife, justice of the peace, sheriff, ambassador, and friend in need.

Maggie's daughter, Minnie Smith, related a difficult birthing situation faced by her mother. A forty-five-year-old Mexican woman was expecting her first baby. Maggie delivered it, but the woman died. Seeing that the family had next to nothing, Maggie wrapped the baby in a blanket and took it home with her. She nursed it for a month until it was doing well and then took it back to its father in Mexico.

Another time, Maggie attended a wedding in Mexico with her young son and her son-in-law. She was always an honored guest on such occasions. A pregnant woman who had ridden twelve miles to attend the wedding went into labor. Maggie found that her helpers had suspended the woman from the ceiling and spread a goat's hide beneath her. Maggie had them cut her down and delivered the baby safely. It was a boy, whom the family named Henry after Maggie's son.

In the life of each of the midwives described above, there was a wealth of warmth and affection shown for her by the community where she lived and worked. "Mamma" and "Auntie" and "Grandma" this or that earned the respect and love of her neighbors, and they seemed to delight in showing it.

For his master's thesis on the attitudes and practices of Mexican-American midwives, Agapito Sanchez interviewed thirty midwives, some working in urban centers and others in rural areas. All of them lived in south Texas counties largely populated by Mexican Americans. Sanchez cited four cultural factors in the Mexican-American population found throughout most of the literature on local medical practices and suggested that these ideas and beliefs are major deterrents to the use of "proper medical health practices." These four themes are cultural folk beliefs about diseases, the traditional role of the family, fear of Anglo medical and institutional practices, and fatalistic acceptance and resignation.[55]

Sanchez's ultimate aim was to suggest changes in these four sets of ideas in order to improve the treatment of children born with congenital defects. This book, on the other hand, simply purports to reveal some common beliefs and practices that may still exist in some areas among Mexican-American midwives and their clients. Despite knowledge in the Mexican-American community of the germ theory, many Latinos viewed these unseeable entities as a kind of Anglo trick.

Sanchez found that although Mexican Americans at the lowest economic level had not accepted the importance of medical prenatal care for the mother, they did view pregnancy as a time of great danger for the fetus. For example, an eclipse or a full moon was considered especially dangerous. A pregnant woman was expected to adhere to many restrictions in her diet and to lessen the amount of water she consumed for fear the baby's head might grow too large. Often the delivery was accomplished with the mother in a kneeling or squatting position.

The mother of a family was considered the primary caregiver for whatever member became ill. From her girlhood, a woman was expected to inform herself about home remedies and to prepare herself for any nursing duties that might arise. If her treatments were not enough, the entire family entered into the crisis, particularly the older female relatives. If it became imperative to seek outside help, curanderos and *yerberos* would be consulted next. The Anglo physician remained a last resort for folks who were really desperate. Part of this attitude stemmed from strong male resentment of having their wives examined by male doctors. Too, the family might feel that hospital restrictions on visitors and visiting hours were obnoxious.

Women Pioneers in Texas Medicine

A real fear of Anglo medicine was present in some Mexican-American communities—the same attitude held by many Europeans in the days before Semmelweiss hunted down the unsanitary causes of childbed fever. To them, the hospital still represented a place to go to die. *Parteras*, they believed, were more patient and understanding than physicians. The fear was that hurried doctors might be too eager to use instruments to speed along a birth instead of letting nature take its course.

Sanchez discovered that infant and maternal death rates among Mexican Americans were higher than those in the Anglo population. In addition, deaths from congenital malformations were almost twice as high as among Anglos. He cited the Hispanic population's prevailing attitude as believing "that the handicapped must always remain the objects of pity and charity and that little can be done toward helping them become contributing citizens."

STUDIES OF MIDWIVES

In 1924, the Texas Department of Public Health conducted a survey of treatments used by midwives and of reasons why women used midwives instead of doctors. Some of the treatments were bizarre by today's standards: one wonders how they could have worked often enough to have been included in a written list of remedies. For example, besides various kinds of teas and oils, some forms of treatment used to increase labor pains included tying a rope around the waistline and tightening it as labor progressed. Some midwives also administered buttermilk, red onion, wasp-nest and dirt-dauber tea, or gunpowder.[56] It should also be remembered that although the unusual treatments listed in the survey seem heroic indeed in light of today's information, all the remedies were well meant and intended to prevent suffering and assist in a healthful birth.

Some reasons for using a midwife given by twenty-two survey respondents included the belief that midwives were better; some women used one because of convenience or the rendering of "more service" or the lack of a doctor but nevertheless thought they ought to have had a doctor; some just didn't think it was necessary to have a physician present. The fact that midwives are much less expensive than doctors also played an important role in their choices.[57]

Eight black midwives in Brazos, Burleson, Grimes, Leon, Madison, and Robertson counties were interviewed by a team led by Dr. Ruth Schaffer, sponsored by the March of Dimes and funded by Alpha Zeta of Texas A&M University in 1979. Through 1977, this group found, the number of actively practicing midwives in the six counties studied sharply decreased from the number practicing in 1967. The survey team attributed this drop to three factors: acceptance of black patients in hospitals, increased welfare payments for hospitalization, and an increase in the "status value" placed on hospital care.[58]

A move by Democratic Senator Hector Uribe of Brownsville in 1983 to introduce legislation to regulate midwives spurred the *Dallas Morning News* to print a long, well-illustrated article on the whole midwife "controversy." The *News* found that only a handful of Dallas-area physicians were willing to meet at a hospital a woman who had been using the services of a midwife and had developed serious complications. Even that handful, the article reported, were careful to emphasize that they were not acting as "backups" for the midwives.[59]

In statistics compiled by the American College of Obstetrics and Gynecology, the records of eleven states were compared in 1975 and 1976. Infant mortality rates in home deliveries were at least double those of hospital deliveries. Some of the doctors interviewed had collections of horror stories of home births gone wrong. Some of the midwives challenged the validity of the physicians' statistics; others said that if anything abnormal was happening at a birth, they would immediately go for help.[60]

Although several of the midwives favored self-regulation, they seemed unanimous in opposing Senator Uribe's effort at midwife control. His bill called for statewide registration and a regulatory board. It was endorsed by the Texas Medical Association and the Texas Department of Health.[61] An earlier regulatory attempt was reported in a 1979 Associated Press story in an Austin newspaper, when the Texas House of Representatives passed a midwife registration bill. This was aimed at limiting the midwife's activities and requiring her to disclose to her clients what those limitations were.[62]

In a report on midwifery in Texas, researcher Laraine Benedikt explained that this topic evokes emotional and moral responses: that is, there are "for" and "against" categories. Recently, she reported, "midwifery has become a tense political issue and a feminist issue." While the powerful medical lobby cites the incompetence and ignorance of some midwives and the dangers of home births, the feminists champion a woman's right to choose a method of birth and also the right to choose to practice midwifery as a profession. Benedikt concluded that midwifery has greatly changed, both in philosophy and in practice, in modern times.[63]

An interview with Niki Richardson, who founded the Austin Lay Midwives Association (ALMA), is included in the Benedikt report. Mrs. Richardson and her husband were determined that their second child would be born at home. When their midwife was out of town at the time her labor began, she and her husband delivered the baby themselves.[64]

Mrs. Richardson had strong spiritual convictions about giving birth. She explained that childbirth is a normal bodily function, not an illness. This was her justification for handling it in a nonmedical way. She stated that with a midwife one can take a "holistic approach" and make the birth experience rewarding for the whole family. The ALMA organization offers preparatory classes as well as birth and postpartum care. A prenatal program was in the planning stage at the time of this report.[65]

CURRENT PRACTICES

Ruthe Winegarten, citing the Texas State Department of Health midwives survey quoted above, found an increase in the use of midwives during the late 1970s. She reported that this midwife movement developed "with the rise of the women's movement in the 1970s . . . based on a growing desire of some women to return the birthing process to women." Mentioning that Mexican-American women have preferred midwives for many reasons, Winegarten named Mrs. Sarah Castro as the first of three licensed Mexican-American midwives practicing in the San Antonio area. Mrs. Castro has also organized a group for Mexican-American midwives.[66]

In the sixty-sixth session of the Texas Legislature, Senator Uribe saw two of his efforts to pass regulatory legislation concerning midwifery die: one bill perished in committee and the other, passed by both House and Senate, was vetoed by then-Governor Clements. A companion bill introduced by Senator Brooks in the sixty-sixth session was also defeated. Two sessions later, however, in 1983, the sixty-eighth session passed SB 238, an act amended by the seventy-third session to become current Texas law concerning the practice of midwifery. There is a sunset clause attached to this act that will make it expire by September 1, 2005, unless steps are taken before that date to extend it.

Under this law, a nine-member midwifery board is provided, to be appointed by the Texas Department of Health. This board must consist of three lay midwives, only one of whom may be a licensed health care professional; one certified nurse-midwife; a licensed pediatrician; a licensed family practitioner or obstetrician-gynecologist; and three persons not practicing or trained in a health-care profession. These three are to represent the public interest. One of the three must be a parent with at least one child born with the assistance of a midwife.

The midwifery board must further provide, or approve of, manuals of instruction for midwives and training courses for them. Midwives who have taken some approved form of basic training are eligible (for a fee) to take a written or oral examination, which the board must provide in both English and Spanish. The board makes public a roster of documented midwives. Included in section 16 (e) (f) (g) of the Texas Midwifery Act in a list of midwives' duties are admonitions to "encourage a client to seek prenatal care . . . [and] to seek medical care if the midwife recognizes . . . [a] complication . . . to childbirth." Midwives must disclose to each client their legal limitations and requirements. This disclosure must be in both English and Spanish.

Among the prohibited acts are use of prescription drugs (except under a doctor's supervision), use of forceps, and assisting at any childbirth other than a normal one unless the life of the mother or child is in immediate danger. This Texas Midwifery Act (Article 4512i, Vernon's Texas Civil Statutes) was amended most recently on November 22, 1993, by the seventy-third legislature. Most of the wording in the amendment concerns spelling out requirements and restrictions on midwifery board membership. It also more specifically allows the board to establish a minimum number of hours of continuing education required of midwives in order to renew their documentation. It is up to the board to "determine key factors for the competent performance of the midwife's professional duties." A few other technicalities were added, but the substance of the midwife's duties and prohibitions was not changed by the amendment.

According to Belva Alexander, administrative assistant to Cecelia

Nobles, midwifery program director in the Division of Women's Health, Texas Department of Health, midwives practicing legally in Texas today are not licensed but documented. This documentation must be renewed annually. The current fee for documentation is $200, and there were about 245 documented midwives in the state after the January, 1996, deadline. To become documented, a midwife must have successfully completed one of six approved courses. Two such courses are offered in El Paso. Tyler and Grand Prairie each have one. The two remaining courses are based in Austin and in Claremore, Oklahoma. These latter two are correspondence courses available to anyone in the state.[67]

chapter 2

NURSES AND NURSING

From prehistoric times, societies have needed to care for their sick and injured. Family members or others who showed a natural ability and willingness to devote themselves to this service acquired reputations as caretakers and were frequently called upon to succor the suffering. For most of history, the only training available in nursing skills was the practical experience gained at the patient's bedside. The coming of the Christian era with its ideals of compassion and self-sacrifice inspired the beginning of religious groups that dedicated themselves to nursing. Several orders of monks and nuns in the Roman Catholic Church were dedicated to nursing. Deacons and deaconesses in the Protestant Church assumed as their main concern the care of the sick and needy. In 1836 a young German minister named Theodore Fliedner and his wife, Fredericke, started the Institution of Protestant Deaconesses at Kaiserswerth on the Rhine, and it was there that Florence Nightingale received her only formal training in nursing. In turn, she developed the concept of nursing as a secular vocation.

Some pioneer nurses in Texas, as well as some doctors, acquired their titles by self-appointment. There were no doubt a number who were as disreputable and hazardous to their patients' health as Dickens's infamous Mrs. Gamp, but there were many others who through skills gained by experience and by genuine concern earned the everlasting gratitude of their patients.

In Texas as in other states, nurses with professional degrees sometimes devoted their life work to particular hospitals. Years of dedicated effort as the first obstetrical nursing supervisor at Saint Joseph's Hospital in Houston taught Stella Kinzy to rely on her own practical in-

Mrs. Lillie Jolley seated with aide. Courtesy Memorial Hospital
Southwest, Houston, Texas

tuitions. "She was using the La Maz method before it was invented," remarked an obstetrician friend who had relied on her expertise many times.[1] Also in Houston, Lillie Jolley became superintendent of nurses at Memorial Hospital, where she was a main force in the development of the nursing school. Texas nurses served in time of war, and some gave their lives in the service of their country. Others, like Louise

Dietrich, May Smith, and Helen Moore, dedicated their lives to using their special talents to bring about important changes in nurses' training and practice. And the female religious orders of the Roman Catholic Church suffered many casualties as they selflessly endured dangers and hardships in establishing and staffing many of Texas's earliest hospitals.

UNLICENSED NURSES

A few of the names and deeds of the earliest pioneer nurses in Texas have survived. Without any scientific training, they cared for their patients using a mixture of common sense and compassion. The following examples of a Native American, an African American, an Anglo-American, and a Jewish American could, of course, be multiplied many times.

SARAH RIDGE

Sarah Ridge's mother was the Princess Susannah, the daughter of the last hereditary chief of the Five Civilized Tribes, whose territory ranged from north to near the Great Lakes, south to the Gulf of Mexico, west to the Mississippi, and east to the Atlantic Ocean. Sarah was educated in the Cherokee mission schools and at a seminary for young ladies in Winston-Salem, North Carolina. On her family's plantation she learned the Cherokee methods of treating illnesses with herbs and also the white man's use of medicine in taking care of the family and the slaves.

Sarah married George Washington Paschal, a lawyer, and in 1848 they moved to Galveston. During the terrible outbreak of yellow fever in 1850, Sarah's reputation as a healer became legendary. She threw open her house to the sick, filling the rooms and halls with beds. Sending the slaves to collect large quantities of leaves from the orange trees in Galveston, she made an orange-leaf tea to stop the inflammation of the stomach and bring down the fever. It was said that she never lost a patient, and Dr. Edward Randall, a local physician, gave her credit for saving many lives.[2]

MARY MADISON

Mary Madison, a free African American, was one of the first nurses whose name was recorded in the history of the republic. Arriving in

Galveston between 1841 and 1843, she won the respect of the citizens of the area, who petitioned the legislature asking that she be allowed to remain among them as a "free woman of color." Eighty-two signatures were on the petition, which attested, "She is a very valuable citizen, in a variety of ways: especially in the capacity of a nurse in cases of sickness: and many citizens and strangers who have been afflicted with disease, have experienced her kindness, her attention and watchfulness when such qualities are really needed."[3] On December 3, 1851, the legislature passed an act to permit Mary Madison to remain in the county of Galveston, citing as reasons evidence that she was law-abiding, had demeaned herself with becoming propriety, and had "rendered services as a nurse to the sick."[4]

ANNIE ELIZABETH BROWN

When it became evident that the country was on the brink of civil war, Annie Moore Brown and her husband, Benjamin Brown, converted their Louisiana property into money and began a long journey to California, where they planned to settle. When they reached Texas, however, they found they could not go through El Paso because of hostile Indians and because the Mexican government would not allow them to travel through that country. Benjamin Brown tried freighting and farming to support Annie and himself and their two children, who were born in Texas. When Indians ambushed and killed their neighbors and stole the Browns' horses, Benjamin went to Fort Worth to seek employment. While there he died of typhoid fever, leaving Annie to care for the children.

These were hard times for a young woman who had grown up on a rich Louisiana plantation. She took in boarders, including Bigfoot Wallace, the famous scout and Indian fighter. Hearing from him and others of the bounteous land around Bandera, she decided to move there. For six months of the year she taught school and for the other six months she did nursing. Later she was employed as a full-time nurse for three years at the Maverick ranch. When the Mavericks moved to San Antonio, she went with them and continued in her profession of nursing for thirty years under the supervision of doctors in that city. She also traveled by stagecoach to Boerne and Kerrville to perform nursing duties there. Late in her life she turned to ranching and made a comfortable living at it.[5]

During the Civil War, many women used their practical experience to fill the urgent need for nurses. Such a woman was Rosanna Dyer Osterman, one of Texas's earliest and most generous benefactors. In 1836, her brother Major Leon Dyer had escorted the defeated Mexican general Santa Anna to Washington, D.C., and it was Leon Dyer who persuaded Rosanna and her husband to come to Galveston to set up a general store in 1839—a venture that proved to be highly successful.

When the yellow fever epidemic of 1853 broke out in Galveston, Rosanna Osterman created a temporary hospital on the family grounds where she nursed victims of the disease. She also acted as a volunteer nurse during the yellow fever epidemics that occurred between 1854 and 1866. After Galveston was blockaded during the Civil War and business came to a standstill, most Jewish families left for the mainland. But Rosanna chose to stay and opened her home as a hospital where she nursed both Confederate and Union sick and wounded. She also acted as a courier of military information to Confederate officials in Houston. In gratitude for her nursing services, the Eighth Texas Infantry Regiment published a letter of thanks to her in the Galveston *News*.

In February, 1866, Rosanna Osterman drowned in a steamboat explosion on the Mississippi River. Her will provided generous bequests to various Jewish charitable organizations in Houston and Galveston. It included benefits for Hebrew benevolent societies, widows' and orphans' homes, schools, synagogues, and the Galveston Sailor's Home.[6]

Nursing Schools

Professional nursing began in the 1850s with the work of the English nurse Florence Nightingale. After the Nightingale School of Nursing was established in London in 1860, its graduates traveled all over the world to teach nursing. The first nursing schools in the United States were opened at Massachusetts General Hospital in Boston, Bellevue Hospital in New York City, and the New Haven (Connecticut) Hospital in 1873. Miss Nightingale's reforms were slow to reach the South. Untrained male attendants (with the exception of nuns) took care of the patients in Texas hospitals, and most doctors thought this was the way things should remain. It took an accident suffered by a beautiful little girl and a group of determined Galveston women to change the status quo.

When the child, Ella Goldthwaite, a member of the prominent Sealy family of Galveston, broke her hip in a fall, she was taken to a hip specialist in New York. On her return to Galveston, she was accompanied by Dorthea Fick, a graduate of Mount Sinai's School of Nursing. By the time Ella died in January, 1890, after a long illness, Fick's abilities had convinced a number of influential women in Galveston that a training school for nurses should be a part of the newly opened John Sealy Hospital. Forming a board of lady managers with Ella Goldthwaite's mother as president, they set out to overcome the antipathy of many older doctors to having white women working in hospitals. When their words made no impression, the women threatened to boycott these older doctors by calling in younger physicians to deliver their babies. They also used their ingenuity to raise money for the training school by extracting subscriptions from Galveston citizens and by an extensive round of bazaars, luncheons, banquets, and operatic and musical extravaganzas.[7]

Thanks to the efforts of these indefatigable women, the first training school for nurses in Texas opened on March 10, 1890, at John Sealy Hospital in Galveston with Nurse Dorthea Fick as its director. The board of lady managers had recruited the first class of eighteen freshmen with difficulty and only after weeks of continuous statewide advertising to persuade the public that nursing was a respectable occupation for young women. The students were required to be of good moral character, in good health, between the ages of nineteen and thirty-five, and able to read, write, and do simple arithmetic. Lectures in various branches of medicine were given by the doctors of the hospital, but the basic training for these first nursing students involved hands-on experience in taking care of patients. On May 2, 1892, six of the original eighteen enrollees remained to receive their diplomas.

In 1897, when the University of Texas took over the school, it became the first school of nursing in the United States to be an integral part of a university. The board of lady managers was thereby relieved of the arduous task of maintaining the school. Courses, which were taught by the faculty of the medical school and the superintendent, included for the first year anatomy, physiology, elementary medicine, materia medica, and surgical nursing. In their second year the nursing students studied obstetrical and gynecological nursing; pediatric nursing; dietetics; urinary diseases; nervous diseases; diseases of the eye, ear, nose and throat; massage; and hygiene. Ward duties still took up most of the students' time. During the first year they served as assistants on the wards; in the second year they performed duties assigned them by the superintendent either in the hospital or as private duty nurses. Instruction and training, meals, lodging, and laundry were all free, but their time was not. Duty hours for day nurses were from 7:00 A.M. to 7:30 P.M.; for night nurses, from 7:00 P.M. to 7:30 A.M. with an "occasional" afternoon off. They received seven dollars a month to cover the cost of textbooks and of the uniforms they were required to wear.[8] In 1907, the two years training course was lengthened to three years.

Over the years, the school expanded to become the University of Texas System School of Nursing with schools in six major cities before it was disbanded in 1976. Eight years after the opening of the nursing school at the University of Texas Medical Branch at Galveston, the El Paso Hotel Dieu School of Nursing opened its doors in 1898. The school of nursing at Saint Paul Hospital in Dallas was established in 1900, and in 1902 nursing schools were started at Seton Infirmary in Austin and at King's Daughters Hospital in Temple. A year later, the Santa Rosa School of Nursing in San Antonio was founded, and in 1904 in Fort Worth Saint Joseph School of Nursing opened.

That same year, the Scott and White School of Nursing began operation in Temple. The student nurses, who lived at the hospital, received fewer than 150 clock hours of instruction over their two-year training period and worked twelve to sixteen hours a day on the wards. The superintendent of nursing services was also the training director, and graduate nurses—later called registered nurses—trained the students. For the first three decades of the school's existence, the typical trainee was a young woman who had grown up on a farm or in a small town and had about eight years of formal schooling. Good health, strong backs, and sturdy feet were physical essentials, and the most desirable potential nurse was "a keen learner, but not too cocky; quick to respond, but not too aggressive; cheerful, but able to take her work seriously."[9]

First nursing students graduated from Temple Sanitarium.
Courtesy Scott and White Hospital Archives, Temple, Texas

Early nursing schools in Texas were run to suit the needs of the hospitals or of the doctors that established them, and there was a great disparity in the quality of training. Also, many nurses still learned their skills by simply apprenticing themselves to a doctor who taught them his preferred methods of nursing. In 1903, North Carolina, New Jersey, New York, and Virginia had become the first states to enable qualified nurses to become registered nurses, or RNs, as they were called.

On February 22, 1907, nineteen nurses met in Fort Worth to form the Texas Graduate Nurses' Association (TGNA), whose first objective was to persuade the Texas Legislature to pass a law governing licensing procedures for nurses. When such a law was passed in 1909, Texas nursing education was officially standardized, and the profession took a giant step forward. Thanks to the efforts of the association, Texas nurses could achieve the coveted RN status. During the next five decades, one of the outstanding leaders of the organization would be a dedicated Yankee who had come to Texas by happenstance.

A. LOUISE DIETRICH AND THE TGNA

Born in Ossining, New York, in 1878, A. Louise Dietrich was one of eleven children. After graduating from Saint John's Riverside Hospital School of Nursing in Yonkers in 1899, she did private duty nursing in New York City for three years. On a train trip to California in 1902, she had a layover in El Paso. Apparently the city instantly attracted her, for she moved there that same year and remained in El Paso for the rest of her long life. Her employers quickly recognized her leadership qualities, and after serving as directress of nursing at Providence Hospital for seven months, she was promoted to superintendent of the hospital.[10]

In 1908 Louise Dietrich attended the Texas Graduate Nurses Association's second meeting in San Antonio. The members wasted no time in putting her talents to use: she gave the response to the welcoming address, presented a paper on "The Use and Abuse of the Uniform," was appointed to the nominating committee, and was chosen to represent the organization at the National Associated Alumnae meeting in San Francisco. Two weeks later at the national meeting, she suc-

The Temple Sanitarium, Temple, Texas.

The Temple Sanitarium, about 1912. Courtesy Scott and White
Hospital Archives, Temple, Texas

cessfully applied for and secured membership for the Texas group. In writing the history of the TGNA, Jennie Cottle, its first president, commented that in electing Louise Dietrich as their representative they had "builded better than we knew."[11]

Louise Dietrich continued to serve the TGNA in various capacities: as secretary-treasurer, first vice-president, president, chairman of the Red Cross Nursing Service Committee, and council member. In 1929 she became full-time general secretary of the association and continued in that role until 1955. During those years the association office was located in her home with her address on its letterhead. The minutes of the annual meetings almost always listed a paper presented by her on some phase of nursing, and they also revealed that she led the way in setting up many of the organization's projects. These included initiating a public health course at the University of Texas and conducting institutes throughout the state as a form of continuing education for nurses. The TGNA bestowed several awards on Nurse Dietrich

LEFT TO RIGHT: *Instructor Catherine Clark, Miss Eden (a student) with Charlie the Skeleton, Hermann Hospital School of Nursing, Houston, Texas, 1938–41. Courtesy Hermann Hospital Archives, Houston, Texas*

and honored her for her many contributions by establishing in her name a fellowship that provides financial aid to enable graduate nurses to further their careers.

In addition to the TGNA, Louise Dietrich, who never married, devoted her enormous energy to health care. With Emily Greene, another nurse, she opened Saint Mark's Hospital in El Paso, and for several years she was in charge of the El Paso Public Health Center. Her activities spilled over the border of her adopted state when she and Greene undertook to manage the Baby Sanatorium at Cloudcroft, New Mexico, during the summer months. For eight years, from 1913 to 1921, they took turns ministering to the needs of the hundreds of babies who were brought to the cool, bracing heights of Cloudcroft to escape the heat and dust of El Paso, where so many of them succumbed to "summer complaint" (diarrhea) or other epidemics in the days before mechanical refrigeration and air-conditioning.[12]

In 1923, when the Texas Legislature enacted the Nurse Practice Act, which included the position of educational secretary for the Board of Nurse Examiners of the state, Louise Dietrich was named the first secretary. One of her responsibilities was to evaluate schools of nursing throughout the state, and in one six-months' period she traveled over thirteen thousand miles and wrote more than 780 letters—without any secretarial help.[13]

Beyond her nursing interests, she took an active part in a number of other organizations, including the Texas League of Women Voters and Saint Alban's (Episcopal) Parish. When she died at the age of eighty-three in 1962, the Texas Legislature passed a resolution recognizing her contributions to nursing.[14] And at Saint Alban's, a stained-glass window incorporating in its design a likeness of A. Louise Dietrich's nursing cap and training-school pin was installed. It is called the Resurrection Window.

MAY SMITH AND THE BABY CAMP

When seven nurses gathered for tea in Dallas on a rainy Saturday in March, 1913, they naturally talked shop. They dreaded the coming of hot weather and the inevitable infant epidemic of summer diarrhea (viral enteritis) with its high death toll from dehydration in babies of indigent families. Old Parkland, the only hospital available to the parents of these children, was overcrowded and dirty with no special facilities or staff to care for children. Sparked by the impassioned pleading of May Smith, the nurses decided to meet the problem head on by setting up a "baby camp" where they could volunteer to care for sick infants whose parents could not afford private medical care.[15]

Born in South Carolina in 1874, May Forster Smith received her nursing degree from Cooper Hospital in Philadelphia, and in 1908 she came to Dallas to work at a sanitarium. Appalled by the infant mortality rate, she lay awake nights trying to think of a solution. Encouraged by the backing of her fellow nurses, she persuaded the Red Cross to lend four tents and received permission to set them up on the grounds at Maple and Oak Lawn Avenues where the new Parkland Hospital was being built. The nurses improvised beds from laundry baskets, tore up old sheets for diapers, and solicited donations of baby clothing. In addition, May Smith used her own funds to supply vital equipment. By April 6 the tents were ready: one was to be used for administrative purposes, one for nurses' sleeping quarters, one as a diet kitchen, and the fourth as the baby ward, equipped with eight sleeping baskets.[16]

In addition to providing treatment and care for the babies, the nurses instructed the mothers in the proper preparation of milk and bottles, the eradication of dirt and flies, and in general hygiene and sanitation. When the weather turned windy and rainy, May Smith and her nurses turned out to tighten the tent stakes and rope down the flaps. In good weather the nurses set up a "sun room" under an oak tree with cribs draped with mosquito netting. The legs of the cribs were set in tomato cans filled with kerosene to repel ants. That summer three premature babies were saved using an improvised incubator made of a washboiler placed on an inverted dishpan warmed by bricks heated on a potbellied stove.[17]

Dr. Hugh Leslie Moore, Dallas's first pediatrician, was one of May Smith's chief allies. Dr. Moore, who had studied at the Great Ormond Street Hospital for Sick Children in London, had an office in downtown Dallas and taught at Baylor Medical School (which moved to Houston in 1943). He encouraged the nurses in their efforts and volunteered his services to check the babies in the camp each day. Others were also impressed by the work of the determined nurses and gave support. The City Federation of Women's Clubs offered to donate operational expenses if the city would provide a permanent structure, and the Texas Graduate Nurses Association pledged to have two nurses on duty at all times. Plans were drawn up for a small frame cottage to be located one hundred yards from the main building at Parkland.

Despite rain a large crowd turned out on May 16, 1914, to admire the new building with its fifteen foot wide screened porch, diet kitchen, bathroom, and sleeping quarters for nurses. Twenty white double metal cribs replaced the baskets, and light blue woodwork and muslin-curtained windows replaced the blank tent walls. A year later, further improvements at the Baby Camp included adding another nursery room, glassing in the front porch, and building a screen sun porch across the back of the building.

By 1917 the Baby Camp had become a year-round operation with May Smith as its director. Operating on a shoestring budget, she struggled to keep it solvent, begging and borrowing funds wherever she could. Despite its precarious financial situation, the Baby Camp continued to expand and even opened a pediatric nursing school for third-year nursing students. In 1923 when the Community Chest adopted the Dallas Baby Camp and Hospital as one of its agencies, the financial burden eased.

Director Smith was pleased that they could now have better medical equipment, but she was not satisfied that they were adequately serving the needs of Dallas's babies. She continued to campaign for a "real" baby hospital. In 1929 her dream came true when Tom L. Bradford, chairman of the board of Southwestern Life Insurance Company, donated $100,000 to build a hospital at the corner of Maple Avenue and Turtle Creek Boulevard. May Smith had become acquainted with the Bradfords when she nursed their daughter Elizabeth through infantile paralysis (poliomyelitis). When sometime later she nursed Mrs. Bradford through a serious illness, Mr. Bradford was impressed with her professional skill and with her devotion to caring for needy infants.

Local newspapers rejoiced when the Bradford Memorial Hospital for Babies opened on January 1, 1930, calling it "beautiful and magnificently well-equipped" and pointing out that it was the only baby hospital in the United States south of Saint Louis. It had a red tile roof, stuccoed walls, and stained-glass windows; the top floor contained an operating room, a dining room and kitchen, and a private apartment for May Smith. The ground floor contained several large wards and an incubator room plus rooms for private patients whose fees would help defray the cost of the free care given to babies of indigent families. It was, indeed, an impressive building, but the timing was bad. The Bradfords suffered a stunning financial setback in the stock market crash two months before the grand opening and were unable to endow the hospital as they had intended.

Again May Smith found herself begging, pleading, and cajoling the public into supporting the hospital because although the doctors donated their services, other costs including staff salaries, utilities, drugs and medical supplies, equipment, food, and formula had to be covered. And she insisted that the hospital continue to expand its educational function. In 1930 she wrote, "No hospital does its duty to the community which supports it unless it is a center of health education in the locality from which it derives its support."[18] So under her direction Bradford Memorial continued to operate a school for senior nurses, as well as an outpatient clinic and a weekly well-baby clinic.

In the face of opposition, she and the members of the Bradford Board of Trustees insisted the hospital accept children regardless of race, color, or creed, and despite their financial difficulties during the Depression, they cared for many African-American and Hispanic babies. As an example of May Smith's practical approach to problem solving, after a group of gypsies abandoned a baby girl at the hospital and radio broadcasts and other publicity failed to locate them, the baby was moved into May's apartment and cared for by her and the other nurses until it was adopted at the age of six.

When May Smith died of pneumonia in 1938, Dallas newspapers eulogized her as "a modern Florence Nightingale."[19] Children's Medical Center was built adjacent to Parkland, the old building was demolished, and the third floor of the center designated the Bradford Memorial Hospital for Babies. It was a far cry from the tent Baby Camp of 1913, but its goals remained the same as those that motivated May Smith and her fellow nurses back on that rainy Sunday: to save the lives and serve the needs of the infants of the community.

HELEN MOORE: ACTIVIST

A number of Texas nurses went on to have successful careers in other fields, and some, like Helen Moore, used these occupations to the advantage of the nursing profession in their state. Helen Moore was an activist in the best sense of the word: all of her life where she saw a need, she stepped up and did something about it.

Women Pioneers in Texas Medicine

When the Moores arrived in Texas City in 1906, there was no doctor in the city, so for five years Mrs. Moore used her training as a nurse to perform emergency medical services for the community. Discovering that the city had no public library, the Moores donated books and furniture to establish one. In 1916 Helen Moore organized the Texas City Red Cross Branch and served as its first president.

Among the mementos of Helen Moore at the Moore Memorial Public Library in Texas City is a yellow button saying, "I will March for Full Suffrage June 7th, Will You?"[20] Woman Suffrage was a cause dear to Helen Moore. Together with Minnie Fisher Cunningham of Galveston (the first woman in Texas to receive a degree in pharmacy from the University of Texas Medical School and president of the Texas Equal Suffrage Association), she worked hard to get the suffrage amendment passed. When Mrs. Cunningham asked Helen Moore to chair the district organization, she wrote, "I am not going to pretend it is an easy work that I am calling you to, but I believe you are the woman for it. I know your spirit and your fire, and they are irresistible."[21] The determination of like-minded women across the state did prove irresistible, and in March of 1918 the women of Texas gained the right to vote in primaries—two years ahead of the national amendment. In 1924 Helen Moore served as president of the Texas League of Women Voters, and she was a representative to the Democratic National Conventions in New York City in 1924 and in Houston in 1928.

During the two terms she served in the Texas Legislature (1930–32 and 1934–36), Moore worked for legislation to improve hospitals and correctional institutions. She visited every state institution for the insane and mentally ill at her own expense, filed reports on the terrible conditions she found, and introduced bills to alleviate them. She also sponsored legislation for improvements in orphans' homes and schools for the physically handicapped. As chairman of the eleemosynary committee and a member of the appropriations committee in the 1930s, she was instrumental in establishing the Galveston State Psychopathic Institute at UTMB. In 1936 when she left the Texas House, the House *Journal* called her "a pioneer in the humanitarian history of our state."[22]

During wars, women have always nursed and comforted the sick and the wounded just as Rosanna Osterman did in Galveston during the Civil War. The few women in the Alamo while it was under siege had to use all of their skills. Susanna Dickinson, who had her baby with her, cooked and nursed and eventually became the messenger of defeat when Santa Anna sent her to give Sam Houston the news of the Alamo's fall. Another woman, Andrea Castanon Villanueva, a Mexican, reportedly nursed James Bowie, and some fifty years later she was granted a pension by the Texas Legislature.[23] During the Spanish-American War in 1898, there were female nurses under contract on duty at Fort Sam Houston in San Antonio.[24] When the Mexican Revolution began, Leonor Villegas de Magnon, a graduate of Mount Saint Ursula in New York City, was teaching kindergarten in Laredo. She transformed the kindergarten into a hospital and nursed the wounded from both sides of the border. With her friend Jovita Idar she founded La Cruz Blanca (the White Cross) in 1913, joined Carranza's forces, and was awarded five medals for her efforts to help the suffering.[25]

During both world wars, nurses served in the army at home bases such as Camp Travis in San Antonio and with Red Cross units at home and overseas. Murle Wann (Heaton), a graduate of the University of Texas School of Nursing in Galveston, was one of the army nurses who served at base hospitals in France in 1917. Numerous Texas nurses served in all branches of the armed services in World War II. Two nurses who were graduates of the Scott and White School of Nursing in Temple were held prisoner by the Japanese for three years after the fall of Corregidor.

In World War II, aeromedical evacuation using flight nurses provided rapid transfer of the wounded from front lines to hospitals and significantly increased the survival rate of injured servicemen. An airvac nurse, Jeanette ("Tex") Gleason, bailed out of an airplane in the China-Burma-India theater of war and survived. Texas flight nurse Lt. Reba Whittle of Rock Springs was shot down and taken prisoner by the Germans. Because of her nurse's flight wings pin, she had difficulty persuading her captors that she was not a pilot.[26]

Another flight nurse, Wilma ("Dolly") Vinsant, graduated from the

Alice (Kight) Morris, 1944 graduate, wearing U.S. Cadet Nurse Corps uniform. Courtesy Hermann Hospital Archives, Houston, Texas

University of Texas School of Nursing in May of 1940. In 1942 she enlisted in the Army Nurses Corps and was graduated from the army air force's School of Air Evacuation in 1943. She was sent to England, where she completed her required quota of missions, but she insisted on going on one more dangerous evacuation flight despite her commanding officer's objections. This one cost her her life when her plane was shot down. On the campus at UTMB Vinsant Dormitory was named in her honor, and in her hometown of San Benito a hospital known as the Dolly Vinsant Memorial Hospital was established in her memory. President Truman posthumously awarded her a purple heart and a personal citation for bravery.[27]

La Verne Farquahar was another nurse who answered to the nickname "Tex." A 1933 graduate of the King's Daughters School of Nursing of Temple (est. 1902), Tex Farquahar joined the Army Nurses Corps with the "relative" rank of second lieutenant in 1942.[28] Assigned as a surgical scrub nurse, she served in North Africa and was then sent to Anzio, Italy, with the Thirty-third Field Hospital—an important part of the Allied assault. Because it was a vulnerable location on a beachhead near stores of anti-aircraft batteries and gasoline and ammunition dumps, the area was subject to frequent hits by the Germans and had earned the name "Hell's Half Acre." On the evening of February 10, 1944, Lieutenant Farquahar was working in the operating tent while German long-range artillery bombarded the area with 8mm shells. When the operating tent suffered a direct hit, Tex Farquahar was killed instantly. Posthumously she received the Purple Heart, the American Campaign Medal, the European-African–Middle Eastern ribbon, and the World War II Victory Medal.[29]

Roman Catholic Religious Orders

In the Roman Catholic Church a charismatic healer, Vincent de Paul, founded the nun-hospitalers as a special order for nursing services in 1668. Following this example, a large number of ecclesiastical nursing orders formed and spread throughout the world as part of the Roman Catholic world missions. During the Civil War, three Catholic orders— Sisters of Saint Vincent, Sisters of Charity, and Sisters of Mercy— supplied most of the nurses for the United States Army Sanitary Commission. In the latter part of the century, various orders of nuns arrived in the eastern states as missionaries to set up orphanages, schools, and hospitals.

Nuns trained as educators and nurses were invaluable in establishing schools and hospitals throughout Texas in its early days. Arriving in the raw state in the nineteenth century as missionaries in the service of God and mankind, their purpose was to save bodies as well as souls and minds. Before 1900, nine orders of nuns had arrived and established numerous schools and hospitals.

Ursuline nuns, who had been in New Orleans since 1727, were the first order to volunteer for service in Texas after it became a state. On January 19, 1847, Mother Superior Saint Arsene Blin arrived in Galveston with six nuns, and by February 8 they had opened the first Catholic school for girls in Texas. During the yellow fever epidemics of 1848, 1853, and 1858, they served as nurses, and during the Civil War they turned their school into a hospital for casualties from both sides. When devastating hurricanes struck Galveston Island in 1875 and 1900, the nuns nursed the survivors. And again, when fires wreaked havoc in 1854 and 1882, they used their nursing skills to alleviate the suffering of the victims.[30]

The second group of nuns, Sisters of the Incarnate Word and Blessed Sacrament, arrived in Texas in 1852. Besides opening many academies and parochial schools, they operated the Burns Hospital in Cuero and Huth Memorial Hospital in Yoakum.[31]

The first two Sisters of Divine Providence came from Alsace-Lorraine (France) to Texas in October of 1866 to open the first Catholic school in Austin. As their numbers increased they opened more schools in Louisiana, Oklahoma, and Texas until they were operating sixty-nine academies and schools with a combined enrollment of nearly ten thousand, including the academy that became Our Lady of the Lake College in San Antonio. Eventually the sisters operated three hospitals and four clinics in addition to their schools.[32]

In 1875, two Sisters of Mercy from New Orleans arrived at Indianola to start a school, but no sooner was the school opened in September than it was destroyed by a hurricane. The sisters then moved the school to Refugio, where they established a motherhouse. In 1894, they founded Mercy Hospital in Laredo and later operated hospitals in Cuero, Slaton, and Brownsville.[33]

The first hospital established by the Daughters of Charity of Saint Vincent de Paul was the Hotel Dieu in El Paso in 1892, and their second hospital in Texas was Saint Paul in Dallas. Arriving in Dallas in 1895, the four sisters occupied a small cottage on Hall Street. Groundbreaking for the building was held on November 13, and while it was under construction the sisters provided hospital and nursing services for patients in their own living quarters. Sister Mary Bernard Riordan, the mother superior of the group, directed the builders, and in July of 1898 the new 110-bed hospital opened. It was very up-to-date with both gas and electric lights and radiators as well as fireplaces. Room rates, which included medical attention and nursing care, were advertised as one dollar and up. Some of the first patients were wounded soldiers returning from the Spanish-American War.

In 1900 the sisters began a school of nursing in the hospital; their first graduating class consisted of three nurses. In 1915 an annex increased the total number of beds to three hundred. But even this capacity was insufficient when the flu epidemic of 1918 reached Dallas, and the government asked the Daughters of Charity to supply hospital facilities for area soldiers. When all the rooms and floor space were filled, sixty-three army tents holding four beds each were erected on the hospital grounds to take care of the convalescent soldiers. As soon as that emergency ended, another arose as thousands of Hispanics streamed into Dallas. They were escaping the aftermath of the 1920 revolution in Mexico and hoping to find jobs in the big city. Of course there was not work for all of them, and the Daughters of Charity opened a soup kitchen to feed the homeless, starving Mexicans. They also rendered health services to them.

Saint Paul Hospital has continued to serve the community throughout the twentieth century. When four million dollars was raised in 1958 to build a new Saint Paul in the Southwestern Medical Center complex, a prediction made by a Dallas paper in 1896, commenting on the original hospital, was recalled: "Its success is guaranteed in that the Sisters of Charity will assume its management."[34] Today St. Paul Medical Center includes a cancer center, a patient-care tower, and a center for the elderly.

Shortly after the turn of the century, the Business Men's Club of Waco asked the sisters of the Order of the Daughters of Charity of Saint Vincent de Paul to organize and run a hospital for that city. Providence Hospital opened its doors on January 1, 1905, and it has continued to grow and expand its services to the Waco community throughout the century.

SISTERS OF CHARITY OF THE INCARNATE WORD
Galveston: St. Mary's. The Sisters of Charity of the Incarnate Word was the most active order of nuns in pioneer medical service in Texas.

By the turn of the century, they had established hospitals in Galveston, Houston, San Antonio, Fort Worth, Beaumont, and Amarillo. In those early years they needed every scrap of their faith, dedication, and determination to overcome the obstacles thrown at them by man and nature from the time they arrived in Texas from Lyons, France, in 1866. On April 1, 1867, the Sisters opened Charity Hospital (later known as Saint Mary's Infirmary and renamed Saint Mary's Hospital in 1965) in Galveston, which is today the oldest private hospital in Texas. During the yellow fever epidemic of that year, Mother Blandine Mathelin died, leaving the other two sisters to carry on the work. In 1868 six more Sisters of Charity made the long journey over the Atlantic to join the Texas group, their transportation paid for by the Empress Eugenie, wife of Napoleon III.

Communication was a big problem for these early missionaries, who, as one nun reported, learned a "fair—if not elegant—speaking knowledge" of English from their patients.[35] The patients also suffered culture shock and sometimes resisted the attentions of the nuns with their "outlandish" costumes and their passion for cleanliness. At that time most sick people preferred to remain at home, cared for by family members. But there was a growing class of self-supporting people such as clerks, waiters, and other workers who lived in boardinghouses or hotels. To meet their needs and improve its own financial standing, Saint Mary's instituted a primitive insurance policy. Flake's *Semi-Weekly Bulletin* (August 7, 1869) explained the plan to the public:

> Any person paying the small amount of 25¢ a week—a dollar a month—in advance during health, is entitled to a bed for himself when ill, with medical attendance, nursing, food and all necessaries. We all know that next to a wife or a mother, the Sister of Charity is the best of all nurses. . . . Housekeepers will make subscriptions for one or more beds that they may have good accommodations for a sick servant. Benevolent individuals will do the same that they may have provision for any poor friend or stranger that may be thrown on their protection. It is insurance against sickness, and will save many an unfortunate from suffering.

Under this plan, in conjunction with its growing reputation for providing excellent nursing care, Saint Mary's Infirmary began to prosper.

Galveston's outstanding architect, Nicholas J. Clayton, designed two three-story buildings for Saint Mary's in 1875 and 1879.

The terrible hurricane of September 8, 1900, devastated Saint Mary's Infirmary as it did all of Galveston. Although the main buildings were of solid brick, the hospital's location at the eastern extremity of the city where the island narrows between the gulf and the bay made it vulnerable when the waters of the two met. All of the frame buildings around the infirmary were completely demolished, and in the main buildings all of the windows were shattered, walls were caved in, and part of the roof was torn away. In one building some of the sisters stood in the rising water, pulling to safety people who were helplessly floating by, until the first floor became completely inundated and everyone was forced to the second level. Terrified refugees found their way to the hospital until some fifteen hundred people jammed the buildings. When the storm subsided, many destitute citizens used the building shells as a temporary home, and the sister in charge of the kitchen set up a tent to serve them while other sisters arranged to have tar paper put over the damaged roofs. Total damage to the infirmary was estimated at eighty thousand dollars. As the nuns struggled to rebuild, they were saddened by the knowledge that on the opposite end of the island, ten of their sister friends and ninety-two children at Saint Mary's Orphanage had been swept away by the storm.[36]

In 1965 a new nine-story hospital replaced the 1875 Clayton building, and in 1983 a new hospital wing and a parking garage were added. In 1987 Saint Mary's became an operating division of the multi-institutional Sisters of Charity of the Incarnate Word Houston Health Care System.

San Antonio: Santa Rosa. In 1869 a cholera epidemic decimated the population of San Antonio. Since only a few doctors and midwives remained to care for the victims, the need for a hospital and nurses in that growing city became urgent. The Sisters of Charity of the Incarnate Word agreed to expand their mission to San Antonio, and Mother Madeleine Chollet and two other nuns set out on the journey by the slow stagecoach from Galveston. Traveling over rough terrain and stopping at every little village, it took them three weeks to arrive at their destination, where they were greeted by the news that the new building that was to have been their hospital and home had burned to the ground a few days earlier. Undaunted, the sisters resolved to help rebuild from the ashes and petitioned the people of the city for support.

The Reverend Mother M. Madeleine Chollet, foundress of the San
Antonio House and first superioress general.
Courtesy Incarnate Word Archives, San Antonio, Texas

Apparently their appeals were answered, for on July 20, 1869, the San Antonio *Daily Express* reported, "Donations to the new Catholic Hospital have been more than liberal."

Santa Rosa Hospital was named after Saint Rose of Lima, the first canonized saint of the New World. It was a two-story adobe structure combining convent and hospital with a few wards and private rooms for patients and a small chapel. Despite the generosity of the natives the hospital was heavily in debt, and following its opening, various San

Antonio groups sponsored benefit entertainments such as fairs and concerts. In addition to their nursing duties, the three sisters did much of the necessary work of running the hospital: scrubbing floors, washing linens, and preparing the patients' meals. Santa Rosa was still struggling in 1891 when the Rev. Mother Saint Pierre reported: "Our resources are none, the debts being greater than the income but . . . we trust to Divine Providence."[37] Providence did look kindly on the hardworking sisters, and Santa Rosa has continued to expand since its founding over 125 years ago. Today it consists of a large number of facilities providing programs and services designed to meet the needs of the ever-growing population of San Antonio as it approaches the twenty-first century.

Houston: Saint Joseph's. In the spring of 1887, a small group of the Sisters of Charity traveled from Galveston to Houston to establish Saint Joseph's Infirmary. Houston's mule-drawn streetcar took them to their destination on the corner of Caroline and Franklin Streets, where they found a large house and two small cottages in a state of disrepair. It took three months and the assistance of many local people to clean, repair, and furnish the house. By June 1, however, it was ready to receive patients and boasted such up-to-date conveniences as oilcloth on the floors and a bathroom on each floor with running water from the city's mains. The two cottages were fashioned into a chapel and a dormitory for the nurses. The rapidly expanding hospital soon included a converted church (old Saint Vincent de Paul made into a ward for men) and a cottage lent to the group by Houston dry-goods merchant W. L. Foley, which was transformed into a ward for women patients.

In December of 1890, when a smallpox epidemic struck Houston, construction of a pest house in an abandoned city cemetery called Old Potters' Field was hastily begun. As soon as it opened, four sisters went to the smallpox hospital to work and remained there for the three months the virulent disease raged. Praising their dedication, a doctor told a *Houston Post-Dispatch* reporter: "What these women have done for the sick, dying and dead at the grim old hospital will probably never be told. They not only took care of the living, but on several occasions are known to have assisted at the interment of the dead. No task was too great for them to undertake."[38]

The Houston City Council passed a formal resolution thanking the

Sisters of Charity of the Incarnate Word "who, without money and without price, amid scenes of desolation calculated to appall the stoutest heart, literally took their lives into their hands and by their devoted ministrations proved themselves veritable angels of mercy among the stricken sufferers during the recent Small Pox Epidemic."[39]

By the summer of 1894, patients were moved into the new three-story Saint Joseph's Infirmary, which was equipped with telephones, electricity, and other modern conveniences. The sisters were delighted that they would be able to give the patients every comfort available. But on October 16 at 2:00 A.M. a fire broke out in a boardinghouse on the same block. Although firemen arrived promptly and did their best, the flames spread rapidly; water pressure was low, and most of the buildings on the block, including the new hospital, were destroyed. The nuns, with the help of ambulatory patients, were able to get the bed-ridden patients out of the buildings, but two sisters lost their lives and a third was seriously burned. Again the citizens of Houston responded generously: many stores contributed 5 percent of their sales on two consecutive days; others sent groceries, linens, furniture, and other necessities; the *Post* sponsored a vigorous campaign to raise funds; and collections were taken up by benevolent associations.[40]

A new Saint Joseph's Infirmary was built on a block of land facing Crawford, LaBranch, Pierce, and Calhoun Streets, purchased by the order's council for $7,200. Designed by Nicholas J. Clayton, the building was a familiar landmark until it was demolished to make way for a new 700-bed hospital on the site. In view of today's encroachment of skyscrapers and expressways, it is startling to read the *Post*'s description of the location: "There is nothing to keep the southern breeze from the place. It is situated far from the noise and dust of the city and is especially adapted as a place for the sick."[41]

Beaumont: Hotel Dieu. In 1896 it was decided that the Sisters of Charity should build a hospital in Beaumont, a growing lumber town of about nine thousand in East Texas. Two sisters were accordingly sent there to select a site and make arrangements for purchasing it. Donations by lumber mill owners were generous, and on January 1, 1898, the Hotel Dieu—a three-story building with wards containing twenty-four beds, two rooms for private patients, and living quarters for the sisters—opened on the banks of the Neches River. During a smallpox epidemic the following year, the sisters isolated the victims and nursed them. Malaria occurred frequently in the low-lying area. When the Lucas oil gusher at Spindletop brought thousands of boom followers to town, a second frame building was hurriedly erected to care for fever victims as well as for sufferers of oil-field accidents. In 1909, the Hotel Dieu began a school of nursing, which continued until 1967.[42]

Temple: Santa Fe. Toward the end of the nineteenth century, the history of the Sisters of Charity of the Incarnate Word became intertwined with the history of railroad building in Texas. The Gulf, Colorado and Santa Fe Railway Company originated in Galveston, and its employees were accustomed to the high quality of the medical care they received from the sisters at Saint Mary's Infirmary. It was natural that when it was decided to build hospitals in other cities for the benefit of the railroad's employees, the sisters were chosen to operate them. Their nearly six decades of service at the Santa Fe Hospital in Temple exemplifies their dedication and superior skills in the field of nursing.

When five nuns stepped off a train in Temple in February of 1891, they found themselves objects of curiosity in the rough and rowdy farm and railroad town. Ignoring the stares, they went to work to equip a modest wood-frame building with meager supplies and set about treating the sick and injured that came to them from all up and down the railroad lines. The hospital's good fortune in acquiring the services of outstanding doctors, combined with the skillful nursing of the sisters, earned it a reputation for excellence. After a few years, the railroad replaced the original wooden structure with an impressive red-brick building with a white-pillared portico. The fourth floor contained the sisters' living quarters and a small chapel, along with the operating rooms. The number of sisters staffing the growing hospital increased steadily as they filled the positions of nurses, druggists, housekeepers, and administrators. The women also ministered to the emotional and spiritual needs of their patients, offering counseling and praying for the welfare of their souls as well as that of their bodies. When it was announced in 1948 that the Sisters of Charity of the Incarnate Word would leave the Santa Fe Hospital in Temple, the railroad board offered the order more money and pleaded with them to stay, and railroad employees signed petitions begging the nuns not to leave. But their long years of service in Temple had ended, and they departed to serve in other areas.[43]

Fort Worth: St. Joseph. Early in 1885 when the managers of the Missouri Pacific Railroad Infirmary in Fort Worth asked the Sisters of Charity of the Incarnate Word to take charge of the hospital, Mother Saint Pierre wrote, "We had firmly resolved not to take any more establishments for a time, but with this opportunity of doing so much good we could not refuse." And she added prophetically, "It is certain that this work will have its cross and contradictions; it would not be God's work if it did not meet with opposition or suffering from some source."[44] The eleven nuns who traveled from San Antonio to Fort Worth found a small wooden building with few conveniences situated so far from the center of the city that a horse-drawn trolley was used for the long commute. During its first year the little hospital was completely destroyed by fire, but all of the patients were carried to safety. The sisters set up beds for the sick in a temporary building and began negotiations with the Missouri Pacific Railroad for a fifteen acre tract of land to build a new hospital. Four years later when this new sixty-bed hospital was complete, they named it Saint Joseph's Infirmary, after the patron saint of the working man.

Patients were charged ninety cents per day or a dollar if an ambulance was necessary. Behind the building, the sisters raised fruits and vegetables. They kept chickens for eggs, cows for milk, and two horses for the ambulance. Besides all their other duties, they did the hospital's laundry by hand. In 1896 a three-story brick building replaced the original structure to meet the needs of the growing community, and in 1904 a school of nursing was established and housed in the original brick infirmary building. During the century following its humble beginning, Saint Joseph Hospital expanded rapidly under the direction of the governing board of the Sisters of Charity of the Incarnate Word. Sister Teresa Martin summed up their forward-looking attitude on the occasion of their centennial celebration. "I enjoy reminiscing about the past," she said, "but I believe we must all go with the times. I live for the present and look to the future."[45]

Amarillo: Saint Anthony's. When the railroad reached Amarillo in the Texas Panhandle, the town became, almost overnight, a major cattle shipping center for the many ranches in the area. The need for a hospital was urgent, and the Sisters of Charity of the Incarnate Word were invited to organize one. Consequently, on a blustery cold day in February of 1901, four sisters stepped off a train in the little town with the purpose of founding a hospital to serve the large area known as the High Plains of Texas. The owner of the Frying Pan Ranch had donated a plot for the building, which turned out to be a two-story red-brick structure standing alone on the wide-open prairie. Six weeks later, the nuns had transformed this stark building into a fourteen-room hospital and dedicated it as Saint Anthony's Sanitarium. There was no gas heating, electric lights, telephones, or adequate sewage disposal system. Nor were there paved streets or sidewalks, and patients arrived at the hospital by horseback or horse and buggy. Water was piped in from a windmill, but when blizzards howled and pipes froze, the sisters melted snow and boiled it to supply water for the patients. Increasingly, trains brought more people into the Panhandle to farm or ranch, and as Amarillo grew so did Saint Anthony's. In 1909, a two-and-a-half story addition was annexed to the hospital and a school of nursing started. Over the years more buildings were added until the little horse-and-buggy sanitarium became a jet-age sprawling complex near the heart of the city—still under the care of the sisters.[46]

These few examples of the work of the pioneer Roman Catholic sisters in Texas could be multiplied many times. In accordance with their vows, the nuns' salaries were turned over to their congregations. After providing for the sisters' needs, the religious congregations used the remainder of their earnings to establish more schools, hospitals, and orphanages and for other charitable work throughout the state. As the *Houston Post-Dispatch* said of the nuns who risked their lives during the city's smallpox epidemic, it is equally probable that the story of the dangers and difficulties endured by all the dedicated pioneer sisters as they selflessly ministered to the welfare of early Texans will never be fully told.

chapter 3

DENTISTRY
AND PHARMACY

Closely allied with the general practice of medicine are dentistry and pharmacy, each once embedded in a general practitioner's repertoire. Dental health and hygiene have, perhaps, been easier to separate from medical practice, partly because with modern technology so many specialized fields have developed within dentistry alone. The sole woman pioneer dentist discussed here covered—as much as she could in her practice—all the dental fields from orthodontics to oral surgery. She lived and worked in those dreadful times when a dentist would say, "Better have them all out at once," and the patient would have to agree. Those days are over now for most if not all dental patients. We are keeping our teeth cleaner, healthier, and, in most cases, for a lifetime. The toughness and durability of a Mary Shelman inspire awe and wonder in a generation more and more accustomed to expecting painless dentistry and miracles of preservation.

Emily Teed Hicks scored a unique achievement by becoming the only woman orthodontist in Texas, a title she held until 1960. She and her husband, Dr. Hardy Hicks, had practiced general dentistry together for a number of years before Emily decided to specialize.[1]

Another related area, one essential to modern medical practice, has established itself separately from the individual physician. Since the days when a doctor ground and pounded out his own concoctions and pills in his office, a giant pharmaceutical industry has replaced him, international in scope and, sadly, materialistic in outlook. On the other hand, wonderful, effective drugs have been and are being developed daily, and they are nationally regulated by a hard-nosed agency whose assignment is to protect the consumer. Moreover, their prices are at least partially moderated by the influence of supply and demand.

Of the two early women pharmacists discussed, one used her license and the other apparently did not after one discouraging year of equal work for unequal pay. Hettie Cunningham and her husband were as devoted to pure drug laws and quality pharmaceuticals as they were to each other. "Minnie Fish" Cunningham was as deeply devoted, but her energy went to the welfare of women in general. She championed the right to vote and thereby partake of the government that controlled women, their lives, their medical resources, and their medicines.

Women Pioneers in Dentistry

MARY LOU SHELMAN, D.D.S. (1866–1955)

All eleven children of Alexander and Catherine Hardesty Shelman of Kentucky were encouraged to study and learn; in fact, Alexander built a school for his children in their small farm community. When Mary Lou wanted more education, her parents enrolled her in a nearby convent. She did not stay there long, for she found the "menial tasks" and strict regime uncongenial. Some of the Shelman siblings branched out to Texas and New Mexico after their father died in 1890 and the estate was divided. In those days, one could obtain a teaching certificate by passing an examination. It is probable that Mary Lou taught in one of those states for a time. Years later, she remarked that many of her students were older than she was.[2]

Her teaching experience made Mary Lou want to learn more. Her mother's example of helping others may have turned her attention toward a health-care career. Catherine Shelman's daughter-in-law remarked that Catherine was "the most loved person in her community. She would get on a horse at midnight in case of illness . . . and go to help anyone." People in trouble would always send for "Aunt Kate."

Dr. Lucy Hobbs, the first woman to graduate from a dental school in any country, finally won admittance to Ohio Dental College in 1866, the year Mary Lou was born. Dr. Jessie Estelle Castle, formerly of Michigan, opened a dental office in Dallas in 1897, just a year before Mary Lou received her certificate from Texas's board of dental examiners. (Dr. Castle did not have to pass the examination since she had graduated from the University of Michigan Dental School in 1896.)

Until 1905, dentists who had graduated from reputable dental colleges were permitted to register their diplomas and practice without examination. Since Mary Lou Shelman did pass the four-day dental examination and receive her permanent certificate in 1898 from the State Board of Dental Examiners (with her name given as "M. L. Shellman"), it seems clear she did not attend dental college. If she served an apprenticeship, records of it have not been discovered. She always gave the year 1898 as her licensing year. She was the first woman to receive certification by examination to practice dentistry in Texas.

Dr. Shelman kept current in her profession by attending postgraduate training sessions and dental conventions and by working with dentists who were well known for certain techniques. She completed postgraduate study at the Chicago Post-Graduate Dental College in 1902, and

Mary Shelman, D.D.S. Courtesy Wanda Keller Sivells, granddaughter and Texas Woman's University, Denton, Texas

DENTISTRY, PHARMACY

in 1911 she went through a training session with Dr. Price Cheaney in Dallas. She enrolled her daughter, Loren, in kindergarten there, and the two of them stayed with the Cheaneys for this session.

Her share from her father's estate enabled Dr. Mary, as she came to be called, to finance a horse and buggy and a gun. So equipped, she collected dental supplies and began a search of central Texas counties for a place where a woman dentist might be accepted. She registered in eight counties; she settled in practice first at Rising Star, Eastland County, and later at Cross Plains, Callahan County. The two communities are about fourteen miles apart. Mary Lou, born left-handed, had learned to write with her right hand so as to avoid being kept after school, but her left was the stronger hand, and she used it to extract teeth. In both locations she made house calls when needed during the horse-and-buggy days. When cars became numerous, anyone wanting a home visit had to come and get her.

Dr. Mary wore spotless, starched white linen dresses, and her shoes were always polished. She had no assistant, but her reception room, operating room, and laboratory were "scrupulously clean." She made her own crowns, inlays, bridgework, and dentures. She enjoyed telling the story of a woman patient who went to a doctor for a physical examination. The doctor told her that her ailments must be caused by her teeth and advised her to have them all out. The woman promptly removed her teeth—a real-looking set of dentures made by Dr. Mary![3]

Butter, eggs, chickens, and other produce were given as payment for dental services in the early days. Dr. Mary found that people who had no dentist available used home remedies including spirits of camphor, snuff, chewing tobacco, kerosene, oil of cloves, liquor, and hot poultices. Before nerve-blocking techniques came into use, Dr. Mary kept a bottle of whiskey handy for those who needed fortification against the pain of treatment. That bottle was used strictly medically; Dr. Shelman was against drinking. When she hired a first-class builder who was known to have an alcohol problem, she made him sign an agreement not to get drunk while he was building her home.

In 1905 Mary Lou Shelman married a building contractor, Samuel Esau Graves. Their only child was a daughter, Loren, who remained with her mother when the couple separated in 1913 and were divorced the following January. Years later, after Loren's marriage, Dr. Shelman had her maiden name legally restored. Probably not many of her patients noticed the change; she had become "Dr. Mary" to all of them.

Through her working years Dr. Shelman kept up to date by taking postgraduate courses and attending dental conventions. Often she was the only woman at those sessions. She carried a Harrington and Richardson six-shooter in her black bag during long trips over lonely roads. The only time she was known to use it, however, was when she was alone and some "mischievous boys" decided to frighten her. She took care of that problem by firing a few shots into the air.

After she had spent time in Lincoln, Nebraska, learning orthodontics in order to prepare braces for Loren, Dr. Mary opened an office in Canyon, Texas. From there she traveled once a week to a small farm community, Happy, where she had a temporary office in the back of a drugstore. In Canyon Dr. Mary provided (mostly free) dental work for World War I soldiers. It may have been this connection that led the draft board in World War II to summon her repeatedly to join the military. At first Dr. Shelman thought these notices were a joke, and she threw them away. When their tone became threatening, she finally wrote to the board, explaining that although she loved her country, she was a seventy-year-old woman and she didn't believe she was the kind of dentist the armed forces needed. She never heard from the draft board again.[4]

Returning to Cross Plains in 1918, Mary Shelman continued her practice in spite of poor health. Finally, she convinced a doctor in Brownwood to perform six simultaneous major surgical procedures on her. It took her almost a year to get over this operation. It is no surprise to learn that this spunky woman pulled her own teeth as needed and made herself a set of dentures that lasted her over twenty-five years.

Although a bad fall down some stairs forced her to use a crutch, Mary continued to practice (eventually graduating to a cane), until 1936, when she sold her office and practice and retired. She then renovated her home to provide six rooms she could rent to supplement her income. The last two years of her life were spent with her daughter and granddaughter. Mary Lou Shelman died on a visit to her granddaughter in Wharton at the age of eighty-nine.[5]

HENRIETTA MANLOVE CUNNINGHAM (1852–97)

Texas's first registered woman pharmacist lived only forty-five years, but she managed to pack her short lifetime with useful work and unusual accomplishments. Not the least of these was her successful marriage and partnership with a heroic Confederate veteran thirteen years her senior.[6] Henrietta Manlove was born in Indiana on February 11, 1852. Her mother, Mary Emily Pease, had been sent to the wilderness as a teacher by her home state of New York. In pioneer Indiana she married William Manlove and bore four children. She died in 1857. When Mr. Manlove moved to Texas is not known; he died in Llano County in 1892.

Henrietta, usually called "Hettie," married into a true Texas pioneer family when she took James Louis Cunningham for her husband. His father, Leander, had come to Bastrop with two brothers in 1833 when Texas was still Mexican territory and settlers expected occasional harassment from hostile Indians. Leander, educated far above the average for his day, was a man of deep intellect and varied talents. He became a lawyer, a judge, an alderman, a mayor, a builder of schools and churches, a postmaster, a merchant, a railroad agent, and a heroic soldier. He was also a friend of Sam Houston, a pronounced prohibitionist, and a profoundly religious man.

James Louis Cunningham was born at Bastrop in 1839, one of six children. Although his father did not want James to become a doctor, James was in medical school and twenty-one years old when the Civil War began. He enlisted at once in Company G, Seventeenth Texas Infantry. He went into one engagement as second lieutenant and came out a captain. When his right elbow was shattered in the Battle of Pleasant Hill, James fought off doctors who predicted gangrene and wanted to amputate his arm. He insisted on having his arm bandaged in a sling at a right angle. Released from the hospital, he served out the remainder of the war in the quartermaster's department.

After the war, James reentered medical school and began rigorous exercises that eventually restored full use and dexterity to his right arm. He received his degree as a physician and surgeon and, in deference to his father, became a pharmacist. After he married Hettie Manlove, they built a two-story frame house and opened their first drugstore as part of Miller's General Store at Waelder, Texas.

Hettie taught all grades of school in the Masonic Lodge building, which had also been commandeered as Waelder's first church. For awhile she also taught summer school for adults and children at Possum Trot (about seven miles away; later called Prickly Pear, and finally Seguin). James would drive her over on Sunday evenings, and someone would bring her home on Friday evenings in a wagon or a buggy. Hettie took her four children along, and the townspeople competed for the honor of having them stay the week.

James kept up with medical advances and took an interest in state politics. He became the House reading clerk for the Constitutional Convention of 1876, where the present Texas Constitution was adopted. The Cunningham home became a forum for political discussion. When the Fifteenth Legislature convened in the summer of 1876, James was calendar clerk for the session. He also became a Royal Arch Mason and, in Houston, joined Dick Dowling Camp, United Confederate Veterans.

Hettie could hardly have helped becoming interested in pharmacy: James, who was horrified by the existing situation in which anyone could stir up and sell any concoction he or she could think of, was working hard for a uniform pharmacy law. Candy manufacturers had at last been stopped from adding Paris green to their products, but in general there were no laws governing the safety or contents of medicine and no requirement that advertising had to be truthful. Finally, a law that left much to be desired was passed in 1889. The year before, the same year her fourth child was born, Hettie passed the state pharmaceutical examination and officially became the first woman pharmacist in Texas.

Having Hettie as an active partner made it easier for James to attend meetings of the Texas State Pharmaceutical Association, which he joined in 1890. That year, along with R. H. Walker, he presented a paper that suggested restricting the sale for medical purposes of a list of dangerous drugs. The paper indicated that dry-goods merchants and grocers in small towns and large were handling such potentially potent products as calomel, laudanum, paregoric, hair tonic, nearly all chill tonics, and cough syrups. The association adopted a resolution to restrict such sales.

Hettie joined the association when it met in Houston in May, 1891. Later that year she was nominated to be third vice president, but "at the request of Mr. Cunningham" her nomination was withdrawn. When the association met in Dallas in 1893, however, Hettie Cunningham was one of two delegates elected to represent the Texas group at the American Association and World Congress, which formed part of the world's Columbian Exposition in Chicago.

Hettie took their thirteen-year-old daughter, May, and five-year-old son, Ben, with her to Chicago. The other delegate from Texas seems not to have arrived. Her report to the Texas Association was given in Austin in 1894, and in 1895 Hettie was elected third vice president by acclamation. This time she accepted the honor. Their children seem never to have been forgotten during the busy Cunningham days. May remembered her childhood as a happy time of taffypulls, lawn croquet, sing-alongs around the piano, and church activities. Often the minister or out-of-town friends joined the family for Sunday dinner.

In 1892 the Cunningham family moved from Waelder to Houston and established a pharmacy on Liberty Road (later listed as 1118 North San Jacinto). Its name was first The People's Drug Store; later it became Cunningham's Drug Store. Four years later, James's father died at age eighty-six. Free of filial obligation at last, James was listed in the 1897–98 census as a physician and surgeon living on Liberty Road. Hettie kept a boardinghouse at that address. Perhaps this was necessary to augment their income while the new medical practice grew.

In October, 1897, Henrietta Manlove Cunningham died of yellow fever in an epidemic that raged through Houston. Her devoted husband died nine months later—May maintained it was simply from a broken heart.

Five years later, another female became the first woman to receive a pharmacist's degree from the University of Texas Medical Branch at Galveston. Although her name was Minnie Fisher Cunningham, no kinship between the two distinguished pharmacists has been discovered.

MINNIE FISHER CUNNINGHAM (1882–1946)
"A 21-year-old ball of fire" is the way a journalist characterized Minnie Fisher Cunningham, formerly of New Waverly, in 1903, one year after she became the first woman in Texas to receive a pharmacy degree from the University of Texas Medical Branch in Galveston. This descrip-

Minnie Fisher Cunningham between friends. Courtesy PICA 16817,
Austin History Center, Austin Public Library

tion characterized her whole-hearted plunging into the suffragist movement that was then building steam in the Lone Star State.[7]

Minnie Fisher proved the worth of the home schooling her mother
had given her by passing, at sixteen, a state examination to earn a teaching certificate. After teaching a year, she enrolled in the University of
Texas Medical Branch pharmacy school. After graduation, she worked
as a pharmacist in Huntsville for a year. She later remarked that the
inequity in pay she experienced there "made a suffragette out of me."
In 1902 Minnie married Beverly Jean (Bill) Cunningham, a lawyer and
an insurance executive. The marriage was an unhappy one, perhaps
because of her political activism and his alcoholism. She became a
widow in 1927.[8]

Since Texas was under Mexican rule until 1836, Spanish law regulated the status of Texas women until then. A woman's property became her husband's when she married; so did anything of value she might acquire later. Women were barred from witnessing wills, along with "a minor under fourteen, a dumb person, a homicide or similar offender, a Moor or a Jew."[9]

After the Civil War, when a Republican convention rewrote the state constitution, a "radical" element actually dared to suggest universal suffrage. This motion was tabled, and in 1875 the convention specifically barred from the vote "women, children, idiots, lunatics, paupers, and felony convicts." Although the Women's Christian Temperance Union joined the cause of woman suffrage, not much had been accomplished by 1903.[10]

In Houston that year, the three Finnigan sisters formed an equal-suffrage league. This inspired Minnie Cunningham to form her own ad hoc committee in Galveston. Minnie Fish, as her devoted followers soon dubbed her, declared, "Opportunity . . . must be snatched off the griddle by women who see the issues of the day."[11]

Early enthusiasm soon cooled in confrontation with the hard reality that although most women might sympathize with the suffragist cause, they lacked the courage to come out and say so. Former president Grover Cleveland typified the more arrogant of the opposition when he remarked, "Sensible and responsible women do not want to vote. The relative positions to be assumed by men and women in the working out of our civilization were assigned long ago by a higher intelligence than ours." In the words of a journalist reporting this remark "activists readily acknowledged the existence of an intelligence infinitely higher than that possessed by Cleveland."[12]

Minnie Fish put the female franchise on the legislative calendar of Texas once in 1911 and twice in 1913. The most recent of these attempts fell only three votes short of passage. Minnie was elected president of the Texas Woman Suffrage Association (subsequently the Texas Equal Suffrage Association) in 1915, which then included chapters in twenty-four cities. By 1915, American women in a dozen states had won limited voting rights. All but one of these states was west of the Mississippi, but Texas was not one of them.[13]

Knowing that passing a constitutional amendment required getting a clear majority from an all-male vote, Texas suffragists chose instead to put pressure on legislators to tinker with the law in order to allow women access to primary elections. They went to work on the legislators one at a time. In March, 1918, Governor Will Hobby signed into law the Primary Election Bill, turned, and handed the silver pen to a triumphant Minnie Fisher Cunningham. Although it was not the full suffrage they wanted, this foot in the voting booth was nevertheless a giant step forward for women striving for equality.[14]

Minnie Fish continued serving as president of the Texas Woman Suffrage Association until 1920. She also worked in the national suffrage movement through the Washington, D.C., organization. Minnie continued to work for the cause until the Nineteenth (or Susan B. Anthony) Amendment to the Constitution of the United States was passed on August 26, 1920.[15]

Ten years later, her name and those of Annette Finnegan of Houston and Eleanor Brackenridge of San Antonio were unanimously nominated by the state board of the League of Women Voters to be inscribed on a memorial tablet in Washington, D.C. Criteria for receiving this honor were their "ability, courage, and God-given vision to lead the fight for suffrage by serving as state president in the days when suffragettes were ridiculed and maligned."[16]

During World War I, Minnie Cunningham chaired the Texas Woman's Anti-Vice Committee and the Liberty Loan Committee. She was first executive secretary of the National League of Women Voters, and in 1923 she organized a Women's National Democratic Club. In 1928 she ran for the United States Senate, and she ran for governor of Texas in 1944.[17]

Truly, this first woman pharmaceutical graduate proved powerful medicine for the cause of Texas women's rights. She is said to have chosen this epitaph for herself: "Born a woman, died a person."

chapter 4

MEDICAL PRACTICE, RESEARCH, TEACHING

Specialization was not a choice available to many of the early licensed women physicians, since they lived in and served areas where their services were often the only medical help available. With both men and women, in the early days of specialization it often happened that a practitioner would switch his or her choice of specialty during internship or residency or even after beginning private practice. Sometimes the physician would practice one specialty a few years and then decide to switch to another.

This changing of fields was a common occurrence with women doctors. Then too, in decades past the specialty labels were fewer, and each covered a wider range of activity. A physician like Dr. Grace Danforth, for example, might be referred to as a "psychiatrist" because of her employment in a mental institution instead of by virtue of her training.

Sometimes the individual doctor's special interests would lock her into an area other than her stated specialty. Elva Anis Wright, for example, who spent her life fighting tuberculosis, had planned for a much broader general career in public health. At other times, a special need within her medical institution or a scientific breakthrough would cause a doctor to become a specialist. Such a physician was Dr. Claudia Potter. Intending to be a general practitioner, she became the first woman anesthesiologist in Texas. As another example, Dr. May Owen had planned a nursing career but became a pathologist because the need for such a specialist, combined with her natural bent, changed her course.

Given such Protean characteristics in the nature of specialization, the women practitioners and their teachers are grouped by the area of human need where they have given most of their service, instead of by specialty. Some of the women who made the earliest breakthroughs are called simply "Pathfinders." Public-health physicians are grouped as "In the Community," and so is Lena Edwards, whose contribution was individual, isolated, and independent.

The section "In the Hospital" includes the kind of practitioner whose services would mainly be found in a hospital setting. "In the Clinic" includes physicians in private practice or in practice with others, though obviously part of their time would be spent in the hospital also.

"In the Classroom" includes those who worked and made important discoveries in research laboratories, for all these exemplary researchers also taught, and most or all of their important findings were made with the help of their students. Easiest to classify because of the dissimilarity of their fields are the three psychiatrists, who are grouped in a section called "In the Mind."

Not easily classified, but certainly deserving not to be forgotten, are those women physicians who looked their male colleagues in the eye and demanded recognition through membership in medical organizations. Acceptance of the first licensed women physicians by all-male medical societies could be bitterly difficult; however, in 1888 an article on feminine physicians in *Daniel's Texas Medical Journal* boasted that Texas could claim the honor of being the first to receive a woman into fellowship without a dissenting voice. Dr. Florence E. Collins, the "lady applicant," was the first one to join the Texas State Medical Association, and she was accepted into membership by "a rising vote."[1] Dr. Collins was secretary and treasurer of the Travis County Medical Association.

Probably not the first woman physician in Dallas but certainly the first one to be accepted into the Dallas County Medical Association was Dr. Grace Danforth, a graduate of Women's Medical College in Chicago. She had little success in building a Dallas practice, however; perhaps the male doctors' chivalry did not extend to sending referrals her way. The Texas Legislature appointed her as assistant physician in the lunatic asylum at Terrell. Sometime later she moved to Granger to resume private practice. In 1895, when she died suddenly of a brain hemorrhage at Circleville, the *Texas Courier–Record of Medicine* reported that her death was supposedly caused by an overdose of acetanilid taken to relieve headache.[2]

Dr. Margaret Ellen Holland, the first woman to practice in Harris County, like many early licensed women doctors, was a graduate of Women's Medical College in Chicago. Her move to Texas happened because she was engaged as private physician to the invalid wife of Major R. B. Baer. Dr. Holland cared for the invalid until 1919, while she maintained a busy practice as well.[3]

It may be difficult to imagine a woman who was only thirty-four in 1980 as a pioneer, but Judith Craven broke new ground in three ways in that year when she became the youngest person, the first woman, and the first African-American woman to head the city of Houston's Department of Health.[4] A year younger, Shirley Marks-Brown is another African-American achiever. She was the first African-American woman to train at New England's oldest psychiatric hospital, McLean, in Belmont, Massachusetts. A staff psychiatrist and ward administrator at the VA Hospital in Houston in 1978, she also became an assistant professor of psychiatry at Baylor College of Medicine. Of her career, she reflected, "At times it's really difficult to sort out whether certain obstacles have been put in front of me because I'm a woman or because I am black."[5]

Readers should bear in mind that the following examples of pioneer women physicians are just that: a few samples extracted from a large pool of medical women whose achievements deserve public notice. One of the considerations has been the desire to indicate by inclusion that women of all races and creeds have contributed to women's equal standing with men physicians in that noble endeavor: the art, craft, and practice of medicine.

Pathfinders

SOFIE DALIA HERZOG (HUNTINGTON), M.D.
(1846–1925)

In Brazoria County Dr. Sofie Herzog was as famous for her colorful personality as she was for her medical skill, and many years after her death people were still telling "Dr. Sofie" stories. A favorite was the one about the necklace she wore made out of twenty-four bullets she had extracted from patients suffering from "lead poisoning." And many

Dr. Sofie Herzog, 1911. Courtesy Brazoria County Historical Museum, Angleton, Texas

remembered seeing her flying down the railroad track on a handcar, hanging onto her hat and her medical case as a rail hand pumped furiously to get her to a medical emergency on time. Then there were her collections: intricately carved and gaudily painted walking sticks from all over the world, deer heads, stuffed birds and reptiles, and animal skins covering the floors and walls of her office. If that wasn't enough to keep her patients' minds occupied, there was her medical display in jars of alcohol, including fetuses—which she considered supported her belief in the theory of evolution, a belief not shared by many of her contemporaries.

Sofie Dalia was born on February 4, 1846, in Vienna, Austria, where her father was a prominent physician. When she was fourteen or fifteen Sofie married Dr. August Herzog, the chief doctor at a Vienna hospital. She gave birth to fifteen children, including three sets of twins, but as so often happened in the nineteenth century, many of them died in infancy. Dr. Herzog's reputation had reached the United States, and in 1886 when the United States Naval Hospital in New York offered him a position, he and Sofie moved there with their seven surviving children.[6]

Since their household included four servants and a tutor, Sofie found time to follow her dream of studying medicine. She took classes in New York schools, but realizing that Vienna was far ahead of the United States in offering women equality in medical training, she made the long commute to study there. On her final trip to Vienna to receive her degree, she took with her the last surviving twins, Rene and Raul. On the voyage they died of diphtheria and were buried at sea.[7]

After receiving her degree from the University of Gratz in Vienna, Sofie practiced medicine in Hoboken, New Jersey, for nine years. August Herzog died around 1895, and although her medical practice was quite successful, Sofie was restless. Her children were grown, and at almost fifty, she still had enormous vitality and a desire for new experiences and challenges. Her youngest daughter, Elfriede Marie, had met and married Randolf Prell, a merchant from Brazoria, Texas, while he was on a visit to Philadelphia where Elfriede was teaching. After a visit to the newlyweds at the turn of the century, Sofie decided to move her practice to Texas.

Situated on the Brazos River, Brazoria, established in 1828 as a port and trading center for Stephen F. Austin's colony, was a far cry from the cities of Vienna and New York. Deep woods of oaks festooned with Spanish moss surrounded the wooden houses on dirt streets. Along the Brazos bottom the high-pitched scream of the panther and the deep boom of the alligator as well as the warning rattle of the dreaded rattlesnake often shattered the quiet. Saloons abounded, and frequently quarrels were settled with the guns that were a common part of men's apparel.

The natives never forgot the shock waves created by Dr. Sofie Herzog's arrival in that small community. Most of them had never seen a woman doctor *or* a woman with cropped hair *or* a woman riding a horse astride like a man. Oblivious to the stares and the gossip, Sofie continued her habit of solving her problems in practical ways. She had thick, naturally curly hair, and the easiest way to manage it was to cut it short with the ringlets hanging down from her man's hat. When she discovered that a carriage was often unable to travel on the muddy trails leading to her patients' homes, she bought a good horse and had a seamstress make her a long split skirt for ease in riding. When the trails were dry, she used a carriage and a driver to make her rounds, and her bemused neighbors often heard her call to her carriage driver in her strong German accent, "James, be sure not to forget to throw the horses over the fence some hay."[8]

At first Sofie set up her office in the Prell's home, where Elfriede assisted her in performing operations and in taking care of patients. Her medical skill and her dedication to her patients won their goodwill, and she soon became affectionately known as "Dr. Sofie." But her interest in doing research and in discovering new cures caused her to go too far for her son-in-law. One day as she was testing a new ointment on a smallpox patient she had smuggled into her office, Prell broke in, demanding to know how she dared bring the victim of a terrible, contagious disease into his home. Equally furious, Sofie demanded to know how he dared come into her office while she was treating a patient. As the argument raged, the terrified patient fled.[9]

After a cooling-off period, the two made up, but Sofie decided she needed an office where she would be completely independent. Consequently, she had a long building constructed on Market Street with space for an office and drugstore where she could mix medications, as well as an emergency operating room and a rear bedroom. Worried about her living alone, Prell brought her a gun, but she refused it on the grounds that she might shoot someone with it. Instead she kept her poker near her and told her son-in-law that it had proved to be quite effective in warding off unwelcome visitors.[10] In this building Dr. Sofie would practice medicine for the rest of her long life.

Here she was free to experiment and to add to her exhibits. She was especially fascinated by rattlesnakes and encouraged her patients to bring her the snakes they killed. Hanging them on the side of the carriage house, she skinned them, and after they had dried she mounted the skins on red satin ribbons to hang in her "museum." Ignoring her son-in-law's warning that she could be poisoned by handling the snakes, she continued to add to her collection until one day she developed a rash and a swelling that spread over her body. Fortunately a skin specialist in Houston, although astonished at the cause of her malady, was able to cure it.[11]

MEDICAL PRACTICE, RESEARCH, TEACHING

Sofie's passion for collecting animal hides and skins put her in danger another time when she expressed her desire for an alligator to add to her collection. In a few days an acquaintance came dragging a hideous seven-foot alligator into her office. He dumped it on the floor, and after taking time out to admire it, Dr. Sofie continued her work. That night after she had retired, she heard a loud crash and opened the office door to find the beast moving its tail. Grabbing her trusty poker, she climbed on her bed and kept watch for the rest of the night until she could get help to make sure the alligator was ready to join her collection.[12] Many women in the early nineteenth century owned alligator handbags, but Dr. Sofie's was as unconventional as its owner. Made from one small alligator, it still has the feet attached and can be seen at the Brazoria County Historical Museum in Angleton.

Dr. Sofie was an active member of the Texas Medical Association, attending local meetings and conventions, making speeches, and taking a lively part in debates. No doubt in her early years in Texas, she was an object of curiosity to the male physicians, who themselves had met few women doctors and certainly few as well-trained or as colorful.

A few years after Dr. Sofie's arrival in Brazoria, railroads began to proliferate in the states, and the Saint Louis, Brownsville and Mexico Railway began laying track in South Texas. In the raw country the work was hazardous, and workers suffered frequent accidents or illnesses. As a result, Dr. Sofie was often called to construction sites that were difficult to reach. Undaunted, she used any available transportation, riding train engines, boxcars, and cabooses as well as handcars at any time of the day or night. Railroad workers and local officials came to know they could depend on her to answer their calls no matter what the difficulties. They passed along their appreciation of her work to their superiors, so that when the job of chief surgeon of the railway opened up and Dr. Herzog applied for it, her application was readily endorsed. When, however, the eastern officials discovered it was a woman they had appointed to the post, they wrote her a letter respectfully asking for her resignation on the grounds that it would be too difficult an assignment for her. Dr. Sofie indignantly refused to resign, telling the official that if she failed to give satisfaction, they could fire her, adding that she asked "no odds" because of her sex. She remained a highly valued employee of the railroad (through its incorporation into the Missouri Pacific Line) until her resignation a few months before her death.[13]

Besides delivering babies and treating illnesses and injuries, Dr. Sofie was often called upon to extract bullets. She was proud of the skill she had acquired since coming to Texas in digging out these lead pellets and boasted that only twice had she failed to find the bullets for which she probed. When she had collected twenty-four bullets, she took them to a jeweler in Houston and had a necklace made with the pellets separated by gold links. She wore this necklace as a good-luck charm, and at her request it was placed in her coffin when she died.[14]

Besides being a dedicated and successful doctor in her community, Sofie Herzog was also a respected business entrepreneur. She invested heavily in choice real estate in the Brazoria area, and she built a hotel, the Southern, across the street from her office. During the grand opening of the hotel a shot was fired at Dr. Sofie by the demented wife of a former employee of the railroad, who believed the doctor had caused her husband's discharge. Although the bullet barely missed her, Sofie showed neither fear nor alarm and later related the incident as a good story on herself. Many prominent visitors, including Bernard Baruch, stayed at the Southern when they came to Brazoria County to explore opportunities connected with the Freeport Sulphur Company or in real estate. It became a local center for social activities and remained in use for many years after Dr. Sofie's death.[15]

Dr. Sofie also built a church in Brazoria. When she perceived a need, she seldom stopped to consult anyone else but went ahead full speed with her own plans. Distressed at the condition of the Catholic cemetery with its weeds and broken-down individual fences surrounding family plots, she decided to make it look more like the orderly cemeteries she was used to. She proceeded to enclose the grounds with a new fence and remove the rickety ones and the weeds. She quickly found herself involved in a bitter quarrel with the parish priest and other protestors who wanted the cemetery kept as it was. Frustrated, Dr. Sofie left the Catholic church and joined the Episcopal congregation, to which the Prells belonged. Seeing the need for a new church, she built and furnished one for the grateful Episcopalians, who continued to use it until it was destroyed by a hurricane in 1932.[16]

As cars became more common, Dr. Sofie decided she needed to update her mode of transportation. As usual she ignored the warnings of friends and family as to the dangers involved and purchased a

Ford Runabout. After taking a few lessons from the salesman, she made her rounds in style, tooting the horn and calling greetings to everyone she met.

An even more radical change in her life was her marriage at the age of sixty-five after almost twenty years of widowhood to Col. Marion Huntington, a seventy-year-old twice-widowed plantation owner. On her wedding license she carefully crossed out the "Miss" or "Mrs." designation and wrote in "Dr.," but she added the name "Huntington" to her business cards. The main house at Ellersly Plantation was a two-story brick structure with white columns and a long, curving driveway. It was located about seven miles from Brazoria, and for the rest of her life she drove daily between the plantation and her office.

Many people who knew Sofie Herzog Huntington well have commented that she seemed to have a dual personality, and this ability to change roles may be why she was able to so successfully combine her career and her family life. From the blunt, no-nonsense doctor or businesswoman, she slipped easily into the role of the typical, doting *grosmama*. Her crochet basket was always at hand in her office, and between patients she snatched a few minutes to work on the miles of doilies, shawls, scarfs, and bedspreads she made for her children and grandchildren. Her grandchildren adored her, and she talked of them and of her children constantly. When she felt she might be boring her friends, she apologized by explaining that when she couldn't see them, she had to have the comfort of talking about them.

Dr. Kenneth Aynesworth of the University of Texas Board of Regents certainly could not have had Dr. Sofie Herzog in mind when he wrote a letter in 1933 to Lillian Bedichek, stating that he would not encourage women to study medicine because "they simply cannot follow the profession of medicine and be a wife and mother."

Dr. Sofie remained active in her profession and in her private life until shortly before she suffered a stroke at the age of seventy-nine and died in a Houston hospital on July 21, 1925.

FRANCES DAISY EMERY ALLEN, M.D. (1876–1958)

In May of 1897 the *Fort Worth Gazette* enthusiastically described the graduation exercises of the charter class of the Medical College of Fort Worth University, and the reporter noted, "Among the graduates in the front row of seats appeared a bright winsome little woman, a fair

Minerva whose presence in the class was a feature of unusual interest."

The winsome Minerva was Frances Daisy Emery, one of two cum laude graduates in the class of sixteen men and one woman. As Dr. O. L. Fisher, president of the university, presented Dr. Emery's diploma, he commented on her "refining influence" on the class. He naturally did not remind the audience that three years earlier when Daisy Emery had applied for admission, there had been some resistance among members of the surprised board of the new medical school. However, since the admission policy did not specify men only, they had felt compelled to admit her.[17]

Daisy was the ninth of twelve children born to Elizabeth and James Wallace Emery. Her father, who had a background in classical literature and a master's degree from Bowdoin College in Maine, was an outspoken advocate of emancipation for slaves in the 1850s, and he instilled in his children a strong sense of personal justice. From her mother, Daisy inherited her petite size, pretty features, and characteristics of great energy and perseverance. At the age of four, Daisy announced her intention of becoming a doctor. Her commitment never wavered as she acquired her basic education in her early years in the public schools in Kaufman County, Texas; then, after the family moved to Fort Worth, she attended Fort Worth University. The opening of the medical school at the university in 1894 when she was seventeen seemed a heaven-sent opportunity.

Following her graduation, Daisy Emery went to live with a sister in Maryland so she could take her internship and residency at the Women and Children's Medical Center in Washington, D.C. The nation's capital was an exciting place for a young woman at the turn of the century. In her diary, Daisy recorded that she had gone "on wheels" to hear Jessie Askerman talk about Africa and the Boers, adding, "I never heard such eloquence from a woman." The next week she attended a lecture by Susan B. Anthony sponsored by the National Woman Suffrage Association. And a few days later, she went to hear a talk by the daughter of women's rights advocate Elizabeth Cady Stanton. Daisy noted in her diary that she was reading a book titled *Should Women Vote?* and that she had made herself a fine pair of bloomers (popularized in the 1900s by feminist Amelia Bloomer as a statement of women's equality).[18]

When her mother became ill with crippling rheumatoid arthritis,

Daisy returned to Dallas to care for her. She opened a small private practice and joined the faculty of Dallas Medical College as an instructor in diseases of children.

Dr. Walter Allen, a native of Tarrant County, received his degree from Fort Worth Medical College one year after Dr. Daisy Emery received hers. They corresponded while she was in Washington and renewed their friendship when she returned to Texas. The friendship became courtship, and they were married on November 30, 1903, in Dallas.

The Allens moved first to Vinson, Oklahoma, where Walter had established a practice. But six months later, when a tornado-spawned fire destroyed the Allens' home and half the town, they returned to Texas. From 1904 to 1910 the Allens had a joint medical practice in the rural community of Content in Runnels County. In the unincorporated village stood a general merchandise store, a blacksmith shop, a barbershop, a school, and a church. Next to their home was an office with a small pharmacy in back where they prepared prescriptions and dispensed medical supplies. Much of their practice, however, involved making house calls and traveling by horse and buggy or by bicycle over rough dirt roads that turned to mud after heavy rains. Following the birth of their daughter Frances Marion, Daisy needed all of her stamina since there was absolutely no one to hire to do housework: all of the farm wives in the area had their own children and housework plus endless farm chores to manage.

Their means of transportation improved as their practice increased; Walter bought a motorcycle and then a three-seater car, which he assembled. One of the drawbacks of their partnership was that they could never plan to travel together. Both Walter and Daisy attended the 1904 Saint Louis World's Fair—but not together. In order to keep up with the latest developments in their field, they took turns attending medical meetings. Trips to Dallas to replenish their supplies gave Daisy an opportunity to visit her family and also her in-laws, who lived in White Settlement, a small town west of Fort Worth.[19]

When the railroad bypassed Content for the equally rural town of Goldsboro, about ten miles away, the Allens moved there. Here a second daughter, Sheila Emery Allen, was born. In 1912 they moved to Newark, near Fort Worth. They were eagerly planning to accept an assignment in China as medical missionaries in 1913, but first Walter

The doctors Allen. Courtesy Moody Medical Library, University of Texas Medical Branch, Galveston, Texas, and Miss Frances Allen, Fort Worth, Texas

had to have kidney-stone surgery. During the operation in December he died, and at thirty-seven Dr. Daisy Allen found herself a widow with two young children.

Refusing offers by her relatives to reside with them, she moved to Fort Worth and joined the faculty of Fort Worth Medical College as a clinical instructor in pediatrics. After the college closed in 1917, she was free to devote her time to her private general practice, serving primarily women and children. At first her office was in a suite with two male doctors in the Fort Worth National Bank Building, but when the Medical Arts Building opened on a beautiful one-block-square park, she secured a single suite there.

Daisy's reputation grew largely through word of mouth as women patients told other women about the efficient, caring woman doctor in the heart of the city. Even though her practice continued to grow, she continued to give generously of her time to indigent patients. She also donated her services freely to the city-county hospital, and she held free clinics at the Wesley Community Center—often making home deliveries of the babies of clinic patients.[20]

She was a founding member of the Fort Worth Academy of Medicine and a member of the county, state, and national medical associations as well as the American Medical Women's Association.[21]

Despite her heavy medical duties, Dr. Allen was deeply involved in civic and religious affairs. A member of the League of Women Voters, she actively studied political candidates and their backgrounds and statements of policy, and she took her daughters to political rallies. She was also active in the First United Methodist Church of Fort Worth, serving as Sunday school superintendent, church organist, and choir member. She and her daughters had season tickets for Fort Worth's musical programs and frequently took advantage of the city's other cultural offerings. In her later years she enjoyed extensive travels in the Americas and in Europe with her daughters.

Daisy Allen was a good businesswoman and an early member of the Fort Worth Chamber of Commerce. She taught her daughters that the only "real" estate is real estate, and by the time of her death she had acquired a considerable amount of property. While they were still in Content, she had purchased two hundred acres a mile north of the town with one of her sisters and later bought the sister's share. Through the years she also invested in land in Callahan County and in Tarrant

County. Sometimes land was deeded to her by the families of patients who had no cash to pay for medical care, and some tracts of land were given to her by her father-in-law. Eventually some of her real estate did prove to be quite valuable.[22]

Dr. Allen continued in active practice until failing health forced her to end her fifty-three-year career in 1950. Even after her retirement, she continued to see a few longtime patients at her home and still made a few house calls to them. On December 7, 1958, at the age of eighty-two, she died of arteriosclerotic heart disease.

In Fort Worth at 301 East Fifth Street, an official Texas history marker commemorating the site of the Fort Worth Medical College states, "Among those in its small charter class was Frances Daisy Emery, the First Woman Medical School Graduate in Texas."

HARRIET (HALLIE) EARLE, M.D. (1880–1963)

On August 20, 1920, Dr. Hallie Earle noted in her journal, "Suffrage is a fact." That same year she was forty years old, and her net income from her medical practice was $2,226.79.[23] Women's rights and woman suffrage were causes she had supported fervently since she was old enough to understand the meaning of the words. Five years earlier she had begun practicing medicine in Waco, the first woman physician in the county. The same ability and persistence that had earned the respect of her professors and classmates in medical school had begun to build for her a group of devoted patients, even though they were somewhat in awe of this woman who carried a gun in her car and sprinkled her conversations with "hells" and "damns." Many of them also knew that she had such respect for life she refused to allow flies and bees to be killed and that she fed dozens of stray cats daily.

Hallie's independent spirit was encouraged by her colorful father, Isham Harrison Earle. During the Civil War he had served in the Tenth Texas Infantry, rising to the rank of major. After the war he returned to Waco, married Adaline Graves Earle, and helped his brother, John Baylis Earle, operate the town's first cotton mill.[24] When the mill was confiscated by the provisional government in Texas in 1867, Major Earle moved his family to a farm near Hewitt, about fifteen miles from Waco. Like many Texas farms, it was both farm and ranch with cattle, cotton, vegetable crops, chickens, and assorted livestock. The major's main interest was in the fine horses he bred and trained and rode so recklessly

Dr. Hallie Earle. Courtesy Baylor University,
Texas Collection, Waco, Texas

that he was once fined for riding too fast down Austin Avenue in Waco.

Hallie Earle was born on September 27, 1880, in the log house on the farm, the last of eight children. She would live most of her life in this house, which grew over the years into a rambling, spacious country home as assorted rooms, porches, and baths were added. The formal, pillared Greek Revival family home built by Hallie's grandparents in Waco in 1858 was a great contrast and a nice place to visit.[25] But the farm was a delightful place for an adventurous child to grow up. Numerous cousins in and around Waco came by buggy to join the Earle children in spending long days playing in the barn made of hand-hewn logs or along the creek. Hallie was the natural leader of the group, encouraging others to follow her lead in swinging by a rope out of the barn loft to drop onto a pile of hay, skipping rocks in the creek, or picking up snakes by their tails along the bank.

Appreciating her quick, inquisitive mind, her father encouraged her voracious reading in the large family library and taught her to play card games. Although they were far from wealthy, her parents took pride in their roots, teaching their children the family history and explaining the role of their ancestors in establishing the city of Waco. Both Hallie's grandfathers had been doctors, and her father told her that at one time he had seven uncles and uncles-in-law practicing medicine.[26]

She embraced her studies as eagerly as she had done her play, and early in her academic life Hallie decided she wanted to go to college. Baylor University in Waco had an excellent reputation and was convenient, for she could stay with relatives during the week and return to the Hewitt farm on weekends. At Baylor her scholarship won recognition from her professors, and in letters of recommendation they praised her as a "most diligent and capable student" with "careful studious habits and strong mental grasp." In her senior year the president of the university, Oscar H. Cooper, wrote that she was doing the "most advanced work done by any student of the University in math." He added his opinion that she would make a "good high school teacher." Her evaluations also contained the information that she was "a lady of strong personality."[27]

In 1901, Hallie graduated from Baylor with sixteen other students in a class dubbed "the Twentieth Century Class." She stayed on for another year, earning an M.S. degree in 1902. Again her scholarship won high praise, and the administration chose to place her thesis in the cornerstone of the new Carroll Science Building.

She had no intention of pursuing the usual careers—marriage or teaching—open to women of her day. She did, however, teach school briefly in small communities near Waco to earn a little money while she waited for her application to Baylor medical school in Dallas to be accepted. During the half-century since Elizabeth Blackwell became the first woman to enter a medical college in the United States, the restrictions had eased, and many medical schools had 5 percent quotas for female admissions.[28] These quotas were seldom filled as Victorian and Edwardian society generally considered medicine an unnatural career for a woman. Not only would she be expected to cut up cadavers and learn to treat unmentionable diseases, but she would also be exposed to the hostility and off-color jokes of her fellow students.

All of these things and more Hallie endured as she concentrated on her studies with her customary determination to succeed. Her letters home were warm and affectionate and revealed a character of tremendous energy, eager for challenges and capable of rising above the discouragement or disparagement of professors or classmates. During her junior year, her grades ranged from 100 percent in surgical pathology to 85 percent in electro therapeutics.[29] In 1907, at the age of twenty-seven, she graduated from Baylor medical school, the only woman in her class of six.

Dr. Earle chose internal medicine and gynecology as her specialties and traveled to Chicago and New Orleans for postgraduate studies before interning at Bellevue Hospital in New York. She took full advantage of her stay in the city, attending all the plays and operas she could afford and making friends with whom she corresponded all her life.

Returning to Texas, she joined Torbett's Sanatorium in Marlin where her cousin, Lucille Pearré, was a laboratory technician. Noted for its hot mineral waters, Marlin was a mecca for health seekers; it was also conveniently close to Hewitt and the Earle farm, where Hallie's aging father lived. During the seven years Hallie worked in Marlin, she occasionally took leaves to pursue additional postgraduate studies. In 1911 she put an ad in the *Journal of the American Medical Association* inquiring about positions. When her only offers were from an Iowa industrial school for girls and a homeopathic hospital in Houston, she decided to risk going into private practice in Waco in 1915.

Her first office was in the Provident Building, where she stayed for four years, until 1919. She then moved to the Amicable Building, where she remained until her retirement in 1948. Cousin Lucille Pearré moved from Marlin with Hallie to be her receptionist, secretary, and assistant lab technician. Advertising herself as "H. Earle, M.S., M.D., Internist," Hallie kept busy giving free medical care to the poor while she

Women Pioneers in Texas Medicine

86

waited for her practice to build. She did examinations for life insurance companies and also for individual doctors as word spread of her capability as a diagnostician. Her practice slowly grew as women patients especially spread the word of her competence and her caring attitude. Her income was never large, partly because she did so much charitable work, and during the depression she lost some of her investment savings. But living at home on the Earle farm and commuting into Waco in her faithful black Dodge was a big savings.

Hallie considered it vital to keep up with the latest medical developments and continued to study journals and medical papers and to attend medical conventions as long as she was in practice. Her patients knew they might have a considerable wait to see her since she took them on a first-come basis, but they also knew that when it was their turn they would not be rushed and that Dr. Earle would listen sympathetically to all they had to tell her. In those days of relatively unsophisticated medical techniques, she enhanced her medical advice with common sense, advising pregnant women to emulate mother cats: lazing around in their first months and stretching frequently. She also instructed patients (and guests in her home) to put their feet up when they sat, to help their circulation. She herself set an example by propping up her own feet in their neat black shoes on her desk as she conferred with her patients.

After her father died in 1918, Hallie continued to live on the farm with her sister, Mary, and her working partner, Lucille Pearré. The three single women shared a busy, happy life, frequently entertaining family members and friends. Children were particularly welcome and enjoyed exploring the unusual house and playing with the numerous outside cats. They seldom, however, caught a glimpse of King, the autocratic and privileged Siamese, who spent most of his time in Hallie's bedroom. At Christmastime tables were set up in the log room with toys, games, and coloring books appropriate for various ages, and each child visitor was invited to choose his or her own gift. At other times they were served cheese straws, tea cakes, and lemonade along with large helpings of family history, in which Hallie took great pride.

Her energy was seemingly boundless, and she believed in and followed the adage that "a change is as good as a rest." After a long day at the office, she helped feed the farm animals and worked in the garden—hoeing, weeding, and experimenting with new crops such as Spanish melons. After dinner she read and studied far into the night in order to keep up with the latest medical developments. Her father had kept a record of the rainfall and temperature in their area since 1879, a year before she was born, and as his health declined, she took over the task. In 1916 she was appointed a cooperative weather observer for the U.S. Department of Agriculture, and in 1956 she was awarded a forty-year service pin.

After the deaths of her sister, Mary, and cousin Lucille, Hallie decided to retire. Although she was still vigorous and mentally sharp at sixty-eight, she preferred to quit before she lost her skills. And although patients and other doctors begged her to reconsider, she was adamant in her decision. Old doctors, she said, might do harm to the patients who still came to them out of loyalty, and she advised her colleagues to follow her example. At the end of 1948 when she closed her practice, she was still the only woman physician in Waco.

For the next fifteen years, she lived alone on the farm with frequent visits from relatives and friends. She loved to shock new acquaintances by saying that although she had never married, she had five daughters. These were five young women whom she "adopted," taking them to restaurants and entertainments and giving them parties and wedding showers. Hallie also underwrote the education of her surviving brother's two sons, including the medical education of one of them. She continued to monitor the weather, and she kept a farm journal, recording the daily activities of churning, canning, and preserving, After her retirement she refused to dispense medical advice, saying, "Now I am a farmer." She would, however, tell friends when it was time for them to see a doctor for some ailment.

Dr. Earle had little use for chitchat or gossip, but she loved to discuss politics, business, sports, music, art, and agriculture and had strong definite opinions on all these subjects. One of her valued possessions was a picture of Woodrow Wilson and his wife, which hung in her office; the mention of Roosevelt and the New Deal, however, was enough to send her blood pressure soaring. She was an avid bridge player, and weekly bridge games continued to be a highlight of her retirement.

She died on November 1, 1963, a the age of eighty-three. Once when a patient asked her if she regretted "not marrying and living a normal life," Hallie Earle responded, "I didn't miss a thing."[30]

EDITH M. BONNET, M.D. (1897–1982)

When the superintendent of schools handed Edith Bonnet her high school diploma, he said, "Here, Baby." Although it embarrassed the teenage Edith a great deal, his remark was perfectly natural. That superintendent was also a county judge, a banker, an organizer of Boy Scouts, and Edith's father. She later acknowledged that he was one of the finest men she ever knew.[31]

The Bonnets lived in Eagle Pass, Texas. Like her three brothers and two sisters, Edith wanted all the education she could get. Her mother, who had always wanted to be an architect herself, encouraged Edith to study architecture, but Edith couldn't get the mathematics. She liked the sciences so well, however, that she decided to study medicine as a way to go on with them. In 1922 she applied to the University of Texas Medical Branch (UTMB) at Galveston.[32] Being accepted into medical school was easy for this top scholar. Edith just sent in her grades and records, and no interview was required. The difficulty was to decide whether she really wanted to enter UTMB that fall or to marry a "nice guy" she had agreed to meet on her way home from a summer camp in New Hampshire. The young man sent a telegram that never reached Edith. Not having met him as planned, she went, on two hours' notice, on to Galveston and medical school. After she had settled into her studies, the suitor let her know he "wouldn't marry a woman that was a doctor."[33]

Edith encountered a certain amount of teasing and even vulgar remarks from some of the male students and lab assistants. She learned that ignoring them was the best response. In later years, she laughed over the fact that some of these same men subsequently referred patients to her—in some cases, their own children.[34]

Coping with male professors who didn't want female medical students to succeed was a tougher proposition. Edith, who had a scholarship, remembered one who said there was no use in her taking the finals because he would see that she didn't graduate. In another case, the wife of an elegant and aristocratic doctor who couldn't tolerate women in medicine came out in her chauffeur-driven limousine and told the women students that regardless of what her husband said, she hoped they were successful.[35]

Dr. Violet Keiller's father, Dr. William Keiller, who was dean of the Medical Department from 1922 to 1926, also objected to female doc-

tors, even though his own daughter Violet was a surgeon and pathologist. Edith thought the dean had only managed to tolerate having his
colleague Dr. Charlotte Schaefer on the staff because "she looked through
a microscope and that was a nondescript and innocent adventure."[36]

When Edith Bonnet graduated in 1925, there was a set policy that
the nine top-ranking scholars in each graduating class would be accepted as interns at John Sealy Hospital. Edith was actually in tenth
place, but because one of the nine above her chose to go elsewhere,
there was an opening for her. When applications were submitted, she
and the other eligible female, Frances Vanzant, learned that one of the
requirements for being an intern at John Sealy Hospital was "being a
man."[37]

The young doctors Bonnet and Vanzant took their problem to Texas
governor Miriam A. "Ma" Ferguson with the plea that because John
Sealy Hospital was a state institution, it could not discriminate against
women. After newspaper headlines and much unpleasantness, the two
young women were given contracts that made them the first women
ever to intern at John Sealy Hospital. A Galveston newspaper story
detailed certain restrictions in their contracts: ". . . with the understanding that they would not be given certain courses applying to
genito-urinary male patients, but allowed special work in other departments to make up the full year's work."[38]

In medical school, Edith had become fascinated with cancer research
and decided to specialize in pathology. She didn't know just how it
came about, but during her internship she became involved with children and tuberculosis and found herself specializing in pediatrics instead. Her friend, Dr. Frances Vanzant, went to the Mayo Clinic, where
she remained for a number of years.[39]

Another stumbling block for medical women seeking appointments
was the position taken by Harvard Medical School. In 1927, when Edith
applied to its pediatrics department for an internship, she was told that
women were not eligible for appointment to Harvard Medical's house
officer staff because "we have not the proper housing facilities." Perhaps Harvard was even then feeling the winds of change, for the letter
did add that Harvard Medical hoped in the near future to overcome
"this physical handicap."[40]

After the year at John Sealy, Edith Bonnet went to Children's Memorial Hospital in Chicago. Meaning to go for just a year, she stayed for four because that training was "just wonderful." She took every service they offered. Residents then were paid ten dollars a month and given board, room, and laundry. In a brief, unhappy stint in a New York clinic, she found that nurses who "didn't have any sense" were mingling supposedly isolated children in one big recreation room during times when the isolation rooms needed cleaning. Edith reported practices like this to the department head and returned to Chicago, where she served in a children's outpatient clinic.[41]

When the possibilities in Chicago had been exhausted, Edith bought a second-hand car and drove to San Antonio, where she entered practice with a group of doctors. It was tough getting started: the first month she earned eighty-seven dollars and not much more the second month. Later she entered a program offered by a local governmental agency that paid doctors fifty cents per office call and a dollar for a house call. In this program Edith usually saw Mexican patients. Although she went at night into the narcotics-ridden west side district, nobody ever bothered her. When the residents saw her coming with her medical bag, they would knock down anybody who got in her way because they knew she was going to help a sick baby.[42]

In 1939 Dr. Edith Bonnet was appointed to the San Antonio Board of Health by Mayor Maury Maverick, whose own children were among her patients. For the health board, the condition of San Antonio's water supply was a major and continuing concern. During Dr. Bonnet's tenure, the most reliable water analyses available came from Fort Sam Houston. She learned that some of the west side residents simply dipped their water out of irrigation ditches. When Edith asked one mother if she boiled her baby's bottles, the mother replied that she had no stove. She explained, "We build a little fire of sticks in the yard" for cooking meals.[43]

After she officially retired in 1959, Dr. Bonnet worked at various clinics until she couldn't read the street signs and it was dangerous for her to drive. She asked to treat Mexican children because she could speak Spanish. A continuing frustration for her was that more health care was available for needy people than they were taking advantage of.[44]

After spending most of her life in medical welfare work, Dr. Bonnet said that her career, which could not be called satisfactory financially, had been rewarding in other ways. She had enjoyed the clinic work more than private practice because there were no house calls and no bills: "You just went down and saw the babies and did the best you could."[45]

In the Community

ELVA ANIS WRIGHT, M.D. (1868–1950)

"She was a wonderful woman," said Dr. Daniel Jenkins of Dr. Elva Anis Wright, who founded the Houston and Harris County Anti-Tuberculosis League early in her forty-year career as a Houston physician.[46]

As a little girl in Pennsylvania, Elva Wright read about the West, pioneers, and the frontier. Texas embodied much that she admired, including the spirit of dying with one's boots on. Her family members, including two brothers, a sister, and two nephews, understood that as the reason she chose Texas for her home.[47]

Dr. Elva Anis Wright with a fireman in a fire truck. Courtesy Harris County Medical Archive, Texas Medical Center Library, Houston, Texas

Women Pioneers in Texas Medicine

After her graduation from Valparaiso University in Indiana with a
B.S. degree in 1894, Elva Wright received her medical degree from
Northwestern University at Chicago in 1900. To this education she
added postgraduate work at clinics in Vienna and Berlin and at the
University of Edinburgh in Scotland. After an internship at Mary
Thompson Hospital in Chicago, she practiced for ten years at Lake
Forest, Illinois.[48]

Like many of her peers in the early years of women physicians, Dr.
Wright specialized in obstetrics and gynecology. Although she continued this specialization in Houston, more and more of her time and
attention were devoted to the detection and prevention of tuberculosis, especially in children. When Dr. Daniel Jenkins came to Baylor
Medical College as an assistant professor in 1947, he met the seventy-
nine-year-old Dr. Wright, whom he found charming. She had a personality that he described as forceful, adding that Alva Wright could
be austere "if she was cornered" but that she remained charming most
of the time. In many of the groups with which she met, she was usually either the lone woman or one of few. Nevertheless, she generally
expressed her opinions about things well and strongly.[49]

One calamity of which Dr. Jenkins never learned the circumstances
was that Dr. Wright had lost one eye. She wore a prosthesis in its place
as well as glasses, perhaps to hide the loss somewhat. Dr. Jenkins remarked that having one good and one bad eye became a part of her
personality and made her more forceful—"You always remembered who
she was."[50]

When Dr. Jenkins was appointed medical director of the Houston
Tuberculosis Hospital, it contained about 150 patients. Each Tuesday,
practitioners from all over the county who were interested in TB would
come to its staff meetings. Dr. Wright, who was on the hospital staff,
would attend, though her interest in tuberculosis had more to do with
organization than with treatment. She mainly participated at meetings, Dr. Jenkins said, "when we had pregnancy problems."[51]

Dr. Wright's main role in tuberculosis detection and prevention was
in the Anti-TB League, whose Houston chapter she had established
sometime about 1908. In its early days, the league was situated in the
basement of Jefferson Davis Hospital. League staff ran a clinic where
outpatients could get refills of pneumothorax or air (staff doctors rendered that service). Other league work included case finding through-

MEDICAL PRACTICE, RESEARCH, TEACHING

93

out the county and taking skin tests on people suspected of having tuberculosis. The organization also initiated a TB publicity program that became the Christmas Seals program—their main source of funding. Dr. Wright, the chief doctor on the league staff, had charge of most of these activities.[52]

Besides the Anti-TB League, Dr. Wright belonged to the regular state and national medical associations and to two other groups specifically designed to fight tuberculosis. She was a founder and charter member of the Houston Altrusa Club and a life member of the Save-A-Life League. She also belonged to the Woman's Forum and Woman's City Club and was a member of the Chamber of Commerce health committee.[53]

Dr. Wright established the first clinic for children at the city health department in Houston and for years was examining physician for the Harris County School of Girls and the juvenile court for girls.[54]

The Houston and Harris County Anti-Tuberculosis League changed its name in concert with the national organization, which had begun as the National Tuberculosis Association and later was called the National Tuberculosis and Respiratory Disease Association. In 1973 or 1974, the name was changed to its present form, the American Lung Association.[55]

When Dr. Jenkins took over the Jefferson Davis basement outpatient TB clinic and moved it to a clinic attached to the Autrey Building on the grounds of the TB hospital, the Anti-TB League continued to obtain money for tuberculosis detection and treatment. The league was not, however, further involved in the medical part of it. These changes occurred toward the end of Dr. Wright's involvement in the organization.[56]

Streptomycin was the first major drug used against tuberculosis. Developed in the early 1940s, it was injectable. Dr. Jenkins, who had done a lot of early work with the drug, was shocked to find it was not available when he came to Houston in 1947. He "raised a hue and cry" and, with some other colleagues, got the Elva A. Wright Auxiliary to raise the money to provide streptomycin for patients at the Houston TB Hospital.[57]

In a paper she read before the South Texas District Medical Society in 1916, Dr. Wright included some sociological observations describing the poverty-stricken lives of some of her infant patients. She added,

"To be sure there is always the element of ignorance and mismanagement, but who shall say that the 'powers that be' are not largely responsible?"[58]

Reviewing her work in the public health clinic, Elva Wright noted that someone had suggested setting up milk stations in various parts of the city. She declared, "It occurs to me that all milk should be of so high a quality that any one might be able to buy pure milk in the open market for any baby in any part of the city." She also advocated establishing a nursing service in the health department as well as prenatal study classes and infant welfare lecture courses that should attract women from all walks of life.[59]

What did this potent practitioner look like? Dr. Jenkins remembered Elva Wright as being rather short of stature and amazingly agile, even when she was elderly. She had glasses and gray hair, and she always wore gloves. "I can hardly ever remember her when she didn't have gloves on . . . sometimes pink ones."[60]

One of her nephews explained that Elva Wright did not affiliate with any Houston church because she felt the enemy she sought to eradicate was no respecter of persons or creeds. She needed the cooperation of all churches, races, and beliefs to assist her program. She worked with them all. She said of her own death, "My friends can carry on, and only [when] they stop remembering and carrying on our work will I be dead." She did not see the necessity of a granite monument. Instead, she set up the Elva Wright Memorial Fund to assist students specializing in the study of tuberculosis.[61]

Although she did not live to realize her dream of a separate TB hospital, Dr. Wright did get her wish to die quickly and quietly—at home, as it happened, from a ruptured aneurysm, shortly after her return from a meeting of the Anti-TB League. Her nephew was sure she had no regrets. She had said often, "My friends have honored me during my lifetime, and I am so grateful."[62]

Her choice of funeral music, to be sung by her friend the well-known musician Walter Jenkins, was in keeping with her lifelong love of western and pioneer attitudes: "Home on the Range."[63]

LENA EDWARDS, M.D. (1900–87)

"I was born a Negro. I've never cried about it. I believe a person can accomplish anything regardless of color, if they try hard enough." That practical statement by Dr. Lena Edwards sums up an attitude toward life that made her many accomplishments possible and led to her receiving the Presidential Medal of Freedom from President Lyndon B. Johnson in September, 1964.[64]

Setting up grand, distant goals for herself came naturally to Lena Frances Edwards. She was one of the four children of Dr. Thomas W. Edwards, a dentist who taught at Howard University Dental School in Washington, D.C. Lena told her father when she was twelve that she wanted to become a doctor in order to help people. This was in 1912, when to be a female, black, and Catholic were far greater obstacles to worldly success in this country than they are today.[65]

In an article detailing some of the special obstacles black medical women have had to overcome, *The Pharos* (a publication of Alpha Omega Alpha, the medical honor society) noted:

> Another compelling example is that of Dr. Lena F. Edwards, who was told by the chief of staff at Margaret Hague Maternity Hospital during the early 1920s that she was not wanted there because of two handicaps—first, that she was a woman, and second, that she was black. Her reply: "That is quite true, but it so happens that God gave me both of those characteristics, and I don't think there's a human being who has the right to judge me for what He did. You'll find that I do my work properly, so you'll have to find a better excuse for not wanting me."[66]

After her graduation from Howard University Medical School, Lena and her husband, Dr. Keith Madison, a general practitioner, established practices in Jersey City, New Jersey, and Lena specialized in obstetrics and gynecology. The Madisons had six children, two daughters and four sons. By 1943 Lena was a widow with all six children to educate. She stayed in practice in Jersey City until 1954, when she became an assistant professor at Howard University Medical School.[67]

Of Lena's children Marie, the oldest, is a psychiatrist; Edward is a pediatrician; Genevieve is a psychiatric social worker; Paul is a high school teacher; John is an aerospace engineer; and her fourth son, Father Thomas A. Madison, is a Franciscan priest. There are nineteen grandchildren.[68]

Like her desire to become a physician, Lena Edwards's wish to become a missionary came to her years before she could see her way to accomplishing it. In 1944, when she wrote a paper on mortality in childbirth in relation to environmental factors, she became conscious of the need of poor people for good maternity care. She knew, however, that her dream of going out to do missionary work must wait until her own brood was established. One day when Dr. Edwards was visiting her son Thomas at the Atonement Seminary where he was studying to become a Graymoor friar, she remarked that when all her children were educated, she wanted to go into missionary work. A classmate of Thomas's said, "Go to Hereford in the Texas Panhandle and work with the migrant farmers."[69]

Inspired by the example of Dr. Albert Schweitzer continuing his humanitarian work into old age, Dr. Lena Edwards became a member of the Third Order of Saint Francis. At age sixty she came into the Labor Camp, a village of thirty-six converted prisoner-of-war barracks facing the Graymoor Mission of Saint Joseph about two miles southwest of Hereford, Texas. A Franciscan order, the Graymoor Friars maintain a clinic in the Labor Camp as part of their Saint Joseph Mission Church.[70]

"I thought I was in a foreign country," said Dr. Edwards of her first impression of conditions in the Labor Camp, where migrant workers and their families lived. She discovered that women had three choices regarding childbirth. First, they could deliver their babies in the barracks with one other woman helping—usually an untrained person. Second, they could go to a "certain" office, wait outside in the car until delivery was imminent, rest on a stretcher for one hour after the baby was born, and then be sent home with the child. Third, they could go to a hospital where they would pay $150 for delivery, medicine, and laboratory and hospital fees. Dr. Edwards learned that most of the women could not afford the third choice.[71]

For her first ten months, Dr. Edwards lived in the mission. She studied Spanish, kept the same hours as the migrant workers, and lived as much as possible as they did. As she put it, she tried by example to prove how well they could live and how happy they could be with the little they had. She laughed at herself for once having bragged, "When I'm sixty, I'm going to cut my hair, dye it henna and have a fling."[72]

Lena set to work, campaigning for a maternity hospital and working for funds to modernize and enlarge the clinic; $14,500 of her own savings started the fund drive. She made trips back East to solicit funds and to bring back office equipment and furnishings she had used in New Jersey. Later she reflected, "It has taken four years of my life and $30,000 of my savings" to achieve the improvements she initiated. "The people don't want anything free, and it is not a charity hospital, as is believed by so many people," Dr. Edwards explained. Patients paid fees that were prorated to fit their financial circumstances.[73]

Honors came to Dr. Edwards often throughout her career. In 1946 she was named one of the thirteen outstanding women doctors in the nation. In 1955 she was chosen Medical Woman of the Year by the New Jersey District of American Women's Association. Later she was awarded an honorary doctor of laws degree from Saint Joseph's College, Rensselaer, Indiana, for "selfless dedication to her fellow man." The Hereford Lions Club presented Dr. Edwards their Citizen of the Year award in 1963 for establishing the maternity hospital.[74]

Dr. Edwards received notice in July of 1964 that the greatest honor that can be awarded to a civilian United States citizen in peacetime was to be hers. She was one of thirty Americans selected to receive the Presidential Medal of Freedom. Also selected was J. Frank Dobie, renowned author of some twenty books on the Southwest. In September, 1964, President Lyndon B. Johnson presented the award to them in ceremonies during which Dr. Edwards was commended for her creative talents and demonstrated excellence.[75]

Lena Edwards returned from Washington to resume the struggle for the survival of the maternity hospital and the clinic, both of which she had maintained almost single-handedly since her arrival in Hereford. Lena's head was not turned by hearing herself called "the Tom Dooley of Deaf Smith County," nor was she sentimental about the future of the project. She said, "I'm giving myself one more year as a lone worker, but if the community hasn't found some way of continuing my program by then—well, there's no point in my committing suicide."[76]

In 1963 Dr. Edwards suffered a heart attack, and there were more warning symptoms in September, 1964. "I've told the town fathers that I'm just one person," she said. "One priest isn't a church, one teacher isn't a school, and one doctor isn't a hospital. You have to have community help to perpetuate a project like this."[77]

A newspaper report in 1964 pointed out that although Hereford had named Dr. Edwards Citizen of the Year in 1963, some of the influential people in the community insisted on refusing her pleas for federal assistance for badly needed programs to aid the poor in housing, daycare, and health because they didn't want any federal interference. Although she was realistic about her chances of changing the community's ideas, Dr. Edwards remained hopeful as long as possible. "I keep after them. Either they break you or you break them, and I'm not worried about them breaking me."[78]

In 1985, two years before her death from a final heart attack, Dr. Lena F. Edwards was listed in the *American Medical Directory* as living in Lakewood, New Jersey. The last listing for her at a Texas address was 1965.

Even though the funding she pleaded for to secure the program she began and to guarantee the futures of her hospital and clinic never materialized, Lena Edwards's years in the Panhandle unquestionably brightened and lengthened the lives of many she encountered and touched the hearts of those who did not give enough.

CONNIE R. YERWOOD (CONNER), M.D. (1908–91)

In the 1930s it was almost impossible for a black woman to gain admittance to a medical school in the South. Even at Meharry Medical College in Nashville, Tennessee, which had been created to train black doctors, there was blatant discrimination against women. Connie Yerwood and Joyce, her younger sister, like to tell an anecdote about an experience they had when they were both sophomores at the college. At the beginning of the semester, a teacher came into the classroom, perched on his desk, and announced, "I see there're two women in this class, and I want you to know now that I don't believe in women doctors."[79]

Because of the two strikes against them—being black and being women—the Yerwood sisters felt fortunate to have been accepted by the college, and they were determined to overcome every obstacle that was put in the way of their becoming physicians. Fifty years later, in 1983, at their fiftieth class reunion at Meharry, the whole auditorium stood and applauded as the sisters marched together down the aisle. The audience was acknowledging their distinguished careers as doctors and as civic leaders who had helped bring about permanent reforms that benefited their chosen states: Connecticut for Joyce and Texas for Connie.

MEDICAL PRACTICE, RESEARCH, TEACHING

Melissa Yerwood, their mother, who died while they were very young, had been a teacher. Their father, Dr. Charles Yerwood, a native Austinite and a Meharry Medical College graduate, had a rural practice in Gonzales County. As the girls accompanied him on his rounds in his horse and buggy, they were impressed by his affectionate relationship with his patients, many of whom paid him by barter. Dr. Yerwood accepted chickens, eggs, butter, and, on one memorable occasion, a heifer calf for his services.

In their home, among the pictures from Dr. Yerwood's college days at Meharry was one of his lone female classmate. Influenced by their father's career and encouraged by the picture of a black, female medical student, Connie and Joyce decided to become doctors. Foreseeing the difficulties they would have to overcome and fearing that studying medicine would destroy their femininity, their father tried to persuade them to study music and develop their obvious talents in that field. When he realized they were determined to study medicine, however, Dr. Yerwood agreed to pay his daughter's expenses and helped arrange for their acceptance at his alma mater. Upon their arrival at the school, officials there tried to persuade the Yerwood girls to attend the college's nearby school of dentistry instead of the regular medical school, but the sisters were not to be deterred.[80] Charles Yerwood had to admit that his fears had been groundless as he watched his daughters graduate cum laude in 1933, wearing high heels and long gowns. They were both doctors and ladies.

Through friends of their father in Kansas, the sisters were accepted as interns at Kansas City General Hospital. They both took residencies at Wheatley-Providence Hospital in the same city. Joyce decided to specialize in gynecology and obstetrics, and Connie chose pediatrics. At this point, their lives became widely separated geographically.

Dr. Joyce Yerwood set up a practice first in Port Chester, New York, and in the 1950s she moved to Stamford, Connecticut. Over the years she delivered more than two thousand babies. She also became deeply involved in social work, especially in the drug addiction program. She served as medical director of the methadone program and also was on many civic boards. In recognition of her service to the community, the two-million-dollar Stamford Community Center was named for her.[81]

Dr. Connie Yerwood had planned to enter private practice specializing in pediatrics, but a friend, Pansy Nichols, director of the Texas

Tuberculosis Association, interested her in a public-health career by telling her of the great need for black women in the field. Consequently, after attending the University of Michigan's School of Public Health on a scholarship, Connie joined the Texas State Department of Health in 1936. She was the first African-American professional in the department and one of the first female black doctors in Texas.

Her first position was as medical consultant in the Division of Maternal and Child Health, where her particular assignment was to work with local health departments in east Texas to determine what health services were needed. Through first-hand observation she found that the infant mortality rate was shockingly high, especially among African Americans. Since almost all deliveries were attended by midwives, Dr. Yerwood set up a training program for them. She also initiated prenatal and family planning clinics and immunization programs. As she told an interviewer many years later, the rewards of practicing preventive medicine were not as spectacular or as immediate as those of practicing curative medicine, but the satisfaction of seeing long-term results was great.[82]

Dr. Yerwood soon discovered that being employed as a physician by the Texas State Department of Health did not preclude discrimination. Their offices were on the third floor of the Land Office Building, and according to the segregation practices of that time, she was not permitted to use the restroom. Nor could she eat at most of the lunch counters in the area. More disturbing was the fact that she found herself repeatedly passed over as less experienced white male staff members were promoted ahead of her—until the passage of the Civil Rights Act in 1964. Connie was not surprised that the authorities suddenly took note of her ability. When the commissioner of health offered her a promotion she was at first inclined to refuse, telling him she knew the offer was made because of the need "to show some ethnicity in the higher levels."[83] Her staff, however, urged her to take the promotion, and with their encouragement—plus the realization that the position would enable her to bring about needed changes—she accepted. Thus Dr. Yerwood became director of the Maternal Child Health Department and eventually chief of the Bureau of Personal Health Services.

During the forty-one years she worked for the Texas State Department of Health, she did indeed bring about many changes and improvements through her determination and perseverance. She was always willing to serve on boards, committees, and commissions, and she belonged to many related organizations such as the Lone Star Medical Association, which elected her president in 1955–56. She was appointed to the first board of trustees of the Mental Health–Mental Retardation Center of Austin and Travis County and served on the boards of the Austin Child Guidance Center and the Citizens Advisory Center to the Juvenile Board of Travis County.

Dr. Yerwood was also a trustee of Huston-Tillotson College in Austin, her alma mater and her father's. She was a diligent worker for her church, Wesley United Methodist, and for the Order of the Eastern Star of the Masonic Grand Chapter in Austin. She was the first African American on Austin's Human Relations Committee. Over the years she received several honorary degrees, and so many honors and awards were heaped on her in acknowledgement of her civic, educational, and religious activities that a listing of them fills two typewritten pages.[84]

Long before her retirement from the Texas State Department of Health in 1977, Connie Yerwood had won the respect and admiration of her fellow workers. On the occasion of her retirement, the board of health of the Texas State Department of Health gave her an Outstanding Service Award for "41 years of Service to the People of Texas." The commissioner of health presented her with a certificate of merit. And the staff of the Division of Maternal and Child Health, the people with whom she had worked most closely, gave her a gold yellow rose of Texas medallion with a diamond center.[85]

FRANCINE JENSEN, M.D. (1917–)

"She was the strong person, the enduring person . . . on the County side," said Dr. Daniel Jenkins of his longtime colleague, Dr. Francine Jensen. It was she who, representing the Harris County Public Health Department, worked with the Anti-Tuberculosis League during the 1940s and 1950s. Dr. Jenkins, who organized the section on pulmonary diseases at Baylor College of Medicine, was later appointed medical director of the Houston TB Hospital. Dr. Jensen was also on the staff of the TB hospital and worked very closely with his people.[86]

Francine Jensen was born in 1917 in Memphis, Tennessee, because her father's work had taken him there and her mother had left their home in Texas to visit him. After Francine's first six weeks of life, the family returned to Houston, where Dr. Jensen has lived ever since. Francine had a sister, now deceased, and two brothers. The younger brother died in 1936, a victim of the first poliomyelitis epidemic recorded in Houston.[87]

Young Francine enjoyed her science courses in high school and college, but she doesn't know exactly what motivated her to study medicine; she disclaims having had any noble intent. After receiving her B.A. at the University of Texas in Austin, she applied to and was accepted by the University of Texas Medical Branch at Galveston.

She did both her internship and her residency at Jefferson Davis Hospital in Houston. This was not the original hospital located on Elder Street at Washington but the one on Allen Parkway. Francine remarked of the original Jeff Davis that it was so old it had the pesthouse (a place to hospitalize people with infectious diseases) annexed to it. Dr. Jensen also did a residency at Methodist Hospital in her chosen specialty, obstetrics.

A few years convinced Dr. Jensen that private practice was not for her. The last straw was a call at midnight from a man wanting to make a routine appointment for his wife. Dr. Jensen, married only a short time before, repressed her exasperation enough to suggest courteously that the call should be made the next day and that the wife should be the one to call. This episode inspired Dr. Jensen to look about for some work in the medical field that would fit in better with her private life.

During World War II, physicians were scarce. Doctors were especially needed at the venereal disease clinic, then housed in the original old Jefferson Davis Hospital. After she worked there awhile, Dr. Jensen found her interest in the field of public health increasing. It seemed to her that in public health she would deal with not just a single patient but a whole community—an assortment of people having problems that affected not only them but the community as a whole. Consequently, she applied for and was given a position with the Harris County Health Department.

Tuberculosis was rampant when Francine Jensen went into public-health work in the 1940s. The polio problem was growing. Children's diseases like diphtheria and whooping cough were pressing concerns. There were also other problems with children's health and with women's health—particularly that of pregnant women—but those took a back seat to the communicable diseases.

MEDICAL PRACTICE, RESEARCH, TEACHING

Dr. Francine Jensen. Courtesy Harris County Medical Archive,
Texas Medical Center Library, Houston, Texas

Dr. Jensen has witnessed both the decline of tuberculosis and its resurfacing. It was considered to be fairly well under control for a number of years, but now it seems to be on the increase again. At one time the public health department checked children in the schools periodically. When the disease seemed under control, however, TB testing stopped except in suspicious circumstances such as when a family member was known to have the disease.

In public health, the hope is always to eradicate disease. Dr. Jensen pointed out that smallpox, for example, has been stamped out worldwide and that polio has similarly been nearly eliminated. She gave measles as an instance of a disease for which a vaccine exists but that seems to keep popping up again after appearing to be under control. Her conclusion was that eradication, though the goal of choice, is not always possible.

When she started working there, the public health department was held in very low esteem by everybody. Dr. Jensen attributed this to poor leadership, noting that the facilities were "just God-awful. We were trying to conduct health clinics in a facility that was nothing but a hovel. The poorest person in Harris County wouldn't have lived in some of those places we had to use. I don't care how poor I might have been, I would not have gone to some of those places for treatment.... I would have done without. But we did have patients come in. You wonder why, but they did." Tremendous gains were made when directors with adequate training and expertise were hired. As the quality of leadership improved, so did the public health department.

Dr. Jensen never felt that being a woman made her career any more difficult. She does remember that there were not the same accommodations for women doctors that there were for the men. In the hospitals, women doctors lived in the nurses' quarters and used the nurses' dressing rooms. They had no special facilities as did the males. She does not remember that this situation caused any friction between female doctors and nurses. Back in those days, interns made twenty-five dollars a month and residents made fifty. Room and board and laundry were provided in addition to the stipend.

By law, communicable diseases must be reported to state agencies. Knowing that a certain number of cases have been reported (or that so many deaths have occurred), the agency gains an insight as to when a significant problem has arisen. Public health department nurses report on local clinic conditions; sanitarians make the agencies aware of environmental problems. "Sanitarians" include all sorts of trained inspectors of restaurants, hospitals, and (lately) a wider range of places because of the many recent environmental issues that have emerged. Nowadays, for example, such inspections include solid-waste disposal sites, spills, and facilities where hazardous chemicals are disposed of.

There was some friction for a number of years between public-health workers and private practitioners of medicine because from time to time, the public-health workers undertook inoculation campaigns and set up clinics where people could bring their children to get free shots. Some private doctors considered this an infringement on their practices because giving such shots might be part of the treatment they offered. Dr. Jensen remembered being called by a pediatrician who was highly incensed because the public health department had set up an immunization campaign at provided facilities (probably for DPT shots). The pediatrician felt that this was taking money away from her.

The public health department has come a long way from what it was when Dr. Jensen started out. She reached an ultimate personal goal when she became the first woman director of the Harris County Public Health Department. Although she began her career with the county in the 1940s, after several years she became director of Houston's Chronic Illness Control Program (CICP), formed to develop management strategies for such diseases as diabetes, cancer, and heart disease. This kind of endeavor was unheard of in the county health department, which previously dealt only with communicable diseases. After this program was instituted by the Houston Public Health Department, Dr. Jensen went from being an assistant director for the county to director of CICP for the city. She stayed with the city for six or seven years. When the directorship of the Harris County Public Health Department needed to be filled, Judge Elliott of the Commissioners' Court interviewed Dr. Jensen and appointed her to the position. She remained there until her retirement in 1985, at which time she had spent a total of thirty years in public health.[88]

In the Chronic Illness Control Program, Dr. Jensen reported with some degree of pride that she established cervical cancer detection clinics, a first in Texas for chronic illness. The program also performed diabetes detection and employed physical and occupational therapists, offered rehabilitation facilities for people with paralysis, and hired nutritionists who tried to improve public knowledge of the educational aspects of health. These nutritionists established centers meant to attract senior citizens for screening purposes and also to serve as educational and recreational outlets.

A raging epidemic of rabies among the canine population in the 1950s created a tremendous problem that required much community coordination. Whole families came in and had to be inoculated. The number of rabid dogs was enormous, and scarcely a day went by without some family coming in for the rabies vaccine. The public health department launched a county-wide vaccination drive to control the situation. Sites for clinics were widespread. The effort took the cooperation of the veterinarian societies and the city and county health departments, all working together. This task was followed by a problem in getting legislation to control canine rabies by requiring vaccination. The city could pass such an ordinance for control within city limits, but the county did not have ordinance-making power without the assistance of the state legislature.

Dr. Jensen, a calm, soft-spoken woman, admitted being provoked with reporters in the 1950s who insisted on reiterating that people had to undergo twenty-one painful shots if bitten by a rabid animal. She explained that the treatment for bitten humans today is quite different and less difficult.

"Nothing earthshaking" is what Francine Jensen has been doing since she retired. She reads voraciously, especially mysteries. Gardening gives her pleasure in spite of a growing tendency to muscular stiffness, and she keeps up with medical news through her professional journals and the news media.

In the Hospital

CLAUDIA POTTER, M.D. (1881–1970)

In June of 1906 Dr. Raleigh White, who was on a trip to New York, wrote to his partner, Dr. A. C. Scott, in Temple, Texas, "I will be home soon, for I know you have lost your mind if you have employed a woman doctor."[89] The woman doctor in question was Claudia Potter, the sixth woman to be graduated from the University of Texas Medical Branch at Galveston. The position for which she was being hired was as fourth member of the staff of the recently formed Temple Sanitarium.

The doctors Scott and White had come to Temple in the 1890s as employees of the Santa Fe railroad hospital. In 1898, while working for the railroad hospital, they formed a partnership to look after their large and growing private practices; in 1904, they founded their own hospital. They bought a former Catholic convent near downtown Temple, borrowed money for renovations, and named it the Temple Sanitarium. Their patient number soon exceeded the space available, and by 1906 the sanitarium included Cottage no. 1 and two nearby houses. Dr. Olin Gober, who had graduated from UTMB one year after Claudia Potter, had joined the staff, and it was probably he who recommended to Dr. Scott that she be asked to join the group.

Claudia Potter was born in Denton County to Confederate veteran William T. C. Potter, a farmer, and Laura E. Potter on February 3, 1881. In the late nineteenth century many small Texas towns lived or died according to whether railroads were routed through them, so the acquisition of two railroads by the city of Denton that same year was a great boost to the economy. Also in 1881 bonds were sold to build Denton's first public high school, and by the time Claudia had finished Little Elm Elementary School, an impressive three-story building had been erected. It had four belfrylike columns, giving it the appearance of a strong, top-heavy castle. The school was staffed with teachers qualified to give their pupils a foundation in Latin, German, physiology, arithmetic, and other basic subjects as solid as the building itself.[90]

After her distinguished career ended, Claudia Potter was often asked why she chose to become a doctor. Of the other five surviving Potter children, four had become teachers and one a nurse. Medicine was certainly not the usual choice for women of her time. It was not a question she could answer; she only knew that from the time she doctored her dolls, she was determined to make medicine her life work. When Claudia was thirteen, the first appendectomy in Denton County was performed in a house in the woods south of Denton. Operations caused great excitement, and people gathered from miles to watch them, bringing their dinners and spending the day. The surgeries were done on dining-room tables, often with the curtains taken down to obtain maximum light. This enabled the curious to peer in at the awesome sight as four men held lamps for the doctors, whose white gowns were soon splotched with blood. Instruments were dropped into steaming soup kettles and fished out as needed. And the crowds made predictions and laid bets on the outcome as the operation proceeded.[91]

Malaria, smallpox, and typhoid fever were common diseases, and turpentine, castor oil, and coal oil were typical home remedies. Newspapers carried ads for such patent medicines as Grove's Chill Tonic and Black Draught. Diphtheria, which in most cases caused a painful, choking death, was the most dreaded disease of children. In 1896, when Claudia was fifteen, the county health officer brought the first diphtheria antitoxin to Denton, and people rejoiced that there was one less childhood disease to fear.[92]

Denton High School was one of the Texas high schools granted an "affiliation" rating by the University of Texas. This meant that Claudia

Dr. Claudia Potter. Courtesy Scott and White Hospital Archives, Temple, Texas

Potter, the valedictorian of her class, qualified to be admitted as a freshman at the University of Texas Medical Branch at Galveston. The
opening session of the school was a month late that year because of
devastation caused by the massive September hurricane of 1900, which
killed about 6,000 people and destroyed hundreds of buildings. Consequently, Claudia's five years on the island spanned the time of reconstruction as Galvestonians raised their homes, filled in the island, and
began to build a seawall. The medical school, which had opened its
doors nine years earlier, consisted of four buildings: John Sealy Hospital; the Ashbel Smith Medical College Building (known as "Old Red");
the City Hospital Building, used to house black patients and white
nursing students; and University Hall, a dormitory for female medical

and pharmacy students. All of these buildings required some repair after the storm.

Claudia found comfortable lodging at University Hall for five dollars per month for her room plus ten dollars for meals. Textbooks cost from one dollar to ten dollars, and a matriculation fee plus laboratory fees and deposits amounted to another thirty dollars. On Monday through Friday, classes ran from 8 A.M. to 6 P.M. except for the lunch hour and on Saturdays until noon. Saturday afternoons and Sundays were free. The comprehensive curriculum included lectures, recitations, demonstrations, and laboratory instruction. Among Claudia's instructors was Dr. Marie Charlotte Schaefer, who lectured and demonstrated in general biology, histology, and embryology. Dr. Schaefer (profiled separately) had graduated in the spring of 1900 and was the first woman to serve on the UTMB faculty, eventually becoming chair of the Department of Histology and Embryology.[93]

As the only woman among the sixty-two entering freshman, Claudia expected and received resentment from some of the males at the school, who considered her an intruder. In her reminiscences she explained that her method of overcoming teasing or rudeness was to keep her temper and use her "woman's wiles" to win over her antagonists. Her strategy worked, and she was elected secretary of the freshman and sophomore classes as well as treasurer of the student council. More importantly, she made lasting friends of her would-be tormentors and learned to enjoy the male-oriented world she had entered without losing her femininity. For her class pictures she posed with a large bow in her hair, but in her classwork she maintained a no-nonsense attitude. The courses were rigorous, and the survival rate among the entering students was low—at least two thirds were expected to fail, commonly known as being "busted." After the first year, thirty-six out of the sixty-two students remained in her class; after four years, only twenty-three were still on hand to graduate as physicians.[94] The class motto, "Labor and Patience," exemplified the principles that guided Claudia Potter throughout her life.

Clinical instruction was emphasized for fourth-year students, who worked with patients in medicine, surgery, obstetrics, and gynecology. Following graduation, Claudia received a one-year appointment as resident physician at John Sealy Hospital with opportunities to acquire more practical experience in medicine and surgery. She then moved to San Antonio to practice with another woman doctor until the call came for the fateful interview with Dr. Scott.

Not surprisingly, after Dr. Scott informed her that her permanent status would have to await Dr. White's approval and repeated White's question about Scott's sanity in hiring her, the young doctor had felt some trepidation. At their first interview, Dr. White told Claudia frankly that he did not want a woman doctor on the staff but that since his partner had hired her, she could stay on a monthly probation basis. At the end of each month she reported to Dr. White and received another month's extension. After three months he told her she need not report at the end of the month but should understand that she was still on probation. When she retired from Scott and White forty-one years later, she remarked with a smile that as far as she knew, she was still on probation.[95]

Dr. Potter was given the title of "anesthetist"—not because of any training or experience but because that was what the partners needed and wanted her to be. During her training, physicians at UTMB used either liquid chloroform or ether as general anesthetics and cocaine or morphine as local anesthetics. She had heard a few lectures on the subject and had had some experience with ether at John Sealy Hospital and during her brief experience in general practice. It was not until 1939 that UTMB recognized anesthesia as a section of surgery; only in 1946, over forty years after her graduation, did the State Medical Association of Texas recognize anesthesiology as a separate medical specialty.[96] As she set out to become a specialist in her designated field, she found there was little literature on the subject and realized that in the early 1900s, anesthesia was more of an art than a science.

Claudia's salary was twenty-five dollars a month plus room and board. In addition to being the anesthetist for all operations, her other duties included serving as house doctor, special-duty nurse, stretcher bearer, and general flunkey. Because operations at the sanitarium began early in the morning, she arrived at 5:30 in order to have everything ready. When an operation was finished, the patient was placed on a stretcher. Dr. Potter took the head end of the stretcher; one of the surgeons took the foot, and they carried the patient down the stairs, across the street, and onto a bed. On their way back to the operating room they picked up the next patient. On days when no operations were scheduled, she helped make supplies and sharpened scalpels on a whetrock. During the first months, after mornings in the operating rooms as the official anesthetist, she worked in the small laboratory as the official pathologist, examining specimens she had collected and those left by patients. But as the reputation of the sanitarium grew, her services as a full-time anesthetist were soon required.

In the early years of the twentieth century, when the hospital quite literally went to the patient (i.e., the doctors went with equipment), the surgical teams used whatever transportation was available. The weather often added to their difficulties. One icy February morning, Dr. Potter and Dr. White started off wrapped in heavy lap robes in a two-horse buggy with hot bricks at their feet. Their equipment, sterile linen, and instruments were pinned in sterile sheets and packed in two enormous leather bags. In places the buggy wheels cut through the mud and ice half a hub deep. Four hours later they reached the patient's home, where a successful appendectomy was performed. After reheating their bricks, the doctors started the return journey about 6 P.M. After stopping at a country store for cheese and crackers, their first food since leaving Temple, they arrived home at 10 P.M., exhausted and half-frozen.[97] When the weather was freezing cold, the home operations usually took place on a table in a room with an open fireplace. At these times Dr. Potter kept wet towels near the patient's head, administering the highly explosive ether with great caution, watching for sparks, and praying the pillow would not burst into flame.

Difficult conditions sometimes led to innovative solutions. One steamy Sunday afternoon in September, Dr. Potter went with Dr. Scott to operate on a transient cotton picker with acute appendicitis. The man was housed in a dirty shack used only at cotton picking time. Not wanting to open an abdomen amid all the loose dust and cobwebs, Dr. Scott had the side boards taken off a cotton wagon and placed across two sawhorses for an operating table in the middle of the cotton field. Dr. Potter stood at the end of the makeshift table and administered ether while the young attending local doctor gallantly held an umbrella over her to shield her from the sun. She later recalled, "With the sky for the ceiling above and depending upon God's hot sunshine to sterilize the air about us, we began."[98]

The hazards of traveling by early automobiles at times equaled those of horse-and-buggy travel. The possibilities included getting stuck on muddy roads, frequent flat tires, and the uncertainty of carbide lights, plus the usual chance of freakish weather in central Texas. One summer afternoon Dr. Potter went with Dr. Scott and his son, who was home between terms of medical school, to assist in an operation in the country. As they were on their way home after dark, they were caught in a heavy thunderstorm with torrents of rain that turned the dirt roads into treacherous, slippery mud. The carbide lights of the car went out, but they crept along by the illumination of lightning flashes to a farmhouse where young Dr. Scott bought a lantern. Sitting on the car's fender, he shined the light on the road, and when they came to a bridge he stood at its edge, waving the lantern to guide the car. Proceeding at a snail's pace, the doctors finally reached home at 4 A.M.[99]

One of Dr. Potter's favorite anecdotes was of the time she was told to prepare to go to the country for a hernia operation and was warned to bring along plenty of ether as the patient was quite large. The patient turned out to be a fine registered sow with a large abdominal hernia, and Dr. Potter soon found that her ether mask was not designed to fit the snout of a twelve-hundred-pound hog. However, by using several towels and "a lot of ether," she finally managed to subdue the struggling patient, who survived the operation and lived to produce many descendants.[100]

When Dr. George Valter Brindley joined the sanitarium, he and Dr. Potter worked together as a traveling surgical team, frequently riding the Santa Fe Railway cabooses to reach their patients. On one memorable occasion, they used a more up-to-date mode of transportation. The September, 1920, issue of the sanitarium's in-house newsletter carried a story titled "Dr. Brindley All up in the Air—Dr. Potter, Too." The reference was to an airplane trip made by the two doctors one Sunday afternoon in response to a call from a local doctor in the town of Ireland, about fifty miles from Temple. The plane had a stretcher, one seat behind the pilot, and no lights because it was not used for night flying. Their equipment was strapped onto the wing, and Dr. Potter lay down on her stomach on the stretcher while Dr. Brindley took the seat behind the pilot. When the top of the plane was pulled down over her, she could not turn over or raise her head. By hanging it down to the side, however, she could see the ground below. Landing in the designated pasture, they were met by the local doctor, who drove them to the patient's home in his Model-T Ford.

The family took a long time to make the final decision to allow the operation. It was late when the doctors returned to the plane, but although it was nearly dusk, the pilot thought they could make it back to Temple all right. From her prone position, Dr. Potter enjoyed watching the lights come on in the country homes as daylight faded. When Dr. Brindley relayed the pilot's message that they might hang a wheel on the power or telephone lines in trying to land, she replied, "If we land safely, I wouldn't take a million dollars for the trip, and if I die, I die happy." Dr. Brindley, who had a wife and children, said he didn't share her feelings. In the meantime the local doctor had telephoned Dr. Gober that they were on their way. Gober sprang into action, calling some twenty people to come to the airfield to outline the landing strip with their car lights. He then had two immense cotton balls five feet in diameter soaked in kerosene and placed at each end of the field. When they heard the sound of the plane's engine the cotton balls were lighted, and the crowd watched anxiously as the plane descended out of the black sky, hitting the ground with a terrific bump and bouncing to a stop. The doctors had even more reason to give thanks for their safe return when they learned that the plane crashed a few weeks later and the pilot was killed.[101]

Although the hours were long, the work often rigorous, and her salary always far below those of the male doctors, Claudia Potter enjoyed her status as part of the Scott and White family, taking part in the watermelon parties, the annual picnics and Christmas parties, the Sunday dinners at the Scotts, the game parties at the Brindleys, and the dances on the roof garden of the old hospital. She was popular with both the male and female members of the staff and attributed one of her few salary raises to Dr. White's fear that she was about to marry an old friend from UTMB. In the end, however, she preferred to remain single, devoting most of her time to her work and relishing her role of "big sister" to the young staff doctors.

When Dr. White died of a heart attack on March 2, 1917, Claudia Potter was sincerely grieved. After working with him for more than a decade, she had great respect for his ability and had come to believe he was a friend she could approach without hesitation in time of trouble. By the time of White's death, the sanitarium had grown into a 200-bed hospital and clinic that could serve over five thousand people per year. The nursing school had expanded from six graduates in 1906 to thirteen in 1917. In 1922 its name was formally changed to Scott and White to perpetuate the names of the founders. Each year, except for a slight drop during the depression years, the number of patients grew with a concomitant increase in the staff, the specialty departments, and the physical plant. The latter expanded constantly, spreading out in a hodgepodge of new and rented buildings with parklike areas between.

When Claudia Potter joined the Temple Sanitarium, the only choices for inhalation anesthesia were chloroform or ether; she preferred ether and thought it was safer. In 1908 as nitrous oxide gained popularity in the East, Dr. Potter was sent to Johns Hopkins to study its use under Dr. W. D. Gatch, an expert in the field. After her training, Claudia returned to Temple with a Gatch gas machine and began using it at the clinic. Although the results were pleasing to both doctors and patients because the induction was more pleasant than with ether and the recovery more rapid with fewer ill effects, the first machine was crude. It had a mask about eight inches tall made of heavy metal and weighing one pound. Because there was no way to fasten the mask, it had to be held in place by hand; Dr. Potter eventually developed a deformed thumb from holding the clumsy affair in place for hours during many operations. Years later Dr. Potter received credit as the first physician in the state to use gas anesthesia, which marked the beginning of scientific anesthesia in Texas.[102]

She progressed to more efficient machines and gases as they became available. In 1924 she began using ethylene gas, which remained her favorite inhalation anesthetic, although the more powerful cyclopropane (with greater potential side effects) was also in use in the hospital. Also in 1924 Dr. Potter took three graduate nursing students to train as anesthetists. They assisted her and remained in service with the surgical department after she had retired. In November of 1925, she presented a paper before the fourth annual meeting of the Southern Association of Anesthetists on the use of insulin-glucose to prevent postanesthetic nausea and vomiting based on research she had done on 185 patients over an eighteen-month period. The paper was published in the April, 1926, issue of the *Journal of Anesthesia and Analgesia*. At her retirement from Scott and White in 1947, she estimated that she had administered anesthetics to fifty thousand patients.

When Claudia's mother and sister moved to Temple, the three of them lived in a two-story house near the sanitarium. After their mother died, the sisters continued to live together, renting some of the rooms to nurses. Helen Potter taught English and Latin at a junior high school, and she and Claudia were active in the First Christian Church of Temple. When Claudia retired in 1947, she had more time to enjoy her hobbies of gardening and needlepoint, but what she enjoyed most was traveling. Although she loved cars, owning first a Hupmobile and then a Buick, Claudia's reputation as a driver was anything but good. As one doctor put it, "She was renowned for her fast driving and usually on the wrong side of the road."[103] She was in several automobile wrecks, including one serious accident in east Tennessee in which both her legs were broken. Toward the end of her life she suffered a series of strokes, and on February 2, 1970, she died in Scott and White Hospital on the day before her eighty-ninth birthday.

Claudia Potter received many honors in recognition of her contributions to the field of anesthesiology, and she worked with a number of organizations to promote education in her field. She was a founding member of the Texas Society of Anesthesiologists and served as its president in 1946–47. She also held memberships in the American Medical Association and the Southern Medical Association and was a secretary of the Bell County Medical Society. She was an honorary member of Delta Kappa Gamma and a member of the American Association of University Women. In 1952 she was elected to honorary membership in the Texas Medical Association, and in 1954 she received the Golden T award from UTMB for "fifty years of devoted service to the promoting of the health of the people of Texas."

In November of 1961, the American Society of Anesthesiologists passed a resolution making Claudia Potter an honorary member. But perhaps the sweetest praise came from her fellow doctors. At a banquet in her honor on the eve of her retirement, Dr. A. C. Scott, Jr., said: "As a pioneer in gas anesthesia, as our principal anesthetist in the early years, as head of our Anesthetic Department for many years, and as a teacher of some of our best anesthetists, you have been of immeasurable value in making surgery safer for our patients. Thus you have been a potent factor in the establishment of the good reputation this organization bears throughout the South."[104] In a history of the Texas Society of Anesthesiologists, Dr. Charles R. Allen wrote that Dr. Claudia Potter was a pioneer in her field holding "a place of honor among Texas physicians and a very special place of eminence among Texas anesthesiologists."[105]

Dr. May Owen. Courtesy Charles A. Rush, Jr., M.D., Fort Worth, Texas

MAY OWEN, M.D. (1891–1988)

Dr. May Owen never cared for publicity. Toward the end of her long and distinguished career, when she finally agreed at the age of ninety-six to collaborate with a biographer, she warned, "I didn't mind the trip, but wouldn't want it gussied up!"[106] She need not have worried: a simple listing of her accomplishments is amazing enough without any enhancing.

Born on May 3, 1891, in Falls County on a farm "twelve miles from nowhere," May liked to tell the story that her parents were expecting a boy, so when she surprised them, they just gave her the name of her birth month. She also maintained that her Welsh-German heritage accounted for her being "hard-headed and miserly." May was the sixth of the eight Owen children, and by the time she was born the oldest son, Louis, had left the farm to work with a copper-mining company in Arizona Territory. Apparently Louis had strong family feelings, for twenty years later he was the one who would enable May to begin her career.

Meanwhile, May grew up under difficult circumstances. Shortly after her first birthday she developed infantile paralysis, as polio was then called, but because no one understood what caused her painful shrieks when her right shoulder was touched, she was harshly punished for having temper fits. The disease, which left her with a deep depression under the shoulder blade where connective tissue had withered, was not diagnosed until she herself as an adult realized she had had polio. Survival on the farm required the efforts of everyone, and by the time she was two, May was assigned the job of gathering wood for the cookstove. At six she had to pen up the young calves and milk the cows in the morning before walking the three miles to school, repeating the chore in the evening after she returned. From the first day of school she was delighted with the opportunity to learn and to escape for a time the stern rule of her autocratic father, who became even more dictatorial after her mother died. The only book on the farm was the family Bible, which May read repeatedly from cover to cover.

The visits of the doctor who attended her mother during her lingering illness made a lasting impression on May as she watched him come galloping up the dirt road, tie his horse to a tree, and remove his black medical bag. She decided that someday she too would be a doctor with a black bag, riding through a cloud of dust to help her patients. On her ninth birthday she made the mistake of telling her dream to her father, who dismissed it as a "damnfool idea" and ordered her never to mention it again. He did, however, appreciate her skill in working the livestock on the farm and her willingness to spend nights in the barn caring for sick animals. The county veterinarian, who was also impressed with her ability, gave her his old veterinary journals. But when she told him she was thinking of becoming a veterinarian, he had to tell her that he knew of no school that would take a woman.

When thirteen-year-old May finished the seventh grade, she saw no way to continue her education: the nearest high school was in Marlin, twelve miles away, an impossible distance, and she was needed on the farm. So for the next eight years she chopped and picked cotton, tended the garden crops, took care of the farm animals, and cooked the family meals. She loved the animals and the farm, but she never stopped longing for more education. In 1912, when her brother Louis wrote from Arizona that he had arranged for her to attend the preparatory school connected with Texas Christian University in Fort Worth, it seemed like a miracle. Because there was no money for clothes, she dug out some of her mother's old dresses and boarded the train for Fort Worth, prepared to enter high school at the age of twenty-one. A job as dormitory monitor provided money for her tuition, room, and board. The large library especially delighted May, and she promised herself she would read every book in it.

Before she left home her father had told her she was his best hand in the cotton fields. When he wrote that he was desperately short of workers to pick the large cotton crop, May dutifully took the train home on weekends and spent long days dragging her cotton sack up and down the rows from sunup to sundown and even later if there was bright moonlight. On Monday mornings she returned to Fort Worth with hands cut and sore from the sharp bracts that held the cotton balls. Nevertheless she made the highest grades in the academy, earning a scholarship that enabled her to enter Texas Christian University (TCU) when her preparatory schoolwork was completed.

In college May earned her way by grading chemistry papers and acting as student assistant in the chemistry and biology departments. Tall and slender with soft brown eyes and a beautiful face, she did not lack opportunities for dates, but her priorities allowed little time for socializing. She still dreamed of becoming a doctor, and her evenings were needed for studying and grading papers.

During her senior year, she took a job with Terrell Laboratories, a medical laboratory that did tests for physicians and veterinarians. Here she cared for the animals, ran errands, and spent her free time watching the technicians perform tests. Seeing her intense interest and realizing her potential, Dr. Truman Terrell began training May as a technician, and by the time she graduated from TCU at the age of twenty-six, she was dividing her spare time between the laboratory and All Saints Episcopal Hospital. When the Terrells invited her to move into their home, she was delighted. As she told her biographer, "The Terrells were my employers, my friends and now my family."[107] And they and their children would remain her warm, caring family for the rest of their lives.

With the encouragement of the Terrells, she began applying to medical schools but soon found that her sex made her an unwelcome candidate. She persisted, and finally the letter that was to change her life arrived from the Louisville Medical School, saying she had been accepted for the fall semester. She arrived in Louisville, Kentucky, in September of 1917 with great expectations, unaware that she was the first woman accepted by the medical school or that her fellow students had marched to the dean's office to protest having a woman in their class. For weeks she attended classes in an atmosphere of icy disdain, but gradually the male students were forced to admire her quick mind and the obvious ability she had gained from her experience as a laboratory technician. Although May did not approve of the gambling or of the profanity that accompanied the male students' preclass crap games, she agreed to be the lookout to warn them when the professor was approaching, and the thaw was complete. After the United States entered World War I, male students who made poor grades were in imminent danger of being drafted for combat duty. May then undertook to tutor those who were in danger, telling them, "The world needs all the doctors it can get, and I am not about to let any of you get away."[108]

The devastating flu epidemic of 1918 was a crucial factor in May Owen's decision to be a pathologist. Abandoning her childhood dream of carrying a black bag full of cures and riding a horse to attend her patients, she decided to specialize in a field where she could study the causes and effects of diseases. From then on, her curriculum was designed to that end. By the time the class of 1921 was graduated, May had won not only the respect but also the affection of her fellow students, and the entire class stood and applauded when the dean called out, "May Owen, doctor of medicine."

Stepping off the train in Fort Worth, the new doctor was astonished to find that the overgrown country town had become an oil boomtown teeming with new buildings and people. The Terrells and their new daughter welcomed her back, and she found a new office and a well-equipped laboratory waiting for her at the Terrell Laboratories, which occupied an entire upper floor of the Texas State Bank

Building at Ninth and Houston Streets. She plunged into her work with such intensity that Dr. Terrell often had to insist she let up. In addition to working in her own laboratory or in hospital laboratories or in doing autopsies at a local mortuary, she worked with Terrell's North Texas Pasteur Institute. Here, under government contract and supervision, rabies vaccine was manufactured and tissue from animals suspected of having rabies was tested. Her reputation for quick and accurate results spread among veterinarians around the state, and many of them came to rely on her.

After her long working day, she spent the late hours reading medical journals or textbooks but still was not satisfied with her learning. One day she wrote to the Mayo Clinic administrator asking if she might be permitted to observe autopsies and audit lectures. When the clinic invited her to come ahead, she took a leave of absence and went to Rochester (Minnesota), where she had a room in an old hotel connected with the hospital by a tunnel. Whenever autopsies were scheduled in the hospital morgue, she was on the list to be called. The remainder of her time she spent observing tests and techniques in the laboratories and attending lectures, all the while filling her notebooks with copious notes. When the Mayo Clinic offered her an opportunity to work there as a pathologist, she eagerly accepted the job after a telephone conversation with Dr. Terrell.

At the end of a year of rich learning experience at the Mayo Clinic, Dr. Owen returned to Fort Worth by a circuitous route. In Rochester she had met an anesthesiologist from Wisconsin who invited her to come to Madison to study that specialty. She agreed, and while she was completing the course, she earned her living by delivering babies. Upon returning to Texas, she stopped at Scott and White Hospital in Temple to renew her acquaintance with some of the doctors she had met at the Mayo Clinic. The pathologist at Scott and White had not been able to take a vacation for lack of a substitute, and Dr. Owen was persuaded to take over his duties temporarily.

Arriving back in Fort Worth in 1927, she found that Terrell Laboratories had moved to the sixth floor of the new Medical Arts Building. Consequently, she decided to move to the Texas Hotel, which was close to the laboratory and had a coffee shop that stayed open twenty-four hours a day. Always reluctant to spend money on herself, she thought fifty dollars a month for the room "a little steep," but it was such a convenient arrangement she decided to take it. In 1930 she published an article in the *Texas State Journal of Medicine* and one in the *Archives of Pathology* based on her Mayo Clinic research on basal cell carcinoma drawn from the 836 cases she had recorded in her notebooks.

The next year she was called upon to help diagnose a mysterious disease that was killing sheep at the Fort Worth Stockyards. Her research proved the sheep were suffering from diabetes caused by the molasses cakes on which they were being fattened. Her paper, "Diabetic Coma in Feed Lot Sheep," published in veterinary journals, made her known among sheep raisers and veterinarians across the United States and as far away as Australia and New Zealand.

In 1933 another irresistible opportunity for more training in her specialty opened up when she learned that the Medical Examiners Department at Bellevue Hospital in New York was looking for a pathologist. With Dr. Terrell's blessing she applied, and her credentials won her acceptance. Living in New York was an exciting idea for a country girl, and she soon found that the job more than fulfilled her hopes of exploring the city. In contrast to the clinical pathology in hospital settings that had been her previous experience, the forensic pathology to which she was assigned meant she was part of a team from the medical examiner's department sent to investigate death scenes. Their grisly work might take the team to the most sordid slum or to the most luxurious penthouse, and Dr. Owen came to know New York very well indeed. After the bodies were brought to the morgue, she did the autopsies, usually as many as six a day. On Easter Sunday of 1934, she spent the day doing nine autopsies.

At the end of a year she returned to Fort Worth, at last feeling satisfied that she had had the best training available in her field. This fact did not make her egotistical, but it did give her self-confidence in dealing with the few male doctors who still mistrusted the findings of a woman pathologist.

With veterinarians and ranchers she had no problems. Having grown up on a farm, she spoke their language, and over the years she had earned their respect. One Sunday morning at 3 A.M. she received a frantic telephone call from a Hillsboro farmer whose mule had just died. He was afraid it might have had rabies, and in trying to treat it he and his family had all put their hands down the throat of the choking animal. Dr. Owen told them to bring the mule to Fort Worth, where she could meet them. A few hours later, churchgoers who passed by the Medical Arts Building on their way to early mass were astonished at the sight of a woman in the bed of a rusty pickup sawing off the head of a dead mule with a meat saw. After she had removed the tissue she needed, Dr. Owen took it to the laboratory for testing while the farmer and the sons waited. Sometime later she was pleased to be able to tell them that the mule had not been rabid. They went on their way to the rendering plant, and Dr. Owen returned to the laboratory to work for the rest of the day.[109]

The discovery that made Dr. May Owen a celebrity began in 1935 when a Fort Worth surgeon asked her help in determining the cause of severe cramps, nausea, and vomiting in a nineteen-year-old woman who had been successfully operated on for appendicitis almost a year earlier. Examining the fibrous membranes and tumorous nodules the surgeon had removed from his patient in an exploratory operation, Dr. Owen worked through a process of elimination of all the foreign substances that might cause such growths until she arrived at the possibility of the talc glove powder used by surgeons and commonly called French chalk. After research involving 120 rabbits and a year of time, she had proven her theory: even minute particles of the nonabsorbable talc falling into a wound could cause adhesions, scar tissue, and fibrous peritonitis.

In May of 1936 Dr. Owen read her paper, "Peritoneal Response to Glove Powder," at a Texas Medical Association meeting; in November it was published in the *Texas State Journal of Medicine*. French chalk was replaced by a new, starch-based absorbable glove powder, and every patient undergoing abdominal surgery was saved from potential hazards. The Texas Society of Pathologists gave her a Certificate of Meritorious Research, and TCU honored her with a doctor of science degree. May's research brought her no money but much praise and many requests for interviews and speeches. She was uneasy about the publicity until she worked out a way to turn it to advantage in promoting a cause dear to her heart: the recruiting of young people into medicine. From this time on for as long as she lived, she would use her reputation as an example of what a poor farm girl could accomplish. Through counseling, encouragement, and the practical means of financial assistance, she enticed promising young people into medical careers.

The coming of World War II brought thousands of aircraft workers to Fort Worth and pulled many doctors away into military service.

Consequently, Dr. Owen was the only pathologist in town, with five hospitals to serve as well as her work at Terrell Laboratories. She responded by working incredibly long hours until she came down with typhus after examining an animal that had mites. During days of high fever, she remained on the critical and serious hospital lists. As soon as she was slightly recovered, however, she began badgering her doctor to let her return to her laboratory for a few minutes a day. In time she made a full recovery and was back to her sixteen-hour-a-day schedule. Her one luxury was to have Sunday dinners at the Terrells'.

In 1946 Dr. Owen was elected president of the Texas Society of Pathologists, and in 1947 she was made a fellow in the College of American Pathologists. Also in 1947 she became president of the Tarrant County Medical Society, and during her year of leadership the emphasis was on medical education. As director of the School of Medical Technology at Terrell Laboratories, May trained many students who found her a "warm, compassionate human being dedicated to helping people" but nevertheless a strict taskmaster for whom they "dared not do anything less than our dead-level best."[110]

May Owen had always been thrifty: walking to save carfare, spending a minimum on clothing and food, and paying back educational loans the first moment possible. As a result, she had money in her savings to invest in what she considered most important: the education of future doctors. "My professional life insurance" she called the loans she made to promising young men and women, who knew they could turn to her for encouragement, counsel, and friendship as well as financial help.

In the early 1950s Dr. Owen was instrumental in conducting research that was credited with saving the cattle industry in the South and Southwest. When cattle began to die by the thousands from an unknown disease dubbed X, ranchers and veterinarians turned to Dr. Owen for help. For many weeks she spent evenings and weekends climbing pasture fences to examine infected animals, riding hundreds of miles in jeeps, pickups, and other ranch vehicles. And in the laboratory she spent countless hours testing cattle body fluids and organs. Like a detective, she eliminated possibilities until it was established that all of the sick animals showed a pattern of subnormal carotene and vitamin A levels. The cause was traced to commercial feed pellets. Further tests proved the feed was being contaminated both by oil dripping from manufacturing machinery and by mineral oil containing the poisonous substance chlornaphthalene, which had been mixed into the pellets. The disease, which now had a known cause and a remedy, was called hyperkeratosis. As always, Dr. Owen insisted on sharing credit with her associates and with the ranchers and veterinarians who had helped her in finding the cause.

Honors and awards continued to pile up. In 1951 Dr. Owen was named one of the nine outstanding women in Texas, and Vice President Alben Barkley came from Washington to present the awards. In 1952 the Tarrant County Medical Society awarded her its highest honor, the Gold-Headed Cane Award, which she especially cherished because it came from her fellow physicians, who called her "the doctor's doctor."[111] In 1953, when May went to London as a delegate to the first World Conference on Medical Education, the high point of her trip was an afternoon spent with the members of the Welsh Society of London, who welcomed her as a long-lost relative. When she slipped on a curb and broke her right hip, the *Fort Worth Star-Telegram* ran a front-page story on her accident. The next day, however, she was dictating to her secretary, and as soon as she could sit in a wheelchair she was back in her office.

In April of 1960, Dr. May Owen became the first woman president of the 107-year-old Texas Medical Association. At that time she was only the second woman in the United States to serve as president of a state medical association. Not surprisingly, the theme she chose for her administration was education. She also stressed the need to combine modern scientific methods with the personal, friendly touch of the old-time family doctor.[112] Although her position involved many trips to Austin and other cities and towns around the state, she refused to use her expense account, asking instead that the money allocated for that purpose be used to start a benevolent fund to assist needy doctors and their families—a fund still in operation.

In 1961, the Southern Medical Association awarded Dr. Owen a medal for "meritorious and original research work in contributing to medical science." And in 1962 the Woman's Medical College of Pennsylvania in Philadelphia made her a member of the college's national board.

With the passing years her involvement in medical, educational, and civic projects multiplied despite the temporary setback of a coronary occlusion in 1964 at the age of seventy-three. She was one of those who helped bring the Texas Boys' Choir to Fort Worth and served as a trustee for that organization.

May also worked hard to help establish Tarrant County Junior College (TCJC), serving as a trustee. In her travels on behalf of the school, she again refused to use the allocated expense money. One of her pet projects was the establishment of a nursing school in connection with the college, and she donated an endowment of $50,000 to provide scholarships for the TCJC nursing school. In addition, she funded a chair in pathology at the Texas Tech University Health Sciences Center.[113]

Two decades after she had started it, her student loan fund had helped finance the professional careers of more than two hundred doctors, nurses, laboratory technologists, and dentists. And May Owen, who had often walked the five or six miles from the TCU campus to downtown Fort Worth to save the five-cent carfare, took pride in "my boys and girls." When the bookkeeping became too complicated and time-consuming, she proposed that the Texas Medical Association administer the loan fund for which she would put up $300,000. The May Owen Irrevocable Trust was thereby established for the purpose of providing low-interest loans to deserving men and women medical students in Texas.

In the 1960s Dr. Owen spent a great deal of time bringing her longtime dream of a health museum for Fort Worth into being. She visualized it as a place of inspiration for young boys and girls who would become doctors, teachers, and researchers—an educational center explaining life, how it began, and the human body with all its complexities. In 1963, as chairman of the health fair for the Tarrant County Medical Society, she was able to start the efforts that would push the project through to reality; in 1965, the completed Hall of Health Science in Fort Worth was dedicated to Dr. May Owen. Today the Physiology Hall of the Museum of Science and History is dedicated to her.

When Dr. Terrell was forced through ill health to sell Terrell Laboratories, Dr. Owen took a new job (at age seventy-nine) with Tarrant Medical Laboratory near All Saints Hospital. The next year a fall shattered her right hip and broke her left wrist, but following surgery and despite advancing osteoporosis, she bounced back.

Throughout her life Sundays had been workdays, but she had always taken time to attend Episcopal church services each week, even though she was not formally affiliated with any church. She enjoyed the fellowship of the "Breakfast Bunch" that met after early service. When she was eighty-two, she decided to take confirmation classes and was confirmed into Saint Andrew's Episcopal Church.

In 1978, at the age of eighty-seven, May took on a new job as consultant to seven small-town hospitals located within a hundred-mile radius of Fort Worth, while continuing as medical director and pathology consultant at All Saints Hospital. She especially enjoyed the trips into the country, for they allowed her to observe the crops, livestock, and condition of the farms along the way.

In 1986 when another fall and a heart problem put her back in the hospital, the board of trustees of All Saints voted to furnish her with a permanent room at the hospital, an arrangement that delighted her as she had always liked to live close to her work. The Breakfast Bunch from Saint Andrews arranged to meet her for breakfast at the hospital cafeteria after she attended services in the hospital chapel.

Although her body was frail, her mind was as active as ever. She joined the Toastmasters Club to improve her speaking ability and began to study acupuncture. During interviews with her biographer, May expressed a wish to attend the AMA meeting in Chicago and the Kentucky Derby in May.

On Monday, April 11, 1988, Dr. Owen's driver found her waiting in front of All Saints with her usual lunch of a piece of cake and a banana. After visiting Dublin Medical Center and Hico City Hospital in her role of consulting pathologist, she returned to her room. That night she suffered a heart attack and died the next evening, a few weeks before her ninety-seventh birthday. As she had hoped, she had been able to work until the day she died.

When the Texas Society of Pathologists bestowed its highest honor, the George T. Caldwell Award, on Dr. May Owen in 1958, she summed up in her acceptance speech the philosophy that enriched her life and the lives of countless others: "I always believed that we can't wait for things to happen. We must make them happen."[114]

RUTH HARTGRAVES, M.D. (1901–95)
A shoebox full of sandwiches, one suitcase, and five dollars in cash were all the valuables young Dr. Ruth Hartgraves had with her on a five-day train trip from Texas to Boston, where she had finally achieved

Dr. Ruth Hartgraves in her office. Courtesy Harris County Medical Archive, Texas Medical Center Library, Houston, Texas

a hard-to-get internship at the New England Hospital for Women. The year was 1932 and the depression was going full blast, so Dr. Ruth's mother had supplied enough food to last her the whole trip.[115]

Ruth Hartgraves said it was her grandmother who inspired her to become a doctor. "I remember we lived way out in the country, and no doctor could get out there very fast," she recalled. "So when a woman went into labor, my grandmother would jump on her horse and ride out and help that woman." Dr. Hartgraves believed her grandmother delivered more babies than the doctors did.[116]

Ruth was born October 24, 1901, to Frank and Mary Adeline

Hartgraves in Norse, a small west Texas town that no longer exists. Another daughter, Hallie, and a son, Perry, made up the family after a fourth child had died. Her father practiced law in Menard, Texas, where his children attended school. Ruth graduated from nearby Brownwood High School (it was accredited, as Menard's high school was not) in 1919.[117]

Encouraged by their father to pursue medical careers, both Hartgraves girls entered the University of Texas at Austin and then medical school at the University of Texas Medical Branch at Galveston. In those days, it was possible to enter medical school without having completed the B.A. degree. Ruth failed during the 1922–23 school year at UTMB in Galveston, but she was told she could return if she finished her B.A. degree first.[118]

Returning to the University of Texas at Austin, Ruth received her B.A. in 1925. Then, needing money for her return to medical school, she taught science for three years at Matador, Texas. She reentered UTMB in the fall of 1928 and received her M.D. degree in 1932. A classmate who became Dr. Edith Bonnet said of Ruth, "She is a very successful physician down in Houston. I admire her tremendously because she wanted to study medicine, busted out, then went back and made it."[119]

During the years right after World War I, there were more than financial obstacles for a girl interested in medicine to overcome. Dr. Hartgraves remembered that when she wrote about her ambition as a high school senior, the teacher read her paper to the class—in order to ridicule it. Again, at UTMB, Ruth remembered that the admissions officer told incoming students to form two lines: "those who really wanted to become doctors, and those who weren't quite sure." She said, "Some of the girls got in the second line, and then just walked right out the door. . . . I wanted to be a doctor so bad I couldn't stand it, so I got in the first line."[120]

Hallie, whose major problem was always her delicate health, had taken a combination course and spent three years in Austin. She entered UTMB in 1922 and received her B.A. from the University of Texas in June, 1923. She graduated with her M.D. in 1926 but had to rest and regain her strength until the following September before going on to an internship. Knowing her health prohibited the more strenuous specialties, Hallie specialized for a time in ophthalmology, but later she gave up medicine to become an Episcopal nun.[121]

As Dr. Ray K. Daily had discovered earlier, Dr. Hartgraves learned that internships for women were difficult to find. She arrived at the New England Hospital for Women in 1932 and stayed for two years. Applying for residency, she found herself facing regional prejudice. Several hospital administrators, after a single interview, told her they did not consider her training adequate. In 1933–34, however, she served as resident at the New York Infirmary for Women in New York City, and in 1935 she returned to Texas, where she established a private practice in Houston.[122]

From her childhood, Ruth had known that obstetrics and gynecology was the medical field she wanted. Getting started in her specialty, Dr. Hartgraves found that while women were quite ready to accept a female doctor, their husbands were sometimes less adaptable to new ideas. She recalled one man who insisted on sitting in on his wife's physical examination. When Dr. Hartgraves explained that she did not allow spouses to be present during physicals, he ordered his wife to get off the table: he would take her to a male doctor. The couple argued, and Dr. Hartgraves remembered, "She went out of there just screaming and yelling. I never heard from her again."[123]

In those early days, when Houston streetlights were more sparse and less effective, Dr. Hartgraves put a spotlight on top of her car so she could see street numbers on houses at night when she went to deliver babies. In due course, she developed a large clientele in Houston's affluent River Oaks area. One of the future prominent Houstonians she delivered was former mayor Kathy Whitmire.[124]

When World War II took its toll of available men doctors, Dr. Hartgraves was swamped with patients. She remembered sometimes spending days without leaving the hospital. The nurses insisted now and then that she lie down on a movable cot and rest. "I'd sleep for about an hour," she said, "then get up and start working again. It nearly killed me."[125]

From 1943 to 1970 Dr. Hartgraves was a member of the faculty at Baylor College of Medicine, and in 1976 she was made clinical professor emeritus in obstetrics, gynecology, and reproductive sciences at the University of Texas at Houston Medical School. From 1970 on she regularly attended continuing specialty education courses at Baylor, for she recognized the vital necessity of keeping a practice up to date. During those years she held appointments at five local hospitals. Dr.

Ruth was noted for insisting on dressing like a woman, which included wearing hat, gloves, and heels.[126]

By 1966 the exhausting habit common to babies of arriving at inconvenient hours had taken its toll, and Dr. Hartgraves stopped taking obstetrical classes. When she had time to travel, she made four world tours, visiting nearly every country in the world. The archives of the Harris County medical library contain many souvenirs she collected. She was active in her church, Saint Luke's United Methodist, for decades. Also an admirer of the arts, she supported such Houston cultural activities as the opera, the symphony, the ballet, the Museum of Fine Arts, and the Friends of Bayou Bend.[127]

One of Dr. Hartgraves's most pressing goals throughout her practice was to open doors for young women entering the medical field. UTMB now offers a scholarship in her name, and her will provides for an endowed chair in obstetrics and gynecology at that school. She was the first female graduate to make such a testamentary commitment.[128]

Although Ruth Hartgraves did not see herself as a feminist ("I didn't waste any time on that"), she organized Houston's Chapter 42 of the American Medical Women's Association (AMWA) and served as its first president in 1956. She became president of the national group in 1963, and in 1964 the local chapter made her the first recipient of its newly established Ruth Hartgraves, M.D., Award.[129]

When the national AMWA in 1974 gave her the Elizabeth Blackwell Award for her outstanding contribution to the cause of women in medicine, she was the first Texan to receive that honor. For her, the Blackwell Award was doubly gratifying as a rebuttal to those eastern trained women who had once disdained their colleagues from elsewhere. Of all her tributes, Dr. Ruth claimed as greatest the Ashbel Smith Distinguished Achievement Award, which UTMB gave her in 1980. Of its 107 recipients since this award was established in 1965, only five have been women.[130]

In 1993, Dr. Hartgraves made a presentation of her own: she gave to UTMB a bust of herself done by Eugenie Kamrath Mydgal, a Houstonian who, along with her mother, is a former patient of Dr. Hartgraves. The sculptor donated her time and materials to this work of art. In his acceptance speech, Dr. Thomas N. James, UTMB president, called Dr. Hartgraves "an outstanding role model for women and a leader in her chosen field."[131]

National recognition had come to Dr. Ruth as early as 1963, when President John Kennedy named her to his Commission on the Status of Women. Another tribute to her achievements was an honorary doctor of science degree bestowed from Southwestern University of Georgetown, Texas, in 1976. Two years later, the Foundation for Children named her and Dr. Goldie Ham Houstonians of the Year, and Mayor Jim McConn proclaimed November 7, 1978, as Dr. Ruth Hartgraves Day.[132]

In 1994, Dr. Ruth Hartgraves was enjoying life in a Bellaire, Texas, retirement home with the companionship of a former nurse and long-time friend. She spent much time reading her Bible, *Time* magazine, and a newspaper every day. She had remained single during her entire half-century medical career. She commented that she had enjoyed her life's work: "It's essential to establish rapport with a patient, and I relate with each on a one-to-one basis. You might say a patient becomes my friend." In her fifty-odd working years, that is more than seventy-five thousand friends.[133] She died October 17, 1995, at the age of ninety-three.

In the Clinic

MINNIE CLIFTON ARCHER, M.D. (1872–1912)
In a brief mention of female physicians, *The Medicine Man in Texas* quotes "Funny Fern" as saying in *The Standard* (March 26, 1853): "For myself, I prefer prescriptions written by a masculine hand; shan't submit my pulse to *anything that wears a bonnet!*"[134]

Nineteen years later, Minnie Clifton Archer was born to Dr. and Mrs. W. A. Archer of Houston. In 1898, she would become the first woman member of the Texas State Medical Society. After achieving a "perfect record" at Houston High School and at Kidd-Key College at Sherman, Texas, in 1894, she was graduated from the Woman's Medical School of Pennsylvania.[135]

Following postgraduate work in her specialty, eye, ear, nose, and throat, Dr. Minnie Archer set up a well-equipped office in Houston in 1895 and began a practice that quickly grew large. In 1910, she was appointed secretary of the Houston chapter of the American Medical Association's Public Health Education Committee.[136]

Always correctly dressed, young Dr. Archer was an impressive sight as she motored around Houston going to her office and making her hospital rounds in one of the first electric coupes brought to town.[137]

Minnie Archer, who was said to possess a "sweet womanly personality," had only seventeen years to exercise her medical skills, for she died of pneumonia February 8, 1912, only a few days after the death of her mother, whom she had been nursing and from whom she had contracted that disease.[138]

In a memorial address, Dr. T. T. Jackson of San Antonio remarked, "It is enough to be a woman . . . but a woman physician—a woman doctor, a capable, educated woman doctor, who gives her life to this profession—none can be greater. There is a wonderful field . . . a field almost unexplored in the branches of this profession for woman, and thank God, she is coming into her own."[139]

A more personal tribute appeared in her obituary notice in *The Houston Chronicle*: "She was a woman possessed of a splendid personality. Her death causes a gap in the professional life of the city which will be difficult to fill." This is a far cry from the "Funny Fern" remarks of a half-century before.[140]

RAY KARCHMER DAILY, M.D. (1891–1975)

"On dark rainy nights crowds of men, women and children are led through the woods, swamps and rivers till the border of Russia is passed. Who can describe the mental agony that the immigrant lives through in the short time?" These two sentences are part of an essay written by sixteen-year-old Ray Karchmer of Denison, Texas, describing her escape with her family from Lithuania and their flight to America.[141]

The Karchmer family considered themselves Russians and in fact had Russian citizenship, though as Jews they were not permitted to live in Russia itself. Their home and Ray's birthplace in 1891 was Vilna, Lithuania. Years later, Dr. Ray K. Daily's son, Louis, described the family's flight as being part of the "Great Emigration." In those times Jews in Russia and its border states suffered great discrimination, including massacres by the Cossacks. There were frequent pogroms—uprisings against Jews inspired by priests who would tell the peasants horror stories about alleged Jewish customs. "Life was really hell for Jews over there," Dr. Louis Daily comments, adding that the musical *Fiddler on the Roof* paints a realistic picture of their sufferings.[142]

How did the Karchmer family happen to come to Galveston, Texas, when so many earlier European Jews had emigrated to New York and

Dr. Ray Daily. Courtesy Blocker History of Medicine Collections,
Moody Medical Library, University of Texas
Medical Branch, Galveston, Texas

stayed there? Dr. Louis Daily remembered reading in a Jewish magazine that the rich Jewish people who had previously arrived, prospered, and established themselves in New York found that their sheer numbers were creating problems for them. The new people tended to form ghettos, thus fostering segregation and putting the previous arrivals in an anomalous position. To relieve this situation, established New York Jews enlisted the aid of the well-known Rabbi Cohen in Galveston to persuade newcomer Jewish families to spread out more. About ten thousand Jews who came to Galveston were sent by the rabbi's arrangements to various other places in the South and Southwest. Rabbi Cohen selected locations by the demand for specific skills: some cities needed mechanics, some could use garment workers. All the skilled laborers from Europe who passed through the rabbi's hands quickly found work. Soon after this large influx, the United States government tightened its policy toward immigrants.[143]

After Ray Karchmer graduated from Denison High School at the top of her class, she wanted to go to medical school. At that time one could go directly to medical school from high school, but she was aware that this was the last year before a college degree would begin to be required.

Ray earned a scholarship, but she had to be eighteen to enter medical school: she was more than a year too young. Her father said to her, "So you got to be eighteen? You're eighteen!" Who could say anything different? Their harried life in the old country had not left behind any birth certificates. Ray graduated from the University of Texas Medical Branch at Galveston at the top of her class. She was the first Jewish woman to graduate from a Texas medical school.[144]

"It was difficult enough, when I was young, for a woman to get a medical education, and when I graduated from medical school in 1913, it was not easy to get an internship and impossible to get a residency," Dr. Ray Daily later recalled. Since she could not afford to pay room and board even with her scholarship, she interned at Woman's Hospital in Philadelphia because it was the only hospital with a dormitory for women.[145]

When she returned to Texas in 1914, Dr. Ray Karchmer married Dr. Louis Daily, whom she had met in medical school. They decided to set up an office where they would practice the specialty known as eye, ear, nose, and throat. As the partnership evolved, Ray did the ophthalmology and Louis did the ear, nose, and throat work. In summer they took turns going to Europe for further studies in their special fields. Vienna and Berlin, as their son recalled, were then "the Athens of ophthalmology" and of other specialties as well. In 1923, when he was four years old, Dr. Ray took him to Europe so she could study for six months. The boy was later told that he forgot how to speak English during this sojourn. He added that he quickly forgot his German after they returned home.[146]

Dr. Ray K. Daily plunged into the political and social mainstream of Houston early, pressing for issues about which she had strong convictions. She wrote copiously, including many medical articles, and became the author or coauthor of nine books. She was "an officer in all kinds of things," as her son put it. He did not remember that his parents suffered any impediment to their professional advancement from ethnic prejudices. His mother was very active politically and was friends with people of influence such as Mayor Oscar Holcombe and Mefo Foster, editor-in-chief of the *Houston Press*. She was a good friend of Lillie Jolley, a registered nurse who ran the nursing school for Memorial Hospital, then located in downtown Houston. Robert Jolley was superintendent of that hospital.[147]

Dr. Ray began her public activities by joining and participating in Jewish groups and gradually moved into broader-based community affairs. In 1921 Mayor Holcombe appointed her a member of the board of health. She spoke to such groups as the Lions Club, the Menorah Society at Rice Institute, and the Daughters of the American Revolution. She was one of the founders of the Houston Academy of Medicine and of the Open Forum, which was established locally in 1926. Ray also served as president of the College and Professional Women's Organization. As an active advocate of woman suffrage, she participated in marches for that cause. An article in the *Houston Post-Dispatch* quoted Dr. Ray Daily's conclusion as to the impact that woman suffrage had on American society: "Another step in the intellectual evolution on mankind."[148]

In 1928, Dr. Ray Daily ran for the Houston Independent School District Board of Trustees and was elected. She was to remain a member of that body until 1952. About that time she was inducted into the American College of Surgeons in Philadelphia. A United Press newspaper article quoted Dr. Daily: "I strongly advise any woman who loves medicine to go ahead with her work and she will not find her sex a disadvantage."[149]

A money crunch brought on by the depression had its effect on Houston schools as it did across the country. A newspaper of the period quotes Dr. Daily as strongly opposing "the present movement to discriminate against married women"—apparently a measure proposed to spread employment opportunities by restricting jobs to one per couple. Dr. Daily said, "There is a movement growing all over the country to push married women out of jobs. . . . This year more married teachers are being given leaves." She stated her belief in judging teachers solely on efficiency instead of on "whether they are married or can afford to quit teaching."[150]

Dr. Daily fought in the following years to keep the school hygiene budget from being lowered and to float a bond issue so that a federal grant could be secured. In 1940, twelve years after she was first elected to the board, Dr. Daily became the first woman ever to be its president. Her election was unanimous. Eight years later she was still working hard for change and improvement. The board had to decide whether to raise graduation credits for Houston high schools from eighteen to twenty. Stating that it would cost the schools $160,000 a year to raise the number of credits, she proposed an alternative: "Since children don't seem to know what they need in high school, why don't we put that money into an adult education program and let them take what they need there?"[151]

A highlight of her school board career occurred in 1933 during Dr. Daily's presidency. She led a delegation representing Houston schools to a hearing before a joint session of the Texas Legislature, where she made a fervent appeal for more school funding. Ray pointed out that in that dark depression year, many schools had to function on a part-time basis. She promised the legislators that whatever taxes they devised, their voters would support them.[152]

It was Dr. Ray K. Daily who, at a meeting of the school board in 1943, moved for the adoption of a resolution to expand Houston Junior College into what is now the University of Houston. Turmoil followed over the details of separating the university from the Houston Independent School District. Dr. Daily led the opposition to giving the giving the board of regents power to hire and fire all university personnel. Her fear was that the regents, being a lay board, might well have "too limited knowledge" to make the best judgments concerning academic abilities. She wanted such powers entrusted to professional educators. Ultimately, the separation was effected, making the university entirely independent of the district.[153]

Added responsibilities began to cut into Dr. Daily's time: she was elected the first woman president of the medical staff at Houston's Memorial Hospital, and she also served as the president of the charity hospital, Jefferson Davis. These activities limited her attendance at the school board meetings and contributed to her defeat for reelection to the board in 1952.[154]

Honors came to Dr. Ray as she continued to work, write, translate and abstract foreign articles, and produce 16-mm films on surgical procedures for the use of Harvard and other medical schools. The American Academy of Ophthalmology and Otolaryngology elected her vice-president. On June 10, 1970, she was awarded the coveted Ashbel Smith Distinguished Alumni Award from her alma mater in Galveston.[155]

Louis Daily, Jr., does not think his parents suffered much from prejudice in Houston, even though "Jews were treated worse than Hispanics at one time. They couldn't live in River Oaks till about 1938." Still, prejudice in Houston was "not as much as up East." At Choate, he was not invited to debutante balls. At Harvard, he and fellow Jews were in fact segregated to the extent of being assigned rooms all in one section of Wigglesworth, the dormitory where he lived. Dr. Ray Daily's friendship with the outspoken Mefo Foster of the *Houston Press* may have shielded her from some attacks. Foster was the most forthright advocate of civil rights of that time in this part of the country; he actively fought the resurgent Ku Klux Klan.[156]

Dr. Ray was a charming person "when she wanted to be . . . and she could be tough when she wanted to be." She wouldn't tolerate any slackness. She sent her son off to school because she was ambitious for him and because she had wealthy friends who were able to get him in. The Dailys had invested largely in Houston real estate; when after the stock market crash the payments could not be kept up, they lost a great deal. Dr. Ray Daily had four brothers and her parents to support after she became established. As her son remarked about the lean years, "Bad things happened to families during the depression."[157]

In 1950, Dr. Ray took her son to Europe so she could take some courses from a pioneer in ophthalmology at the University of Vienna. They obtained a visa and went to a little atticlike tourist agency in Vienna where they spent the night. When they woke in the morning and had to give their passports to the concierge, they discovered they were in the Russian zone. Dr. Ray became very anxious, since this was the height of the Cold War, and people were disappearing behind the Iron Curtain. She knew the Russians could claim her as a Russian citizen. A family could lose a relative in the middle of the night; this had been happening in Vienna. They immediately went out and found a room to which they could move in the American zone.[158]

These summer study trips bore fruit in the practices of the Daily physicians. When Louis was still a boy, Dr. Ray would find someone to stay with him while she attended classes. The two of them traveled cabin class (never first class) and stayed in small apartments, which was the least expensive way. Visiting a famous cataract surgeon in Prague, Dr. Ray learned the intracapsular method of cataract removal. This was an advance in the cataract surgery of the time, and Dr. Ray used it on a generation of patients.[159]

The elder Dr. Louis Daily died in January, 1954, but the Daily Eye Clinic continued. Young Dr. Louis joined the team as an ophthalmologist. "She loved the work not just as a way to make a living, but for itself," he said of his mother, "and she made me love it."[160]

In 1973 Dr. Ray became very ill, but she would not give up her practice. She would come into the office, rest on the couch for a couple of hours, and see a few patients. About nine months before the end, she became too ill to come to the office at all. She died in November, 1975. An obituary article by Joseph Samuels, publisher of the *Jewish Herald-Voice*, refers to the "absurd McCarthy-type charges" of which Dr. Ray Daily had been "cleared" by some government agency in her last, contentious campaign for a school board position. Editor Samuels had also entered the race for a different position, he said, for the purpose of promoting the creation of an educational television station. He noted, "She did lose the election—and so did I. However, we did get the education television station—Channel 8."[161]

A most fitting memorial to Dr. Ray K. Daily is the fact that fifteen or so years after her campaign for free lunches for poor schoolchildren was defeated, the free-lunch program became a permanent feature in Houston schools.

GOLDIE SUTTLE HAM (HANSON), M.D. (1896–1979)
Almost from the time of her birth in Atlanta, Georgia, in 1896, Goldie Suttle Ham knew she had something to prove. After a son born earlier to her parents died in infancy, her father had desperately wished for another boy. A year later a sister, Bess, was born, and finally the longed-for boy, Gatewood, arrived. By that time, however, Goldie had been deeply hurt by the knowledge that she was a disappointment to her father.[162]

At the turn of the century the family moved to Greenville, Mississippi, where Mr. Ham and his brother established a large furniture store. Despite her childhood rheumatic fever that had left her with a "rheumatic heart," young Goldie became a tomboy. She even rode astride, still not a common practice for girls in those days. She loved biology and sometimes dissected dead animals she found alongside the roads.

Goldie entered Agnes Scott College in Decatur, Georgia, and a year later Bess enrolled there. When Goldie came down with a bout of diphtheria, the illness delayed her graduation with a B.A. in mathematics by a year. Consequently, she and Bess were in the same graduating class, and since Bess came first alphabetically, she preceded her older sister down the aisle to get her diploma. This episode furnished enough sisterly ammunition to Bess for a lifelong family joke.

Goldie continued to be plagued by delicate health, and doctors said she ought to stay in bed. They predicted she would not live long enough to have a career and said she certainly ought not to marry. These dire predictions may have reinforced her father's strong opposition to her desire for a medical career. As he put it, that was not for women. This daughter, however, was as strong-willed as her father, and she later said there was never a time when she did not want to be a doctor. In fact, her family doctor was so impressed with her interest in medicine that he allowed the sixteen-year-old Goldie to "scrub up" and assist him in surgery at a Mississippi charity hospital. Although all she really did was to hand him instruments, it was a powerful experience for her.[163]

Goldie's bachelor uncle volunteered to finance a medical career for her—as long as the medical school was not anywhere up north. When Goldie enrolled as a medical student at Tulane in New Orleans, her relationship with her father broke completely. Nevertheless, despite the great emotional distress this break caused her, she pursued her medical studies successfully. In 1922 she was inducted into Tulane's chapter of the medical honor society, Alpha Omega Alpha.

She was in medical school, living with a family of Christian Scientists at the end of World War I, when she came down with Spanish flu. Some of her classmates brought her a human arm and shoulder so she could catch up with her anatomy class. They hung it in the woodshed, and when a hired boy came to chop wood, he took one look in the shed and disappeared. The family never saw him again.

Dr. Ham's daughter remarked that her mother learned in medical school to overcome her sensitiveness. "She liked to be in control," the daughter remembered, adding, "She also had a wonderful sense of humor." When Goldie was warned of one professor who told his classes he would automatically fail any woman student who cut her hair, she went ahead and bobbed her hair. Although she was prudent enough to wear a beret, her haircut was noticed, and she received a failing grade. Goldie went to the board of regents, proved she had satisfactorily completed the work for that course, and eventually graduated in the top ten of her class.[164]

During her internship at Charity Hospital of Louisiana in New Orleans, Goldie heard good things about Houston as a place to practice medicine. A woman friend told her it was the "city of the future," and Dr. P. H. Scardino, a male friend with a large Houston practice, convinced her to begin there. She became the first woman resident at Saint Joseph's, then the largest hospital in Houston. After her residency, Dr. Ham became associated with Dr. Scardino in general practice, and by 1930 she had "drifted into" a specialty in obstetrics and gynecology.

During her residency, there had been no facilities at Saint Joseph's to allow Dr. Ham to live in the hospital as the male residents did. She lived in a boardinghouse and, during 1925, at the YWCA. Such inconveniences continued after she began private practice. Although Saint Joseph's had a resting room for male doctors who might have to deliver more than one baby per trip, there was no such place for female doctors. It took Dr. Ham until the early fifties to finally persuade the hospital to set aside one small room for the women doctors' use.

Since she had survived past the ripe age of thirty in spite of everyone's expectations, Goldie Ham thought she might as well risk marriage. In 1932, at thirty-six, she married Gordon Bell Hanson, an engineer and the president of Howe-Baker Corporation, whom she had known about six years. She gave her prospective husband the premarital physical herself. Her daughter Ann was born when Dr. Ham was thirty-seven, and she was forty when her second girl, Elizabeth, was born, a difficult birth that brought Goldie close to death. Each time, Dr. Ham worked right up to delivery time.

Dr. Ham kept her own surname because her practice was already established, usually signing herself "G. Suttle Ham" because she hated her first name. Perhaps, too, she used an ambiguous name to avoid antifemale prejudice. She was on both the obstetrical and the consulting staffs of Jefferson Davis and Saint Joseph's hospitals. She actively supported the Planned Parenthood Association, the League of Women Voters, the YWCA, the Houston Symphony Society, the Museum of Fine Arts, and the Houston Opera Association.[165]

Goldie Ham maintained a highly organized home life for her family. Her children always had a nursemaid along with other household servants, but Goldie read to the girls at night. A very strict French governess helped manage their orderly style of life: dinner was a special occasion for which they were expected to dress. Daddy carved, and the meal was served formally. Her daughter Elizabeth said her mother was a firm believer in dressing elegantly for work and that her appearance was always meticulously correct. Dr. Ham sewed "beautifully" (an ability that came in handy for surgical procedures) and she made all her daughters' formals during their school years.

When it sometimes happened that no servants were in the house overnight, Mr. Hanson was away on business, and her elder sister was in college, Elizabeth Hanson remembered that Dr. Ham, rather than leave her alone in the house, would wake her and take her along for a night delivery. Sometimes her mother would be driving home at 4 A.M. with young Elizabeth holding the door open to see where the edge of the road was on a densely foggy morning. In some seasons the Texas coastal area produces real pea-soup fogs; often the murk was so thick Elizabeth could not see ahead. She doesn't know how her mother managed when she was driving alone.

Goldie Ham never turned people away on account of race or lack of funds. She practiced before the days of wonder drugs, and her daughter believed she had a sense for diagnosis and a "sense for healing" more potent than some more modern doctors have time to develop. Mr. Hanson was a man before his time in accepting his wife's profession and its complications. Her daughter observed that Dr. Ham didn't worry about male/female equality because she didn't consider it possible to "bring men up to our level."

In Dr. Ham's early days of practice, the four main Houston hospitals were Saint Joseph's, old Methodist, Hermann, and Jefferson Davis. For a time she had alternating periods on and off duty at the latter. She also lectured occasionally at Baylor Medical College. During World War II she took over the obstetrics and gynecology practice of her friend, Dr. Maurice Meynier. During the baby boom of the 1960s, her waiting room was always full. At one point Dr. Ham had two offices because she was reluctant to abandon old patients by closing the one near Saint Joseph's. She therefore ran back and forth from it to her new office on alternating hours.

When she gave up the obstetrical part of her work, Dr. Ham missed the joyfulness of childbirth and the pleasure of working with well patients. She calculated that she had averaged delivering one baby per day during her thirty-five years' practice. In 1964 she retired fully. Although for many years of her practice women had not been admitted to the Harris County Medical Society, in 1965 Dr. Ham was elected to honorary membership in the Texas Medical Association.[166]

After retirement, Dr. Ham occasionally spoke to students in local schools. She was a board member of the Foundation for Children, and she received the foundation's Houstonian of the Year Award in 1978 along with a colleague, Dr. Ruth Hartgraves. Her retirement years were busy with sewing for seven grandchildren and "hauling friends around town." She could hardly go anywhere in Houston without encountering people she had delivered: there had been almost twelve thousand babies. Before her death at the age of eighty-three in 1979, she had the satisfaction of knowing she had overcome not only her own physical frailty but also any assumptions of inadequacy that some men of her father's generation attributed to women in general. Her daughter Elizabeth claimed as part of her heritage from her mother, "I never thought that I couldn't do something because I was a woman."[167]

CLOTILDE P. GARCÍA, M.D. (1917–)

"Hell on wheels" was the way José Antonio (Tony) Canales described his mother, Dr. Clotilde García. Certainly she has had to be a dynamo to achieve the recognition and honors her grateful state and nation have bestowed on her. Dr. García has delivered ten thousand babies during her almost fifty years as a general practitioner and surgeon in Corpus Christi, Texas.[168]

Born in Mercedes, Texas, in 1917, Clotilde García was one of seven children who were earmarked by their parents for careers in medicine. Her father, José G. García, and her mother, Faustina Perez García, both schoolteachers, set high goals for their brood and furnished the loving, stimulating home environment needed to achieve those goals. Dr. García remembered how competing with her siblings for parental

Dr. Clotilde García. Courtesy Dr. Clotilde García, Corpus Christi, Texas

praise stimulated her desire to succeed. Six of the seven children became medical doctors.[169]

Getting there wasn't easy for Clotilde. After growing up in the depression years, she earned her bachelor of arts from Pan American
University in Edinburg, Texas, and two years later a B.A. from the
University of Texas (UT). During the UT years she did such part-
time work as bookkeeping, sales clerking, and being a library assistant. With her two elder brothers in medical school and younger
brothers and sisters nearing college age, Clotilde knew she would have
to pause in her own education and find a teaching job. For a Mexican-American woman, finding a good assignment was especially
difficult. She got her start in a two-room ranch school, a job that paid
$800 per year.[170] In those days, the average Texas teacher earned $1,000
to $2,000 per year.

World War II brought Clotilde García a soldier husband and a son,

Tony Canales. The marriage did not succeed, and the young mother soon found herself alone with the responsibility of bringing up a youngster. Years after Tony had matured and become a lawyer, Dr. García remarked that "the fulfillment of motherhood and raising and educating my son" was an achievement even more precious to her than her own accomplishment in becoming a doctor. She also felt that, aside from parenthood, being able to improve the care of children through her medical work "has been my greatest satisfaction and my greatest contribution."[171]

When Clotilde doubted that she would ever earn a medical degree, her brother Dr. Hector García encouraged her to apply at the University of Texas Medical School, and she was accepted in 1950. In 1954, she became one of the first Mexican-American women to earn the M.D. degree.[172]

Beginning her medical practice in Corpus Christi, Dr. García found that she must teach as well as treat her patients. Observing that many of them suffered from poor nutrition, she taught them about a healthful diet and proper care for their bodies. More interested in people than in money, Dr. García was especially committed to seeing that babies and children grew into healthy adults.[173]

Dr. García has always been a general practitioner and experiences her greatest happiness when she delivers a baby. She is also concerned for many of the elderly people who visit her office because those who were formerly maids or laborers are often not receiving Social Security.[174]

Clotilde García seems never to have said no to a cause she deemed worthy of support. In 1984, her memberships included five professional associations and twenty-eight civic and charitable organizations. Her membership in the American GI Forum came about at the urging of its founder, her brother Dr. Hector García. This group was organized after World War II to assist veterans in obtaining employment, education, and health care.[175] She became state director of the forum's Committee on Education, and she is also a member of its Ladies' Auxiliary. Many of Dr. García's special interests are rooted in her vital concern for Hispanic Americans and their children: she has worked with the Nueces County Antipoverty Program, the Carmelite Day Nursery (she donated a van for the use of its nuns), Catholic Charities, LULAC, and other groups directly involved in the nourishment and education of less-privileged children.[176]

Another area that has engaged Dr. García's deep interest is the preservation of Mexican-American history and genealogical records. She has written five books on Mexican-American history, and she founded the Spanish-Americans Genealogical Association (SAGA). To help Spanish-Americans trace their family lines, she donated to the Corpus Christi Library a limited edition of encyclopedias of Spanish surnames compiled by Alberto y Arturo García Carraffa. Her SAGA group has developed thirty-two books of computer printouts from parish records in Texas and Mexican towns. Organized alphabetically and by date, these records can reveal their roots to interested Mexican Americans.[177]

In 1973, Dr. García agreed to be one of seven women appointed to the thirty-seven-member State Constitutional Revision Committee. In a Corpus Christi newspaper article, she explained how she planned to cover her medical practice for half a year so that she could work on the revision committee. In spite of her feeling that more women should have been included on the committee, she said, "I wouldn't miss it for anything."[178]

Busy as she has been with her medical practice and all the writing and committee work on the side, Dr. García keeps herself buoyed up by an unfailing sense of humor. Bounding in late because of an inconveniently timed natal call, she announced to members of the meeting she was to address, "I just delivered another Democrat!"[179]

To a newspaper staff writer, Clotilde García revealed some of her extramedical concerns: "My cause is to help people become aware of their rights and privileges. . . . Thank God I'm able to be involved in causes." She strongly supports her Roman Catholic faith, both with group work and with financial contributions. She advocates bilingual education but insists it should be a tool for teaching English to students, not an excuse for them to continue speaking Spanish.[180]

In 1977 she was appointed to a forty-six-member task force to evaluate the state's medicaid program—an appropriate task for one who proudly wears the title "Doctor of the Barrio."[181]

A gratifying instance of public recognition for Dr. García occurred in 1983 when Del Mar College of Corpus Christi named the Dr. Clotilde P. García Science and Health Building in her honor. She served as a regent of the college for twenty-two years. In 1984, a ten-member panel including Governor Mark White named Dr. García one of twelve inductees into the new Texas Women's Hall of Fame.[182]

At a dazzling Texas Gala night on May 16, 1990, Clotilde García received an exceptional international honor: she was given Spain's Royal American Order of Isabella the Catholic. The medal, which is a general Order of Merit, was handed to Dr. García by a representative of His Majesty King Juan Carlos I. Local, state, and national government representatives, including Senator Lloyd Bentsen, added their voices to the chorus of praise for Dr. García's lifetime of achievement. Congratulations from the pope himself were sent through the Most Reverend Rene H. Gracida, bishop of the Diocese of Corpus Christi. An elegant printed brochure gives the story of the historic order awarded to Dr. García and includes pictures of Queen Isabella and the modern Spanish king and queen; of a descendant of Christopher Columbus, who shared the occasion in an open letter praising Dr. García; and of notable persons attending the affair.[183]

Very likely, on her night of triumph, this hardworking, humanitarian doctor thought back to the anxious time when she was a young single parent, short of every advantage except hope, courage, and faith.

In the Classroom

MARIE CHARLOTTE SCHAEFER, M.D. (1874–1927)
From high school to medical school was a possible leap for a bright student in 1894. Marie Charlotte Schaefer, who had been salutatorian of San Antonio High School a year before, taught in San Antonio's public school system one year and then enrolled in the medical branch of the University of Texas at Galveston. She graduated in 1900; by then only a handful of women had received medical degrees at UTMB.[184]

After doing postgraduate work at the University of Chicago and at Johns Hopkins, in 1901 Dr. Schaefer became the first woman on the faculty of UTMB. She served as demonstrator of histology in the medical school and as resident pathologist at John Sealy Hospital. In 1910 she was elected associate professor in biology and histology at the medical branch; in 1915 she was made a full professor of embryology; and in 1925 she became full professor of histology, a branch of biology dealing with the microscopic study of the structure of tissues.[185]

Her superiors described the young professor as methodical, punctual, and economical in the use of her time and effort. She enjoyed remembering good students who later made brilliant professional records, but she also watched with interest and helped those who were not so blessed.[186]

The head of the Department of Bacteriology, Dr. William B. Sharp, described Charlotte Schaefer's impact on students and colleagues this way:

> The students continued through the years to regard her semiseriously as a character. They complained that she rode them hard! Where another teacher might ask them to describe a structure, Schaefer must have it in the minutest detail. . . .
>
> In the eyes of the bacteriology personnel she was a character of different mold, pleasant and gracious, as witnessed by her generosity with facilities. [She had] expert use of carpentering tools, for adding to scant office and laboratory equipment.[187]

Dr. Schaefer's most important contribution to medical literature was probably her paper "Ancylostoma Duodenale in Texas," which was published in the *Medical News* in New York. This article appeared soon after her finding of the prevalence of hookworm infestation in the southern states. This discovery came about when Dr. Schaefer, doing a routine examination of stool for amoebae, found hookworm ova. Further investigations by Dr. Schaefer and her students revealed parasites in the feces of 10 percent of the students, who represented counties from every part of Texas.[188]

Dr. Charlotte Schaefer had a rare opportunity to express her deeply felt philosophy of medicine when in October of 1912 she addressed the entire UTMB freshman student body. To the medical students, she remarked, "The human relations of the physician have expanded from the personal merely to the widely social and even to the racial. This is the day of the practical realization of the interdependent brotherhood of man."[189]

To the nurses, she explained, "The first ministers to suffering human creatures were women—mother-nurses. You young women . . . owe a great debt to the heroic struggles of women before you who have heard the call of suffering and responded to it, though their response required the martyrdom which comes to those who defy unthinking prejudice and sentimentality in hewing a new way."

For the pharmaceutical students, she warned of "the evil of patent medicines purchased by a public educated to an astonished medical gullibility by advertisements of nostrums and quacks, and of the prescribing of manufactured medicines by unscrupulous or half-trained doctors, ignorant of the formulae they are using." She said that the honest druggist must stand against this invasion of the field of the physician and must also resist the encroachments of the manufacturers upon the pharmacist's domain.

Dr. Schaefer died suddenly and unexpectedly, in the midst of her usual daily work. Graduation time was at hand, but out of respect for Dr. Schaefer, all entertainments for May, 1927, were canceled, and the Final Ball was not held. Never having married, Dr. Schaefer was survived by her sisters.[190]

VIOLET KEILLER, M.D. (1887–1958)

According to her first resident, Dr. Jack Pruitt of Lufkin, "about seventy-five pounds" was all there was to Dr. Violet Keiller. That diminutive size in no way interfered with her forty-five-year career in medicine, first at the University of Texas Medical Branch at Galveston and later at Hermann Hospital in Houston.[191]

Violet Keiller was born in Edinburgh, Scotland, in October, 1887. She and her parents emigrated to America in 1891. Dr. William Keiller, her father, had started his college career as an art student but had then become fascinated with anatomy. Having graduated from the University of Edinburgh with honors, he was appointed lecturer in anatomy at Edinburgh just a year before he decided to emigrate in answer to a "professors wanted" advertisement. He became the first professor of anatomy at UTMB.[192]

After graduating from Bryn Mawr in 1910, Violet Hannah Keiller entered the Galveston medical school and graduated in 1918, but not without at least one feminist incident. In 1912, the fifteen female medical students tried to ensure a voice for their sex in the Students' Council by making the office of secretary-treasurer permanently reserved for women. This motion did not pass, but Violet became secretary-treasurer for that year.[193]

Instead of interning, Violet joined the staff of UTMB, working with Dr. James E. Thompson in surgical pathology until his death in 1927. She then accepted the position of pathologist at Hermann Hospital in

Houston, along with a teaching position at Baylor University Medical School when it moved from Dallas to Houston.[194]

During the 1920s and 1930s, Dr. Keiller published some fourteen or more articles in professional journals. One of these, concerning spina bifida, was published in a British journal. During those busy first years in Houston, she also went back to teach at Galveston twice a week.[195]

Dr. Jack Pruitt met Dr. Keiller during his internship in 1943. He later described some of the early days at Hermann. Dr. Keiller had a little laboratory on the east side of the clinic wing of the old building. Their only paraffin microtome (an instrument used to cut thin sections of tissue to study under a microscope) was "a huge sliding monstrosity." Tissues were stained by hand; both Dr. Pruitt and Dr. Keiller frequently suffered severe phenol reactions in this process. To Dr. Pruitt, the ultimate of this primitive method was that Dr. Keiller hand-wrote all the pathology reports at a little desk near the microscope.[196]

Dr. Keiller invited Dr. Pruitt to become her first resident when his state of health prevented him from joining the armed services during World War II. He stayed with her three years. He remembered that Violet Keiller always wore a pure silk dress and a linen apron to work and was spotless despite a persistent slight aura of formaldehyde. She served coffee or tea each morning or afternoon, using her Spode china. All the lab staff and any available medical staff were invited to partake. One day a saucer was missing; Dr. Pruitt presumed it had perished. Later, on a trip to west Texas, he found an exact match for the out-of-stock saucer and sent it to Dr. Keiller. She sent him a most effusive thank-you letter.[197]

A highlight of Dr. Pruitt's residency with Dr. Keiller came when the two of them read about the discovery of the Rh factor in blood. This gave them an explanation of some of the difficulties they had observed in transfusing blood. They relished, too, the frequent visits of their neighbor across the street, Baylor pathologist Dr. Paul Wheeler. "We gave him whatever gross specimens he wanted to use in his teaching, and he took them home in a big tin bucket," recalled Pruitt.[198]

Dr. Pruitt remembered how Dr. Violet Keiller always made herself available to demonstrate surgical and clinical pathology and helped the observers to understand what they were seeing and doing. He added, "I don't know of any intern or resident that did not adore her."[199]

When she retired in 1948, Dr. Keiller by no means quit working. She served as a consultant to the M. D. Anderson Hospital and Tumor Institute and to Hermann Hospital. She had served as chair of the Texas Medical Association's Section of Pathology in 1930; in 1953 she was elected to honorary membership.[200]

Soon after her retirement, former interns and residents of Hermann Hospital established the Violet H. Keiller Award to give the most outstanding student each year an opportunity to pursue further his or her medical education.[201]

Dr. Waldemar Schmidt, who joined the University of Texas Medical School's Houston faculty in 1977, noticed an oil portrait of Dr. Violet Keiller on an out-of-the-way wall. He was intrigued by her face and investigated to find out more about the lady with the bright-eyed gaze and the determined chin. When he learned how much she had meant to the interns, residents, and students who studied under her aegis, Dr. Schmidt proposed that Hermann Hospital's new surgical pathology lab be named in her honor. This was done in 1982. The hospital's executive director, William F. Smith, noted that this was the first time any facility in the Hermann complex had been named to memorialize a physician. A tiny old black microscope that Dr. Keiller had used was displayed in the new laboratory.[202]

ROSE GRUNDFEST SCHNEIDER, PH.D. (1908–)

Two icebox dishes and a cake plate, all purchased from a dime store, helped Dr. Rose G. Schneider become internationally famous in hemoglobin research. In 1948, when she began to study hemoglobin, only a few of the very expensive Tiselius apparatuses for studying hemoglobin existed, so Rose went to the dime store. She used the two icebox dishes as buffer chambers and suspended filter paper between them. Hemoglobin was spotted on the paper. Dr. Schneider used carbon electrodes and B batteries to achieve electrophoresis, or the movement, under the influence of an electrically charged field, of charged particles. This process enabled her to identify several new hemoglobin variants and to become a pioneer in hemoglobin electrophoresis.[203]

Rose Grundfest was born in Minsk, Russia, in 1908. Five years later, she and her parents arrived in New York as immigrants and settled in Kearny, New Jersey. Her father became a merchant and her mother a midwife to help support the little family, Rose and three brothers—all of whom may have been influenced to go into medicine by the mother's deep interest in the profession.[204]

Living at home, Rose was graduated from Barnard College in the depression year of 1929 with a bachelor of arts degree. Lacking money for graduate school, she accepted a position as technologist in the serology laboratory of the bacteriology department of a large medical center. Her hopes for stimulating contacts were dashed when she discovered that her supervisor and sole work companion had only four words to say daily: "Good morning" and "Good night." The gregarious Rose soon found companionship with women in the main bacteriology lab. The "mindlessness" of endlessly recording incubation data from solutions in test tubes, however, drove her to save money and apply to the bacteriology departments of several medical schools.[205]

Accepted by Radcliffe, Harvard's alternative for women, Rose completed her master of arts in bacteriology and immunology in three years. She always said her master's was from Radcliffe until some years after Harvard finally opened its doors to women in 1945. At that time Rose received a letter from the university administration that authorized her to say that her M.A. degree was from Harvard. She married a professor of medicine at the University of Chicago and continued her education, attaining her Ph.D. in pathology from Cornell Medical School in New York. Her second marriage, in 1939, was to radiologist Dr. Martin Schneider. The couple arrived in Galveston in 1941.[206]

Because Dr. Martin Schneider was professor of radiology at the University of Texas Medical Branch, an antinepotism law prevented Dr. Rose from taking a staff position until a kindly professor offered her a position on his grant, which was not considered a part of the university budget. Since this position allowed for some research, she set to work studying sickle cell anemia.[207]

Hemoglobin is a complex protein and iron compound that colors red blood cells, which retain oxygen for later release throughout the body. Variants of this compound can make hemoglobin cells fragile. When enough of such fragile cells break down, anemia or other diseases can result.

As she entered the field of hemoglobin research in 1948 before the existence of abnormal hemoglobins was known, Rose Schneider began her dime-store electrophoresis apparatus and eventually studied about half a million samples, identifying many variants. Before she retired, her laboratories' work developed a method using computer analysis to determine whether a variant is a new one. This eliminates the need of amino acid sequence analysis for such determination.[208]

Dr. Schneider's professional publications add up to over eighty in journals and books and more than twenty abstracts. However, not all of her energy was devoted to serious production. She also found time to contribute to the social and entertainment aspects of UTMB life. For an anniversary celebration, Rose produced a "fantastical historical musical" titled "Twenty-Five Years at the Medical Branch, or Sawbones on a Sandbar." There were two acts. Act I was "Galveston before 1900—with Flights of Fancy Forward," and Act II depicted "Galveston after 1900—with Irreverent Asides." Mildred Robertson, longtime secretary of the UTMB Alumni Association, has good reason to remember Rose Schneider's lyrics. For one of the shows, Miss Robertson sang "Stately Home of Learning."[209]

Outside of her work, a son and two daughters claimed Dr. Schneider's attention. She managed to combine the rearing of this family with her duties as research professor of pediatrics and professor of human biological chemistry and genetics during her years at UTMB.[210]

Other outside concerns of Dr. Schneider were noted in a local newspaper article that mentioned her campaign for reelection to the Board of Regents of Galveston College. She had been on the board since its inception in 1966, and she was also a member of the League of Women Voters and the American Association of University Women.[211]

The press continued to chronicle Dr. Schneider's career with articles describing her presentation of papers in Japan in 1968 and in New York in 1971.[212] The following year, a story described a "massive" education program for Galveston in which Dr. Rose Schneider was quoted as saying that "about 8 percent of Galveston's black population has sickle cell trait." She explained that "sickle cell trait" is thought to have developed in Africa as protection against malaria. If two people with the "trait"—meaning some sickle-shaped cells and some normal cells—marry, their children are more likely to have sickle cell anemia.[213]

In 1970 the *Houston Post* reported that Dr. Schneider had found ten hemoglobin variants, about one-fifteenth of all variants then known. She went on to find "several dozen" new ones and to describe several methods for identifying and studying hemoglobins.[214]

She adopted a practice of naming each new hemoglobin variant for the location where the donor patient lived, a fact noted by the local papers.[215]

In the midst of increasing public recognition and exciting professional events, Dr. Schneider took time in 1971 to make a speech in La Marque, a neighboring city, on the subject of women's liberation. Her title was "You've Come a Long Way Baby—Or Have You?"[216]

At the 129th annual Chamber of Commerce banquet in 1973, Galveston businessmen honored Dr. Schneider at the Moody Civic Center with the Chamber's Citizen of the Year Award. Two reasons for Dr. Schneider's receiving the award were cited: her work with the Sickle Cell Anemia Foundation and her efforts to gain for educators an opportunity to run for public office.[217]

In 1975, another honor for Rose Schneider was the John G. Sinclair Award of UTMB's chapter of Sigma Xi, an honorary scientific research society, for "excellence in the pursuit of scientific knowledge." That same year she was appointed to the Expert Panel on Abnormal Hemoglobins and Thalassemia of the World Health Organization for a three-year term.[218]

Dr. Rose Schneider understood the anthropological and historical importance of her hemoglobin research. One of the new variants she had found was in members of a Texas Indian tribe, the Alabama Coushattas, a group whose gene pool had been shielded from outside interchanges for many years. This same variant exists in donors living in various parts of Asia. Dr. Schneider concluded, "It probably represents a time when there was a land bridge between Asia and the North American continent."[219]

On March 22, 1985, the Texas Genetics Society presented Dr. Rose Schneider with a plaque reading, "The Texas Genetics Society Honors Rose G. Schneider, Ph.D., for Outstanding Contributions to Genetics in Texas." The speaker mentioned Dr. Schneider's avocations, gardening and stone and brass plaque rubbing, as well as her humble beginning in hemoglobin research with dime-store equipment.[220]

In September, 1994, Dr. Schneider was at home in Galveston with her children's promising futures and her own hobbies to look forward to and her great contributions to look back on with much satisfaction and no regrets.

Dr. Katharine Hsu. Courtesy Dr. Katharine Hsu,
Houston, Texas

KATHARINE H. K. HSU, M.D. (1914–)

Dr. Katharine Han Kuang Hsu's approach to fighting tuberculosis in children has been, "When the house in on fire you try to put it out— but why not prevent the fire?" When she arrived in the United States for what she thought would be a one-year work-study opportunity to learn more about the disease that was ravaging Chinese children, young Dr. Hsu had been for five years assistant professor of pediatrics at Chung Chen Medical College in Kiangsi, China.

She was born in February, 1914, in Foochow, South China, and her earliest memories are of times when she and her family had to hide from warlords battling over territory in prerevolutionary China. Her family moved to Peking when she was four. Her father, employed by the Ministry of the Navy, augmented the family income by practicing herb medicine.[221]

Katharine and her elder brother were tutored at home in Confucian classics and Chinese poetry during their early years because their father disapproved of the then-current movement of replacing classical textbooks with "plain Chinese language" and books written in contemporary speech. In 1923 when she was nine Katharine was enrolled in elementary school, and in 1925 she became a student at Bridgman Academy, a Christian middle school in Peking. After graduating in 1931 with honors, she was accepted into Yenching University without being required to take the entrance examination.[222]

Both Dr. Hsu's parents were devout Christians, and the young pre-med student had already experienced deep religious feelings. As she became more engrossed in science, she developed a philosophy that reconciled her spiritual convictions with the wonders of the scientific world. At each major crisis of her life, she has turned for support and guidance to her heartfelt religion.[223]

China's highest-ranked medical school was Peking Union Medical College (PUMC), a project of the Rockefeller Foundation. Young Katharine, who had graduated from Yenching with honors, took the stiff entrance examination although her family could not afford the high tuition. Waiting and praying through a hot Peking summer, she finally received notice that she was one of thirty-five applicants accepted by PUMC that year. A few days later, even more gratifying news came: since Katharine was among the three top applicants, she had been awarded a full four-year scholarship.[224]

After a residency at PUMC, Dr. Hsu moved to Shanghai to become chief resident in Shanghai Children's Hospital in 1941. When the city fell to the Japanese a year later, she received an invitation from Generalissimo Chiang to teach at Chung Chen Medical College in Kiangsi, a part of China not under occupation. Getting there was the problem. Many who tried to move around in occupied China were robbed and killed on their journeys.[225]

Dr. Hsu left Shanghai with a party of fifteen men, women, and children. The most frightening episode of the journey was the arrival of a contingent of Japanese soldiers who ordered the travelers to stand aside and began to interrogate each person as to his or her destination and reason for traveling. The young doctor could feel her heart pounding wildly as a soldier approached—and then, for some reason, turned away. The questioning was over and they could proceed.[226]

After two weeks' travel on foot through the countryside, knocking each night at some farmer's door and begging to sleep on the floor, the little group arrived at a river marking the edge of Japanese-occupied territory. An army with machine guns guarded the banks. They hired a sampan, waiting until the moon had set, and floated downstream in pitch dark. Dr. Hsu prayed all the way, and at daybreak they found themselves in free China.[227]

When Chinese soldiers who met them suspected the travelers of being spies deliberately let through by the Japanese, Katharine Hsu revealed that she was an appointee of Generalissimo Chiang's medical school. The leader became polite and confirmed her story by a call to the school. Before the group could leave, she was asked to treat the local army commandant's son, who was very sick with malaria. Dr. Hsu was able to assure his family that the boy would be all right because she had the needed medicine with her. She and little band of travelers hiked the last month's journey with an armed fifty-man escort provided by the grateful commander.[228]

Hardship and struggle continued for Dr. Hsu during the years until World War II ended in 1945: the Chung Chen Medical College had to move three times because of further Japanese invasions. She was still there in 1947 when news of a fellowship—one per country for twelve countries, offered by the American Society of Pediatric Research—was announced in the journal of the Chinese Medical Association. Dr. Hsu applied, and "so I became a Fellow."[229]

Katharine arrived, intending a one-year study and then a return to China. After eight months' work at Cincinnati Children's Hospital, Dr. Tom McNair Scott, her fellowship adviser, arranged for her to study further at the Henry Phipps Institute for Tuberculosis Research at the University of Pennsylvania, since she was eager to acquire the latest knowledge about tuberculosis, which was rampant in China.[230]

When the outbreak of the Korean War in 1950 prevented her return to China, Dr. Hsu went to work at the Pennsylvania State Tuberculosis Hospital in South Mountain, Pennsylvania. She was still there three years later when Dr. Russell J. Blattner, chief of Baylor University College of Medicine's Pediatrics Department, wrote, and offered her a position in which she would initiate a tuberculosis control program for children in the city of Houston. She later learned that the Pediatric Society of Houston had petitioned Mayor Oscar Holcombe, asking him to do something about the tuberculosis epidemic in the city. Katharine's colleagues had recommended her to Dr. Blattner, to whom the mayor had turned for help. Blattner asked her to start a tuberculosis clinic and hospital for children.[231]

Dr. Hsu remembered that when she arrived in Houston in 1953, tuberculosis was a frightening word. If people in a pediatric clinic waiting room heard there was a tuberculosis patient present, they just left. Starting work in July, 1953, Dr. Hsu discovered that the only building available as an outpatient clinic for tubercular children was a boarding school on the grounds of the Houston Tuberculosis Hospital. Known as the Preventorium, it was used to house the children of adult tuberculosis patients. One vacant room on the first floor of the Preventorium could be used for the children's clinic. The doctor and her helpers borrowed two tables and several chairs, erected a wooden sign in front of the building, and set about their business.[232]

The one room clinic soon became impossibly overcrowded, and since many of the children were too sick to be taken home, a second-floor area in the Preventorium was vacated to make a hospital facility for them. Still, the furnishings and equipment were dreadfully inadequate. There was no air conditioning and no kitchen in which to fix formula for the babies. Dr. Hsu prepared a scrapbook with pictures of the dilapidated furniture and equipment. When Christmas brought an invitation for her to visit the home of Mr. R. E. ("Bob") Smith, a successful oilman, she took along the album. When Smith inquired about her work, Dr. Hsu answered by showing him the album. Shocked by the deplorable condition of the hospital, he sent an emissary to visit and then came himself to determine what the needs were. Within a short time the hospital was transformed into a modern facility with new equipment, new furniture, air conditioning, and a milk kitchen. Not long afterward, the Houston city government constructed a new building adjacent to the hospital to house the outpatient clinic.[233]

Before Dr. Hsu left Pennsylvania, she had witnessed the discovery of a wonderful drug: isoniazid. This discovery opened a completely new door for the treatment of tuberculosis. Streptomycin, which had been invented in 1948, was the most effective treatment known for TB before isoniazid. When isoniazid (which can be taken by mouth) was developed in 1952, it proved to be much more effective than streptomycin. At that time, most of the new drug testing would have been done first on adults, but Dr. Hsu was in a position to start with children.[234]

After Dr. Hsu saw how effective isoniazid was in treating full-blown cases of tuberculosis, the thought came to her, "Why not use it for prevention?" All children who develop TB start with an infection that shows no signs. The parents know nothing about it. Dr. Hsu wanted to kill off the tubercule bacilli and spare the children all the hospitalization and suffering. She thought about it and talked with her colleagues. They all laughed at her, saying, "Whoever would think of treating TB before you see the shadow in the X-ray?" So Dr. Hsu had had no chance to test her theory in Pennsylvania. It was just then that Dr. Blattner's letter arrived from Houston. When she received it, she was quite surprised. Another surprise also awaited her arrival in Texas: when she left Pennsylvania the snow was knee-deep, but when she arrived in Houston the roses were blooming.[235]

Katharine's main effort became to prevent tuberculosis. There are several critical periods during a child's life when tuberculosis infection is more likely to produce the disease. One period is early in life, before age three. Another danger time is during the teenage years. An infected child might remain healthy for years, but then the disease can explode when adolescence arrives. Dr. Hsu saw much of this in Pennsylvania, in a 250-bed hospital built on a mountain to treat the disease. "I saw so many of them die . . . teenage girls . . . beautiful girls . . . they just melt away like wax!" she recalled. Little children frequently died of tuberculosis meningitis because the germ went to their brains. Once it reached the brain, it was uniformly fatal.[236]

She observed that the youngest children also died of miliary tuberculosis. Like millet seeds, the tuberculosis in the blood spreads out in the body. Unlike cancer, it does not go to one location or the other, but travels in all directions like tiny seeds. This is a sort of metastasis, but it is acute, all over the body. That is why, she explains, it is a killing disease. Young children usually die of tuberculosis meningitis or from miliary TB; teenagers usually die of lung (pulmonary) TB.[237]

Dr. Hsu was anxious to find out if her preventive treatment would protect the young children from teenage TB. "I kept watching my children. . . . I couldn't let them go . . . through teenage, to make sure they were protected. That's why it took me so long—thirty years—before I wrote my final report. I wrote my interim reports, of course, to be read to medical conventions . . . but I didn't write my final report until I had watched a generation of children get through teenage. And that was very, very gratifying.[238]

A mother isn't going to fight to medicate a child who is not yet sick, as Dr. Hsu pointed out. Isoniazid must be taken a whole year in Dr. Hsu's regime. TB is a family disease, so the whole family must be tested, and all infected members—including adults—should receive the preventive treatment. Every time Dr. Hsu saw a child with tuberculosis, she offered the adults in the family free X-ray exams. She also offered free skin tests to all the siblings.[239]

Dr. Hsu had to seek out her first preventive medical patients because the children and their parents were unaware of the asymptomatic infection. When a child ill with TB came in, Dr. Hsu would ask the mother, "Who gave your child tuberculosis?" Often the mother wouldn't know. Dr. Hsu would then inquire, "Would you like for me to find out who gave it to your child? And also I am concerned about your other kids. They may have caught it and not yet be sick. I can do something to protect them." With this kind of understanding, the mother would let Dr. Hsu test all the children. In some homes, almost 100 percent of the other children had already been infected.[240]

Dr. Hsu believes the lessening of public tobacco chewing and spitting (witness the disappearance of those old brass spittoons, once prominent features of courtrooms and other public gathering places) helped drive down the incidence of tuberculosis. Spitting on the sidewalk, she maintains, is not as dangerous as indoor spitting because the sunlight will kill the tuberculosis germs. As director of tuberculosis control in the City of Houston Health Department, Dr. Hsu took four years (1964–1968) to recruit and train thirty-four staff. She said we became complacent about tuberculosis before it was really eradicated, and that is one cause of the recent resurgence of the disease. Another important reason for the TB upsurge is AIDS, whose victims lose their immunity to the tuberculosis: as the curve of AIDS victims rises, the curve of TB victims goes right up with it. There is no means of enforcing compulsory isolation for patients with AIDS, a communicable disease, because its victims keep their conditions secret and remain in the community.[241]

Dr. Hsu had always wanted to see the Holy Land. In 1960, the opportunity arose to go with a group of chest physicians who meet in a different part of the world every three years. The conference, at which Dr. Hsu was invited to speak, was in Vienna, where she could indulge her abiding love of great music. After the Chest Physicians Congress, the group went on to Israel. As the Arab-Jewish war was then going on and they were traveling under the aegis of Israel, they were only able to see part of the Holy Land at that time.[242]

When Dr. Hsu again attended the congress in 1963, it was held in India. Afterward she was able to tour the Jordanian side of the Holy Land, including Jerusalem, the Jordan River, Bethany, Golgotha, and Christ's Tomb. Another highlight of the trip was the opportunity to see the Dead Sea Scrolls, some of which, she noted, are surprisingly well preserved.[243]

She found that the tuberculosis situation in India was bad. TB hospitals there and in Europe, like the American ones, were built up on mountainsides because there was no treatment for tuberculosis in the early days except sunshine and fresh air. Many of the patients suffering from tuberculosis of the bone had come from Saudi Arabia; no one seemed to know why that region had more of that particular form of the disease.[244]

Dr. Katharine H. K. Hsu's academic career advanced through the years beyond her specific absorption with tuberculosis control. She served as assistant professor of pediatrics at Baylor College of Medicine from 1953 to 1960, when she became an associate professor and director of Children's TB Hospital and Clinic. Director of tuberculosis control for the Houston Department of Public Health was one of her titles from 1964 to 1968. During those four years, she was also a project director for four United States Public Health Service grants. In 1969 she became a full professor of pediatrics and director of the Pediatric Chest Service for Baylor College of Medicine, where she was still teaching in 1995. Her curriculum vitae lists more than thirty-five articles published in medical journals.[245]

Her choice of teaching methods has been as unorthodox as her thinking about TB prevention. She insisted on being assigned only five students at a time before Baylor's Pediatrics Department adopted small-group teaching in place of the traditional larger classes. In this situation, she can give one-on-one instruction, and the course can be a matter of give-and-take in problem-oriented, two-way discussion. She has followed this plan for thirty-four years.[246]

Ten years before Dr. Hsu published her final report on the thirty-year research project using Isoniazid as a preventive for TB, those in the know began to celebrate the decline of tuberculosis. A 1974 article in *Inside Baylor Medicine* carried an interview with Dr. Hsu titled "Erasing the Threat of Childhood TB." Houston Mayor Kathryn Whitmire and her city council passed a resolution July 20, 1983, thanking Dr. Hsu "for dedicating her life to the enrichment of quality health care throughout the world." Her thirty-year report, "Thirty Years after Isoniazid," was published in the *Journal of the American Medical Association* March 9, 1984. "Tuberculosis Cases Down for First Time," announced an article in the *Houston Post* of the same date. A summary story in *Baylor Medicine* for April/May, 1984, detailed Dr. Hsu's research processes.[247]

With the thirty-year project well in hand in 1974, Katherine Hsu accepted the request of the Baylor Pediatrics Department to establish an asthma clinic to care for children whose asthma was beyond control. Medical thinking about the causes of asthma has changed during the last few decades. A 1959 *World Book Encyclopedia* entry identified asthma as a type of allergy. The *Reader's Digest Family Health Guide and Medical Encyclopedia* in 1970 stated two major causes of asthma. One (which results in intrinsic asthma) is an infection of the nose, sinuses, bronchi, or lungs, such as bronchitis. The other cause is an allergic reaction that is usually hereditary in origin.[248]

Dr. Hsu's years of investigating asthmatic children have led her to conclude that what an asthmatic inherits is a lung that overreacts. She stated that some asthma victims are born asthmatic, some react to allergens and some to chemicals; other cases are the results of viral infections that have damaged the lining of the bronchial tubes, "as if you skinned a knee." Such multiple causes are why the treatment of asthma is so complicated. All aspects of asthma management, such as optimum dosages of medicine and the best drug for a particular patient, have to be fine-tuned; every child is different.[249]

In 1974, Dr. Hsu had as a guide only a set of studies that sought to establish what is normal lung function for American children. The basic flaw in these data was that all the studies were based only on the white race. She wrote a proposal, received a grant, and set up and trained a staff to do studies on normal children of the three groups that predominate in Houston: Caucasian, Hispanic, and African American. To get thousands of children to test, the researchers went to the public schools. To be successful they needed the cooperation of teachers, school administrators, parents, and the children themselves. Dr. Hsu designed a questionnaire to be pinned onto the child for parents to complete and return. State-of-the-art equipment was obtained, and medical teams trained for the testing rolled up to each school in a big van and tested the children. Final results were accurate measurements of normal lung function in children of three races from first through twelfth grades.[250]

Once the new standards were set, they were accepted and printed in pediatric textbooks. At Baylor, every resident carries a copy in his or her pocket. A series of graphs in the textbook gives the pediatrician the ability to select the child's race, age, and lung measurement and compare that with the norm. The studies show that Hispanic children have the largest lung capacity, whites are next, and African Americans have the smallest lungs. Dr. Hsu related these facts to differences in leg length and chest formation in the races. Finding that their results also revealed basic differences between boys' and girls' lung capacities, the group provided a breakdown as to male or female for each of the three races. Dr. Hsu cited as her major publications "Preventive Treatment of Tuberculosis" (a series of articles) and "Normal Lung Function of American Children."[251]

Along with the research to establish normal lung function, Dr. Hsu developed at the Children's Asthma Clinic in Jefferson Davis Hospital a structured program of comprehensive testing, education, medication, and research for early detection and treatment. There is also a parent education program that Dr. Hsu considers particularly important in the treatment of the individual child.[252]

Dr. Hsu's honors include listings in *Who's Who of American Women* and other publications and memberships in distinguished professional groups. In May, 1994, she was presented with a Distinguished Achievement Award from the American Thoracic Society at its international conference in Boston. The Thoracic Society serves as the medical section of the American Lung Association. Their selection of Dr. Hsu was based on "her contributions to medical education, clinical research, and treatment involving lung disease." On the trip to Boston Dr. Hsu was accompanied by the daughter she had adopted twenty years earlier, Dahlia, who is a nurse and "a very good companion."[253]

Although she says she can speak more fluently in Chinese than in English, Dr. Hsu never seems at a loss for words in ordinary English conversation. Her church is the place where she can best exercise her Chinese nowadays, and she is always happy to greet the occasional Chinese medical student. She explains her Chinese name this way: Hsu (promise) is the family name; Han is the tribe name, there being five tribes in China; Kuang means light—"So my parents expected me to be the 'light of my tribe.'" The facts of her life reveal how well she has lived up to that promise and how this petite, involuntarily expatriate doctor has found a home in the hearts of thousands of people whose children are alive today because of her work.[254]

In the Mind

MABEL GIDDINGS WILKIN, M.D. (1896–1980)

Mabel Giddings Wilkin, who succeeded spectacularly in her three careers (journalism, psychiatry, and ranching) was a woman of independent means and ideas. A "reluctant psychoanalyst," she questioned much of the current psychiatric dogma and believed more in short-term analysis and group and family therapy than in years-long sessions with a patient. With her friends and colleagues, Dr. Hilde Burch and Dr. Dorothy Cato, she made an extraordinary impact on the practice of psychiatry in Texas.[255]

Mabel's grandfather Dewitt Clinton Giddings, built his home on family land near Brenham, Texas, and reared his children there. Lillian, Mabel's mother, married James Wilkin and moved with him to Oklahoma. Their three daughters, Mabel, Marion (a family spelling), and Lillian, grew up in Oklahoma City, where their father went into banking with a brother-in-law.[256]

After Mabel's mother died in 1901, James Wilkin persuaded his brother and sister-in-law, Robert and Minnie Wilkin, to live with him and help care for his daughters. Aunt Minnie was a religious fundamentalist who did not allow dancing or anything frivolous. Escaping to Brenham for visits as often as they could, the girls found a far more nurturing figure in a maternal relative, "Aunt Frankie" Foote. When their grandfather died in 1903, he left separate funds for each of the girls and directed Aunt Frankie to maintain the Giddings home for them.[257]

Mabel graduated from high school in Oklahoma City in 1914 and took a bachelor of arts in philosophy from Hollins College in Virginia, her mother's alma mater, in 1918. She went to New York to study journalism at Columbia, rented an apartment, and entered an active social life. An uncle who was administrator of the girls' funds was appalled at the amount she spent on clothes. Marion and Lillian also wound up in New York, taking cooking lessons. The two of them subsequently opened a tearoom in Colorado, where Mabel joined them one summer.[258]

In 1921 James Wilkin's bank failed, and in 1923 he died. The girls' kindest supporter, Auntie Frankie, died the same year. These repeated misfortunes may have been the impetus for a trip to Europe the girls took in 1925. "Those Wilkin Girls" was the name of an anecdotal journal that Marion kept about those days. Lillian's daughter, Mrs. Marian [sic] Fleming, thought of the three sisters as part of the Roaring Twenties.[259]

At loose ends, Mabel enrolled in Rice Institute and earned her master of arts in philosophy in 1931. During her stay in Houston she wrote feature stories for the *Houston Post-Dispatch* on subjects ranging from treasure hunting in Mexico to the need for cleaner bridle paths for well-dressed horseback riders. She also reported on a new airport to be built on Telephone Road, on a gifted teenage Houston artist, and on the life of a "pilot-adventurer." She was the first woman in Houston to be given a byline.[260]

A Houston friend, Dr. Herman Johnston of Hermann Hospital, suggested to Mabel that she enter medical school. From 1931 to 1933 she took prerequisite science courses at Johns Hopkins University, and in 1937 she was graduated with honors from the University of Maryland Medical School. The next ten years saw Dr. Wilkin progress through continuous study and training, including personal analysis, from an internship in pediatrics to being a practicing psychoanalyst. She developed a large practice in the Maryland area with some patients coming from as far as New York, but the pull of home and family never left her. In 1949, she returned from Maryland to Texas to become associate clinical professor of psychiatry at the University of Texas Medical Branch at Galveston.[261]

MEDICAL PRACTICE, RESEARCH, TEACHING

During the Maryland years Mabel was given custody of and later adopted Elmer Grape, a young man whom she brought up and who came to Texas with her. In 1945 she also employed Ira, a manservant from Brenham, and his wife, who cooked. Marian Fleming, then in college in Washington, D.C., often visited her Aunt Mabel and remembered that she lived graciously and enjoyed pretty furnishings. Mabel, she said, always "felt soft and smelled good." Witch hazel was Dr. Wilkin's favorite lotion. The two of them became confidantes; her aunt always gave Marian unconditional acceptance. Two colleagues from those days who remained close to Dr. Wilkin were Dr. Harry Stack Sullivan and Dr. Frieda Fromm-Reichman, both of whom earned international recognition for their psychiatric work.[262]

Dr. Wilkin brought a feminine approach to psychotherapy. In cases where she considered moral support more important for the individual than therapy, she did not hesitate to tell a patient, "You don't need me," or "I think you'll handle this problem very well by yourself." Although she wrote little for professional journals, she produced two papers concerning the training of psychiatric residents. In the first she advised adoption of a curriculum to encourage residents to retain their uncertainty and confusion during early training, as opposed to sinking into premature ideologies by adopting one or another psychiatric school for the sake of simplicity and peace of mind. The one certainty that Dr. Wilkin endorsed about psychiatry was that "the answers are most assuredly not all in." In the second essay on resident training, Dr. Wilkin proposed group analysis for psychiatric residents as a means of shortening the "time of rediscovery" of basic psychological truths.[263]

"I owe my life to Mabel Giddings Wilkin," said Elmer Grape, whose different perspective on the psychiatrist is the result of a doctor/mother–patient/son relationship shared by the two of them for a good many years. This came about when Elmer was bouncing around from one foster home to another, and Dr. Wilkin was asked to work with the fourteen-year-old boy. She decided to take full responsibility for Elmer, and from that point on, he reported, "our relationship was very stormy indeed." Elmer looked back on Dr. Wilkin as truly a pioneer—both in her profession and as a woman in a man's world—who never backed down from her belief that intellectually, women were equal to, if not better than, men. He understood that her profession trained her to look for reasons for every action and reaction "in me and in her patients. . . . Mab [pronounced 'Mob' by the family] needed to maintain control at all times and questioned everything I thought or did." There were years of estrangement after Elmer chose a nonmedical career. At a chance meeting in 1978 at a family Christmas party, a friendly but not very personal relationship was reestablished.[264]

Always well groomed and beautifully dressed, Dr. Wilkin enjoyed socializing with a small circle of intimates. She was noted for using a very long cigarette holder and wearing designer clothes, a mink coat, and diamond earrings. She claimed to have been the first woman in Oklahoma to smoke in public.[265]

At age sixty Dr. Wilkin was commuting back and forth, beginning to transform the inherited Giddings acreage from cotton fields to more profitable cattle ranching. This ranch life became her fulltime third career when she was seventy and failing eyesight forced the close of her psychiatric practice. She loved animals; a big moment in her life came when her F1 heifer won an award. Her two standard-sized poodles slept with her. She rode horseback all her life and may in her early years have taught horseback riding for a brief period in Colorado or New Mexico.[266]

When she had become legally blind, Dr. Wilkin reviewed some of her cases with the aid of a reading machine "to see if I did any good." Diabetes and other ailments began to surface, but Dr. Wilkin refused to seek further medical treatment. She died of intestinal cancer a few days after being taken to the hospital. Some days after her death, Mabel Wilkin was posthumously presented with a Wildlife Conservationist of the Year award from the Burleson-Lee Soil and Water Conservation District.[267]

Based on the way her friends still talk about her, the benefits received by grateful patients, and the difference her ideas made in the training and ideological development of many young residents, it appears certain that she not only did some good: she did a great deal of good.

HILDE BRUCH, M.D. (1904–84)

Hilde Bruch was the middle child of seven in a prosperous German Jewish family. Her parents ran a livestock business, and, though financially conservative, they considered money for good educations a necessity. Hilde recalled that although she behaved well, she was a

Dr. Hilde Bruch holding one of the books she wrote. Courtesy Harris County Medical Archive, Texas Medical Center Library, Houston, Texas

troublesome student because she always asked questions and "never believed a thing."[268]

Hilde's father died when she was sixteen, and the wealth he left his family was destined to be wiped out by inflation. Nevertheless, her Uncle David persuaded Hilde to study medicine. With financial aid from both sides of her family, Hilde received her M.D. degree from the University of Freiburg in 1929. After a year as a research assistant in physiology, she entered a pediatrics residency at the University of Leipzig.[269]

Women Pioneers in Texas Medicine

When the Nazis and their anti-Semitism came to dominate German politics in 1933, Dr. Bruch used the pretext of attending the International Pediatrics Congress in London to leave Germany forever. She went first to Radington, England, for a year, but when an anti-Semitic editorial urged the townspeople not to consult her, she departed for America under sponsorship of a relative who was a United States citizen. Her own escape and the fact that she could not rescue some of her family members from the Holocaust burdened Dr. Bruch for life with feelings of deep depression and "survivor's guilt." Early in her American career she was hospitalized after a suicide attempt. This led to several series of psychotherapy sessions for Hilde Bruch. In turn, her personal analysis deepened her interest in psychiatry and eventually led to her specializing in that field. Another influence in that direction was her work with adolescents who had eating disorders.[270]

From childhood, Hilde had been known as *das Dicka*—"the fat one." In one of her important early papers she demonstrated that several obese children she had studied were not, as had been assumed, suffering from Frohlich's syndrome (a glandular condition) but instead were fat because their mothers had overfed and overprotected them. Her struggles with her own "voracious appetite" and her realization that obesity can be psychological in origin had given Dr. Bruch a major insight that ran counter to conventional medical thinking of the day.[271]

This tendency toward independent thinking and her Socratic habit of questioning accepted standards made Dr. Bruch admired and respected in New York, where she became a psychiatry professor at Columbia in 1943. Perhaps it was those qualities also that made some of her colleagues consider her autocratic, egocentric, selfish, and manipulative. When she became director of a psychiatric hospital in 1954, it was noted that she was an excellent teacher and gifted clinician but a poor administrator.[272]

Although New York living was enjoyable to Hilde Bruch, the increasing crime rate and several episodes of severe winter weather made her want to find a milder climate and a safer home. When Dr. Shevert Frazier, chairman of psychiatry at Baylor College of Medicine, invited her to join the faculty, Dr. Bruch accepted.[273]

When Hilde came to the Lone Star State at age sixty, she resolved not to be intimidated by Houston's many Cadillac drivers. She bought a beautiful 1959 Rolls Royce Silver Cloud, which she said was her "Texas

Stetson." Although she had learned to drive late in life, a circumstance that frequently produces a more cautious driver, she was reckless behind the wheel. During this car's ten-year life span, not many of the psychiatrist's friends were brave enough to join her for the Sunday drives she enjoyed. The Rolls went through a series of disasters and near-collisions, including crashing into a brick wall at her condominium, until it perished in flames during a trip to Salado, Texas, where Dr. Bruch was supposed to attend a Baylor medical faculty retreat.[274]

At Baylor, Dr. Bruch taught residents and continued her work with anorexia nervosa patients. A tall, stout, attractive brunette with a heavy German accent, she became known as the "Grand Dame of Texas." She most often chose vividly striped or checked-print dresses. She served gourmet dinners to a wide circle of friends and colleagues. Dr. Freida Fromm-Reichman and Dr. Harry Stack Sullivan were among her closest confidants. In January, 1946, Herbert, the son of Hilde Bruch's eldest brother, came to live with her. Both his parents died in the Holocaust, and Dr. Bruch adopted the boy, of whom she was very fond and proud.[275]

Texas colleagues with whom Dr. Bruch found pleasant companionship and professional rapport included Dr. Mabel Giddings Wilkin, who had returned to her Texas roots a dozen or more years before Dr. Bruch left the northeast; and Dr. Dorothy Annette Cato, a UTMB graduate practicing psychiatry in Houston. Each of these three questioned many of Freud's conclusions, and each held herself free from tradition-bound thinking in her use of psychotherapy.[276]

Because Dr. Bruch's writings were so numerous, the Houston Academy of Medicine–the Medical Center (HAM-TMC) Library has issued a guide to her professional writings. In an introduction to the guide, Dr. Theodore Lidz mentioned five particularly important books by Dr. Bruch that are also accessible to the lay reader because of her clear and simple style. In order of publication, they are *Don't Be Afraid of Your Child: A Guide for Perplexed Parents,* New York: Farrar, Strauss and Young, 1952; *Eating Disorders: Obesity, Anorexia Nervosa and the Person Within,* New York: Basic Books, 1973; *Learning Psychotherapy: Rationale and Ground Rules,* Cambridge: Harvard University Press, 1974; *The Golden Cage: The Enigma of Anorexia Nervosa,* Cambridge: Harvard University Press, 1977; and *Conversations with Anorexics,* New York: Basic Books, 1985.

In the 1970s Dr. Bruch learned that she had Parkinson's disease. At first the symptoms did not much affect her work, and she kept the condition a secret. Over time, however, the disease and other ailments encroached more and more on her ability to work. Fortunately for the completion of her last manuscript, *Conversations with Anorexics,* she knew in advance that her life was ending. Dr. Lidz recalled, "She told me proudly, 'I finished dictating the book before I went into the hospital.'" That was a few days before she died.[277]

Dr. Bruch received many awards in recognition of her written and clinical contributions to American psychiatric thought. A final distinction came when the Department of Psychiatry at Baylor established the Hilde Bruch Award for Excellence in Psychiatry. This is given annually to a graduating medical student.[278]

A guiding principle of Dr. Bruch's career is expressed in lines she liked to quote from Goethe: "Damaging truth, I prefer it to advantageous error. Truth heals the pain which, perhaps, it evokes."[279]

DOROTHY ANNETTE CATO, M.D. (1916–)

Fate had a lot to do with Dorothy Annette Cato's decision to become a doctor. Born in Houston in 1916, at twenty-one months she developed severe pneumonia. There were no wonder drugs then: one did or did not survive the crisis, and a survivor might well have complications. In her case, pus formed between the chest cavity and the lung. Periodic drainage was the only treatment for that—a horrific experience for a little girl not yet two years old. Dr. Cato recalled that before she was four, she decided, "If you can't lick 'em, join 'em." Her intention to have a medical career never wavered, and making the decision early in life saved her much of the agony that undecided young people go through.[280]

After she was graduated from the University of Texas with a bachelor of arts in biology and zoology and a minor in chemistry, Dorothy Cato worked five years as a lab assistant before she entered medical school at the University of Texas Medical Branch at Galveston. Because of World War II, in 1943 the school had an accelerated program that enabled students to get through in three years. "We had no significant vacation time," Dr. Cato remembered. She enrolled in March, 1943. Four months later, a hurricane partly destroyed the dorm she was living in. With a wartime hiatus on construction, medical students had to continue living on the damaged premises, their number dwindling a little at a time as some of them found other shelter.

A shocking event during Dr. Cato's internship at Galveston was the Texas City disaster wherein two ships loaded with fertilizer exploded. Dr. Cato and others on duty in the hospital just across the waterway heard radio announcers describe the first blast. Warned that a second ship was on fire, they kept their backs turned to the windows as they continued preparations to receive victims. Dr. Cato's memory of the disaster remains vivid: four mattresses on the floor in one room; "everyone" having compound fractures; a two-year supply of plasma depleted; all the blood gone (the nearby army depot sent a planeload when they were down to the last bottle of plasma). There were used bottles all over the place, and it "looked as if a gigantic orgy had taken place."[281]

Dr. Cato was graduated from UTMB in 1946 and followed through with a half-year's internship in San Antonio. She returned to Galveston for the other half-year. She had intended a residency in clinical pathology, but there was no opening in that department at Galveston then. Dorothy therefore took psychiatry, a field that usually requires three or four years' study after one's medical degree. In fact, by taking fellowships and special courses, one could be a perpetual student if one wished. She had found UTMB "tuned in" to psychiatry from the first day of her medical training. Its general approach to the subject was biological instead of dynamic: the emphasis was placed on such physical interventions as electroshock therapy or prescribing drugs to alter the body's chemical balances instead of on mental approaches such as psychotherapeutic sessions. Weapons against mental illness during her early days were Salversan to treat syphilis of the brain, electroshock, insulin shock for schizophrenia, bromides, and barbiturates. Dr. Cato remarked regretfully that the use of shock therapy has become politicized: "When politics comes in, medicine goes out the window."

Psychoanalysis, Dr. Cato explained, is a specialty within a specialty. It is not that the psychoanalyst is necessarily more trained than any other psychiatrist; it is that his or her training is focused down to a sharp point. Dynamic psychiatry is a joint venture between the therapist and the patient.

Although a psychoanalyst is not required to undergo analysis himself or herself, doing so helps the psychiatrist understand how the human mind works with respect to the unconscious and "transfers." As Dr. Cato pointed out, one does not have to be a Freudian psychoanalyst to need an understanding of those phenomena.

When Dorothy Cato came to Houston in 1950, there were only two psychiatric clinics. Before long, Methodist Hospital was built and opened up a psychiatric floor; Hedgecroft, which had been used for polio rehabilitation, became a psychiatric facility. Thorazine, which was new at the time, was used there. Dr. Cato became the first psychiatrist on the staff of M. D. Anderson Hospital. In the 1960s she began working with a continuing education group designed to keep local psychoanalysts up to date. Thirty years later, Women in Radio and TV recognized this work with an award for Dr. Cato as "an outstanding woman physician" and for her contribution to psychiatry.

Professional colleagues and friends of Dr. Cato were Dr. Mabel Giddings Wilkin and Dr. Hilde Bruch. One outstanding characteristic common to these three analysts was their questioning attitudes toward established psychiatric dogma. That Dr. Cato deeply admired both Dr. Wilkin and Dr. Bruch is evident in her conversation; this leads to the conviction that each of the trio received stimulation and support from the ideas of the others.[282]

Sadly, Dr. Cato notes that the commercialization of psychiatry has been a terrible thing. It seems to her that how much money you make is more important than how good your care is. She deplores this trend as a bad turn that might eventually destroy psychiatry as a discipline.

Dr. Cato's work has never bored her. She believes that some of the new psychiatrists coming along may have educations that are too technical and limited by lack of insight into the human element. Working usually with women residents, she helps them see how to work without either losing or playing upon their femininity. As she remarks, "It's pretty tough to be a decent human being."

In February, 1994, the Houston Psychiatric Foundation awarded a plaque to Dr. Cato commemorating her clinical excellence.

chapter 5

NEW FRONTIERS

As the old barriers of space and time have been subdued by women and men in medicine and our technologies have exploded into skills that specialists are fast absorbing, whole new frontiers of medical discovery and application are opening to rising generations of scientists. This section offers glimpses into four new areas of medical investigation.

There are many women in Texas laboratories now, working on equal footing with men. A "fellow" is as likely as not to be female. In fact, listening to some of these new women pioneers, it seems that the research way of life was inevitably theirs from birth. They are also deeply conscious of their predecessors in new discoveries and techniques. For example, it was Dr. Janet Butel who pointed out to us the importance of the work done by Dr. Bettylee Hampil, an early virologist.

"Before there was an identifiable women's liberation movement, there was Bettylee Hampil," noted Dr. Joseph L. Melnick, the first chairman of virology and epidemiology at Baylor College of Medicine. He added, "For several decades, she has been a role model of an accomplished female scientist and has been a strong influence on those about her. . . . She was wonderful with graduate students and could set them straight with just a sentence or two."[1]

Born in Houston around the turn of the century, Bettylee was the eldest of three daughters of Dr. Clarence Charles Hampil, a family doctor, and his wife, Cora, a teacher. After graduation from the University of Texas and a brief teaching experience, Bettylee took a job in a medical laboratory in Houston. Finding the work "absolutely fascinating," she took some science courses at UT and then went to Johns Hopkins, where she received a doctor of science degree from its School of Public Health and remained to teach for nine years. Then she began virology research at the drug company that is now Merck Sharp & Dohme, serving for almost ten years as director of its virus research laboratories and then as director of the Merck Institute for Therapeutic Research. Her career highlights included directing the research team that made the first influenza vaccine tested by the U.S. Army during World War II and preparing the first manufactured lots of Sabin polio vaccine.[2]

When she retired at sixty-five, Dr. Hampil came home to Houston, and Dr. Melnick promptly put her to work at Baylor, where she remained on duty for fifteen years. He explained, "She directed the international efforts to prepare standards for the identification of more than seventy different viruses. Her reagents are now distributed by the World Health Organization for use in every part of the world. Sera which she was instrumental in preparing are in use today in typing enteroviruses and will still be in use into the next century. Bettylee Hampil truly has been one of the outstanding contributors to biomedical science for at least half a century."[3]

It is symptomatic of modern times that one of the four protagonists in "New Frontiers" is a doctor of philosophy in her scientific field, virology, instead of a doctor of medicine. As research and discoveries proliferate, it was perhaps inevitable that some such divisions of expertise and focus must occur. In the long run, those who seldom see a patient because they spend their days in the laboratory over electron microscopes and other apparatuses may well affect the lives and health of more human beings than do doctors with busy practices.

The role of nuclear medicine in helping to identify and treat cancer, heart disease, and other old and new diseases will be explored. Virology, an immense world of tiny little particles with incredibly complex lifestyles and variety, will be investigated. Genetic research will offer a look at the fascinating combinations and codes that control the lives and welfare of us all. The final bow will be to new medical responses to death and dying: the gentle and infinitely kind ministrations of hospice care.

Nuclear Medicine

BETTY JANE MCCONNELL, M.D. (1923–)

When a reporter from Hockaday High School in Dallas asked Dr. Betty Jane McConnell what advice she would give to a young woman interested in medicine as a career, the doctor replied, "Be well-disci-plined, have plenty of confidence in yourself and your ability, study hard, and be willing to burn the midnight oil."[4]

This answer includes some of the traits and habits that have con-tributed to Dr. McConnell's successful career in the field of nuclear medicine, an area that opened up following World War II. It involves the use of radioactive tracers to diagnose disease in patients whose ill-ness suggests an abnormality of one or more organ systems. In the early days of nuclear medicine when Betty Jane McConnell entered the field, she was one of only a handful of women.

Other traits and circumstances also make B. J. (as she is known to friends and colleagues) an extraordinary person—in her work and in her life. One astonishing fact is that she entered the area of nuclear medicine after a hiatus of seventeen years from the practice of medi-cine. During those seventeen years she and her husband, Robert Mc-Connell, reared their six children. Their partnership in the field of nuclear medicine is unique, and the partnership concept extends to every area of their lives.

The first unusual circumstance in B. J.'s life was one she did not originate: she was born a twin. She and her brother, Lowell Emmitt Golter, attended Bond Hill Elementary School in Cincinnati, both skipping the second grade. They went on to Walnut Hills High School and from there to the University of Cincinnati College of Liberal Arts, where they received bachelor of science degrees in 1944. Two years later, they were awarded M.D. degrees by the University of Cincinnati Col-lege of Medicine. Also in their commencement class was Robert War-ren McConnell of Troy, Ohio, a Virginia Military Institute graduate, whom B. J. had married on July 1, 1944.

While they were in grammar school, Lowell had decided that he wanted to be a doctor when he grew up. B. J. thought she might be-come an artist. She enjoyed her art classes so much that from the fifth grade on she began attending classes at the Cincinnati Art Museum on Saturday mornings. At first her father escorted her, but soon she learned to manage the trip, which involved transferring from a bus to a streetcar, by herself. In order to arrive on time, she had to get up very early—a discipline she was willing to endure for the sake of art.

Reading was a favorite pastime of the Golter twins, and they were frequent visitors to the Bond Hill Branch Library near their home.

*The doctors McConnell. Courtesy Scott and White Clinic
and B. J. McConnell, Salado, Texas*

Their mother, Jeannette Golter, who wrote poetry and studied gene-alogy, encouraged this habit. B. J. reflected that her mother was prob-ably the most influential person in her life: from her, B. J. absorbed her fundamental values and attitudes. She also acquired her mother's pe-tite stature and good looks.

B. J.'s father, Lowell Emmitt, had a law degree, but during the de-pression he took charge of the Garlock Packing Company's Cincin-nati office, a position he held until his death. He encouraged the twins to do well in school and saw to it that they always had a quiet time of study. According to B. J., he may have been "one of the first women's libbers." In high school, B. J. did well in her science courses and began to consider medicine as a career field. Her father told her, "Betty Jane, you can be anything you want to be, do anything you want to do." It was a message she never forgot.[5]

NEW FRONTIERS

Walnut Hills High School provided the Golter twins with an exceptionally good basic education. Housed in an impressive red and white building situated on a hill, the six-year college preparatory school required admission tests. Cincinnatians were proud of the fact that it ranked with Exeter and Andover in National Merit Scholarship ratings. Although the curriculum was demanding, B. J. enjoyed a number of extracurricular activities such as singing in the a capella choir, serving as art editor of the yearbook and as president of HI-Y (a YMCA youth organization), and being a member of the Quill and Scroll Society.

The twins had no problem gaining admission to the University of Cincinnati's six-years M.D. program, which consisted of three years at the liberal arts school and three years at the medical school. Classes went all year round. Again B. J. took her studies seriously. In June, 1941, Mr. Golter received a letter from the office of the president of the university congratulating him on "Betty Jane's continued fine work" and noting that her name "appears again on the Dean's List."[6] She was also chosen for membership in Alpha Lambda Delta, an undergraduate women's honorary society.

Despite her determination to do well in all her classwork, she again found time to become involved in a number of campus activities. A member of Kappa Alpha Theta, she participated in many of that sorority's projects. At the end of her sophomore year, she was chosen to be a junior advisor for incoming freshmen women. These "big sisters" were selected on the basis of their leadership ability and participation in activities.[7]

B. J. admitted that meeting Bob McConnell during her first year of medical school was a distraction, but she stuck to her goal of doing well in her medical studies. It was difficult to plan a wedding and keep up, but she managed. Her brother gave her away (her father died the previous year) at the ceremony in the Calvary Episcopal Church on July 1, 1944. After a brief honeymoon over the long Fourth of July holiday, the couple was back in school.

Upon graduation in 1946, B. J. began a fifteen-month rotating internship at Cincinnati General Hospital. When she discovered she was pregnant, it was decided that instead of taking her turn at pediatrics, with the possible danger of exposure to German measles, she should cover psychiatry. Some shocking and even frightening experiences in abnormal psychiatry helped her formulate the reaction, "How shall I respond medically to this situation?" This reaction would prove useful in dealing with traumatic situations in her future career.[8]

With the birth of their first child, B. J. began her extended leave from medical practice. The McConnells moved to Davenport, Iowa, where Bob had the position of head of the Department of Radiology at Mercy Hospital. B. J. spent her time making a home for Bob and their ever-increasing family and being involved in community life. She served as chair or cochair for the benefit dances such as those given by the Mercy Hospital Auxiliary and for the elaborate annual December Crystal Ball, also a benefit affair. As cochair of the Mercy Hospital gift shop, she helped plan its annual bazaar. Participating in the children's activities meant sewing for four daughters, constant chauffeuring "for everything," and being a volunteer "for everything."

Despite all these activities, she found time to read extensively in medical journals, especially those articles dealing with her husband's field of radiology. Interesting things were happening in that field following the development of the atomic bomb and the discovery of ways to artificially produce radioactive isotopes. Unlike X rays, which pass through the body to portray a certain part (such as the chest) on film, radioactive isotopes emitting gamma rays are tagged to specific types of chemical compounds, which, when injected or ingested, localize in specific organs or systems that then may be visualized on film. For example, radioactive iodine is used to diagnose various thyroid disorders and to treat hyperthyroidism and functional metastatic thyroid cancer. Other "tagged" compounds are used to image the kidney and liver and test the functions of these organs, screen for blood clots in the lung, and identify the spread of cancer to bone.

In the early 1950s, few doctors had had any training in or exposure to nuclear medicine. However, courses were beginning to be offered at university hospitals such as Stanford and Cook County Hospital. Bob went to these seminars and also to two training sessions at Oakridge, Tennessee. In 1955, he was licensed by the Atomic Energy Commission to administer small amounts of radioactive material to patients. Nuclear medicine was in its infancy, but as the medical community around Davenport became more aware of its potential, the workload at the Radiology Department at Mercy Hospital relentlessly increased. B. J. watched her husband, always a person of very high energy, become exhausted and frustrated trying to keep up with the demands. In a weak moment she told him "I'll come back to work." So in 1960, she returned to medical practice in the Department of Nuclear Medicine at Mercy Hospital. The job was supposed to be part-time, but her hours grew steadily longer as newly developed radioactive isotopes replaced discarded ones. New equipment, more sophisticated and complicated lab studies, and an ever-increasing patient load made them both much too busy. B. J. said, "I quit," and Bob soon decided that the only way out for him was to quit also.

In June, 1967, they moved to Dallas, where Saint Paul Hospital had invited Bob to head its newly created Nuclear Medicine Department. B. J. set out to increase her knowledge of the field by attending seminars wherever they were held across the country. At home she studied every night and read everything she could get her hands on. Feeling that she needed some formal training to bridge the long gap away from her profession, she took a special internal medicine–nuclear medicine fellowship created for her at Southwestern Medical School and Parkland Hospital. In this program she worked in every discipline in which she was interested and saw patients in the clinic. She reflected, "It was a great learning experience."[9] From 1969 to 1971 she was on the attending staff of the Department of Radiology at Parkland Memorial Hospital in Dallas.

In 1972, the first year that board certification was offered in nuclear medicine, Bob McConnell took and passed his examinations. The following year, Betty Jane McConnell passed her examinations and became a diplomate of the American Board of Nuclear Medicine.

From 1973 to 1976 she was chief of nuclear radiology at the Veterans Administration Hospital in Dallas. And from 1969 to 1976 she was on the attending staff of the Department of Nuclear Medicine at Saint Paul Hospital. When Bob was elected president of the American College of Radiology and had to be away at meetings, B. J. sometimes took over for him at Saint Paul.

Their home on Hallmark Drive was a busy lively place with assorted daughters, sons, and sons-in-law, plus friends, pets (mice, fish, dogs), and sometimes a foreign guest: the McConnells housed a high school student from Thailand and a Japanese English teacher. Sundays were "family days," often with a dozen people around the breakfast table. Family sports included swimming, fishing, golf, and an occasional skiing trip to places like Taos, New Mexico.

After almost ten years in Dallas, the McConnells moved in 1976 to Houston, where Bob had been asked to head the newly formed Division of Nuclear Radiology at Hermann Hospital, a part of the University of Texas Medical School at Houston. B. J. was appointed as assistant professor in the Department of Radiology, Nuclear Radiology Division, at the medical school and was also on the attending staff at Hermann Hospital. She worked closely with referring physicians on patients with various heart problems. An article titled "Nuclear Angiocardiography" in the Hermann Hospital *Medical Staff Newsletter* quoted her as saying, "Although our studies do not show the anatomic details of blood vessels, they show the effects of the narrowing of these vessels on the heart muscle, how well the ventricular wall contracts, if the patient has had a myocardial infarction, and if the infarction is recent or old."[10]

The Division of Nuclear Radiology did occasional studies on heart transplant candidates to provide a baseline for future research. It was also active in providing studies for the kidney transplant program at Hermann Hospital. The patients were then followed closely after transplantation. The acquisition of a computer in 1977 by the department enhanced the McConnells' work by adding the capacity to detect relative function to the ability to study physiologic nuclear images visually.

In December of 1978, when the Hermann Air Ambulance Service acquired its third helicopter, it became the largest civilian air rescue program in the nation. As B. J. noted, "There was lots of trauma in Houston." When the University of Texas Medical School acquired a grant to study trauma, she served as a member of the Central Nervous System Trauma Committee.

In Houston and in Dallas, B. J. was involved in many peripheral activities connected with nuclear medicine. She was a member of the Board of Trustees of the Southwestern Chapter, Society of Nuclear Medicine, and served as secretary-treasurer, vice-president, and president of the Texas Association of Physicians in Nuclear Medicine. As a member of the Committee on Nuclear Medicine of the Texas Medical Association (TMA), she also served as chairman of the Ad Hoc Committee on Volume Reduction of Radioactive Waste, charged with advising the TMA of developments in this area.

During her career, she has been an invited speaker on topics relating to nuclear medicine at numerous scientific meetings in Texas, South

Carolina, Nevada, and California. B. J. has also collaborated on many articles in her field. Frequently, the presentations and articles have been in conjunction with Bob.[11]

In 1982, the McConnells left the busy Houston metropolis to settle in the quiet village of Salado. Both had accepted positions with the Radiology Department of Scott and White Hospital in Temple, fifteen miles north of Salado. B. J. was on the senior staff of the hospital clinic and taught in the Texas A&M University Medical School first as an assistant professor and then as an associate professor. She also worked on several studies (including two on myocardial imaging) for which she planned tests and kept the records.

Since her retirement from Scott and White in 1991, she has been an emeritus member of the staff. Six years later, her fellow workers in the Department of Nuclear Radiology were still expressing their regret at her leaving.

Retirement for the McConnells has meant time to use their high-level energy for various community activities. Both have devoted enormous time and effort to create an outstanding library for the village. B. J. has served as president of the Historical Society. She is active in the local chapter of the PEO (a philanthropic educational organization) and in the Village Artists Association. Keeping up with six children and nine grandchildren also takes a big chunk of time. Even during their busy years in practice, the McConnells found time to satisfy their travel lust and have been all over the United States. Many of their trips were fishing expeditions, especially those to Canada, Colorado, Wyoming, and New England. Recently the McConnells gave the Dallas Museum of Art an antique six-panel screen that they purchased in Japan on their first overseas trip. Since then they have been to Mexico, England, Scotland, and many European countries including Greece and Italy, where B. J. studied art. In January of 1996, they traveled to China.

For over fifty years the McConnells have worked as a team, professionally and domestically. Their partnership has worked because they like as well as love each other and because they obviously have great respect for each other and are willing to compromise when disagreements arise. Bob attributes B. J.'s success as a parent and as a doctor to her "strong, compassionate, maternal demeanor." When she talks to a patient (or family member or friend) she concentrates her full attention on that person, who understands that she really cares about what they are saying. "She never treated 'a thyroid'; she treated a patient *and* their family," he added. He believes that in a sense B. J. was "called" to her profession.[12]

When asked what Bob's influence on her has been, B. J. answered, "He has ever been caring and supportive." She added, "I always thought, 'If he can do it, I can.'" And she has.

Virology

JANET S. BUTEL, PH.D. (1941–)

Dr. Janet Butel, head of the Department of Molecular Virology at Baylor College of Medicine in Houston, was the first woman to chair an academic unit at the college, the first woman to be appointed to one of the college's endowed professorships, and the first woman to be voted a distinguished service professor.[13]

Janet Susan Butel was born in May, 1941, in a Kansas farmhouse near the town of Overbrook. She and her four brothers were brought up on that farm by a father who was a college graduate and a mother who majored in architecture for three years (she was the first and only female in the School of Architecture) before leaving Kansas State University to marry. Mr. Butel had considered becoming a weathercaster but changed his mind and returned to the family farm of about 320 acres. He became deeply involved in his community, serving as a school board member and on the board of directors of the bank and the farmers' co-op. The Butel home was always full of books and magazines. Uncommonly for that time and place, it was "just assumed" that all the children would go to college.[14]

The young Butels attended an all-in-one elementary school that seldom had more than eight or ten students at a time. Their high school, too, was small, with a total of about one hundred students. Janet had about twenty-eight classmates. Her studies came easily to her; she remembered that chemistry offered the most interest and challenge. She started work toward a chemistry major at Kansas State University, but as soon as she began taking the requisite biology courses, she realized that was the field she preferred. Until then, she had never heard of viruses. When she attended the only lecture on viruses offered in one of those biology courses, it seemed to her the most interesting area she had ever heard of. She felt "just entranced."

In June, 1963, Janet Butel graduated summa cum laude with a B.S. in bacteriology and a minor in chemistry. She had had no idea just what she would do after getting her degree. Since one of her university professors had advised her to go on to graduate school, she looked around and discovered that at that time only two schools in the United States—Harvard and Baylor—had a program devoted to virology. She applied to and was accepted by Baylor College of Medicine in Houston.

Dr. Joseph L. Melnick, who gained international recognition for his work on poliomyelitis vaccine, founded and directed the virology program at Baylor. He had employed Dr. Bettylee Hampil, who was making a postretirement career of classifying viruses. Young Janet Butel worked with Dr. Hampil, earning her doctor of philosophy degree from Baylor College of Medicine with a major in virology and a minor in cell biology. This degree was awarded with honors in 1966. She then became a postdoctoral fellow in the Virology and Epidemiology Department. In the next ten years, she progressed to a full professorship in the department. In 1989, Janet Butel became head of the Division of Molecular Virology, and in 1995 she was voted the honorary title of distinguished service professor.[15]

"You can't apply too many superlatives to Dr. Butel," remarked Dr. Melnick of his colleague. "Straightforward" and "fair" are the adjectives he chose as most descriptive of her.[16]

Dr. Butel married a man she met in graduate school, Dr. David Graham, who is now chief of gastroenterology in the Department of Medicine at Baylor. According to his wife, he "does wonderful, very important work" and has received much recognition for it. In academia, where people sometimes move around a lot, it is uncommon that both doctors have found such good jobs in the same institution. Marriage complicated the professional lives of these two teaching doctors. Dr. Graham did not want to move where winters are too cold, and neither of them pursued job opportunities when there was not a suitable post for the other one. They have a son and a daughter, both now in medical careers.

"I remember being tired all the time," Dr. Butel recalled of the first several years after the children were born. She had flexible hours and was able to spend time with them in the mornings before going to work; she then would stay up late, working on papers after the children were asleep. She was able to participate in a carpool to get the children to and from school and to attend their special school activities. Their daughter, Kathleen, graduated from Southwestern Medical School in Dallas and in 1995 was doing her residency at Denver. The son, David, at that time had just started medical school at Baylor.

Like another celebrated Kansas farm girl, Dr. Butel has spent much of her life in a wonderland of strange creatures: in her case, the whole world of microorganisms, tiny living things one cannot see. They are mostly bacteria and viruses, a fascinating area to Dr. Butel. The viruses are so tiny they can be seen only through an electron microscope, and they can reproduce themselves only by infecting cells in some other organism. There are viruses that infect bacteria, viruses that infect plants, and viruses that infect every kind of animal. They take advantage of the process of living cells to duplicate themselves. There is huge variety in the structure of viruses, in their strategy for their transmission from one host to the next, and in their taking over control of the cells in order to reproduce themselves.

In their process of survival, viruses sometimes do damage to their hosts. It is because they cause diseases that viruses were first recognized. Many viruses do not cause disease. Some, however, Dr. Butel explained, cause rabies, the common cold, measles, chickenpox, and herpes lesions. Others can cause neurological diseases as well as cancer, hepatitis B, and diarrhea. Virology is a very young discipline: Pasteur, though he made an attenuated rabies virus, did not know what he was working with. The study of viruses required the ability to culture them in some way and to work with them in the laboratory, and this has been possible only in the twentieth century.

Molecular virology, to Dr. Butel, means understanding in a very detailed way what viruses are and how they work. Another area is diagnostic virology. She predicted that in the not-too-distant future there will be more antiviral drugs as well as speedy tests available to the diagnostic laboratories. The tests that were used in the past took so long that the patient was well (or dead) before the results came back. It took days and sometimes weeks to get results. With new techniques like the polymerase chain reaction, one can get quick results from small samples. Results that are more timely may influence treatment of the patient.

Dr. Butel defined basic science as doing experiments "to learn things when you don't know if any practical application will come out of that work." Biochemical experiments can be done. Scientists can make antibodies against an agent of disease, and over time "you get an antiserum. There are all kinds of antisera that people have or that you can buy; and you can use the antibodies to test and see if you have a particular agent. Things are easier now that we have genetic engineering and cloning."

Newspapers talk about "emerging viruses" as if they had not existed before, but Dr. Butel explained that probably these viruses did exist—they just hadn't done anything that made it possible for scientists to recognize them. When a disease outbreak occurs that indicates "something going on here," scientists will investigate and know the organisms are out there. Also viruses may jump species, and when a virus gets into a new species, it may behave very differently. This changing of hosts apparently does not happen very often, but when it does, the results can be dramatic. Current thinking about the origin of HIV is that it probably was a primate virus in Africa that somehow got into the human population. Although it might not have caused disease in its former host, in human beings it very often does. In that sense, viruses are changing and evolving, but they are not being created out of the air.[17]

Dr. Butel's own research is focused on cancer-causing viruses. Papilloma virus appears to be involved in causing cervical cancer. It is a tumor virus in the same family of viruses that cause warts. There are about seventy-five viruses in this family. This virus is very complicated in the way it has designated its strategy to reproduce. It has a mechanism that causes the cells it infects to start proliferating, each reproducing the virus in the new cell. Dr. Butel explained that normally skin cells do not grow very much. Cells have complex regulatory pathways that let the cells know when to grow or not to grow, and the tumor viruses have a viral protein that disrupts this regulatory machinery to encourage the cells to divide. The cells start dividing, and in that process they duplicate the viral nucleic acid and become tumors.

Dr. Butel's interest has always been tumor viruses, but nowadays she finds herself spending less time in the laboratory and more in writing applications for research grants. Job security for laboratory assistants is a terrible problem: she calls it "the biggest challenge of my whole career." The funding picture has been bleak for the past five years, and many scientists fear it will continue so into the future. As head of the department, Dr. Butel finds herself worrying about all of the people in her department: "The funding situation is just a nightmare." About four students a year get into the virology graduate program. There are also fellows who come from all over to train. They have an interest in the project, but they have to have some support.

Every experiment, said Dr. Butel, should ask a question; one hopes it will give some kind of answer, which then leads to another question. "We have long-term goals for our projects: we break those down into smaller aims, then we try a series of approaches to get at this general question. The approach will be made up of a series of experiments. These should be thought out so that you have the right controls so you can interpret the results that you get. That helps you design the next experiment, so that you take a lot of little baby steps toward a goal you have."

Dr. Butel's group has received a National Institute of Health institutional training grant that will keep a number of laboratory researchers on the job for a time. There is no long-term funding security for any of their work. With the explosion of discoveries in molecular biology, there are many opportunities to do experiments, to ask questions, to find out new information. "[There were] things we couldn't do ten years ago because we didn't have the tools. Now we have the tools, we know what needs to be done, we know how to do it—and now comes this money crunch. Programs are not getting funded, so they have to shut down, they can't continue—it's really too bad."

Being in a new, rapidly developing field has meant for Dr. Butel an enormous output of writing and lecturing. Her scientific contributions are clearly reflected in her publications of almost 150 papers appearing in first-class journals that are reviewed by the researcher's scientific peers. She is listed as the first author in twenty-two of these publications. In addition, she has made significant contributions to thirty-eight books or symposia, in eighteen of which she is the lead author.

Her honors include participation grants, graduate fellowships, and research awards. She was the first Joseph L. Melnick Professor of Virology for Baylor College of Medicine (awarded in 1986), and in 1988 she was voted a fellow of the American Association for the Advancement of Science. In 1996, she was a nominee for the ICN International Prize in Virology, a $50,000 prize awarded annually by ICN Pharmaceuticals. Dr. Butel's nomination was for her "contribution to basic understanding of viruses." Her wishes for the future put the welfare of her department and the continued top quality of Baylor College of Medicine ahead of her personal feelings, but she did say, "I still feel that I have things to contribute in the areas of the tumor viruses that I am working on."

Genetics

HUDA Y. ZOGHBI, M.D. (1955–)

Civil war in Lebanon during the late 1970s eventually brought Dr. Huda Zoghbi to Baylor College of Medicine in Houston, where in 1993 she and her research teams announced that they had identified a "killer" gene: one that causes spinocerebellar ataxia type 1, or SCA1.

Born Huda Y. El-Hibri in Beirut, in June, 1955, she was one of five children. Both parents encouraged her interest in sciences and supported her decision to become a doctor. She graduated from the American University of Beirut with a bachelor of science in 1975 and enrolled in that institution's medical school.[18]

Because of the civil war in 1976, young Huda's first year in medical school was spent in the school's basement, where she ate, slept, and studied while bombs exploded outside. During that hectic period she met William Zoghbi, also in his first year of medical school. The following summer "for a respite" she and a younger brother were sent by their parents to visit a sister in the United States. When it was time for them to go home, they found that the Beirut airport was closed and they could not return. Being cut off from home and medical school without any preparation was the worst experience of her career.[19]

Meharry Medical College in Nashville, Tennessee, accepted Huda's application six weeks into the semester. She entered as a second year medical student, was inducted into Alpha Omega Alpha (the honors medical society) in 1978, and graduated in 1979. Two honors were awarded her during her student days: the Seibels R. Green, Jr., Memorial Award in Internal Medicine and the E. Perry Crump Award in Pediatrics, both in 1979.

She married William Zoghbi, who had come to America in the early 1980s when both were in fellowship training. "We lived within our means, a very simple life," Huda recalled, which was easier because of outside support. Huda described her husband as a "fantastic

Huda Y. Zoghbi. Courtesy Baylor College of Medicine, Houston, Texas

person" who gives her unlimited support. She considers him "the ideal husband . . . what every man should be like." They have two children: Roula was twelve years old in 1995 and Anthony was ten. Both are "good kids." All four Zoghbis now have both American and Lebanese citizenship. Dr. William Zoghbi does echocardiography, using sound waves to form a picture of the heart, a procedure which has day-to-day impact on patient care.

From the beginning the Zoghbis hired a full-time babysitter—a considerable financial load during their fellowship training period, but both felt having such help was important. A major change for the two doctors was learning to set schedules that allowed time with their children. Of her lifetime achievements, Huda Zoghbi rated rearing her two children and sharing life with her husband as the most important.

It was Huda's idea that pediatrics would be "fun" as a medical specialty. She did a three-year residency in pediatrics at Baylor College of Medicine, followed by a one-year residency in neurology and then two more years in pediatric neurology. Then she became intrigued in her neurologic studies by how the brain works. "Thinking how we can get up in the morning and think, and how we eat . . . it's fascinating."[20]

It was when she realized the impact of hereditary and genetic defects on brain function and how these cause many neurologic problems and untreatable diseases that her interest in genetic research emerged. She wanted to "figure out how disease is happening through genetic defect." Huda spent three more years training in molecular genetics in the laboratory of Dr. Arthur Beaudet at Baylor from 1985 through 1988.

As the young doctor progressed at Baylor College of Medicine to a full professorship in the Departments of Pediatrics, Neurology, and Molecular and Human Genetics as well as the Division of Neuroscience, she earned several more awards for research, teaching, and scholarship. The two most recent were the Michael E. DeBakey Excellence in Research Award in 1994 and the Kilby Award in 1995 for "extraordinary contributions to society through science, technology, innovation, invention, and education."[21]

Under Dr. Beaudet's guidance, Dr. Zoghbi began to study families afflicted by spinocerebellar ataxia type 1, a neurodegenerative disease found in about one in 25,000 Americans. Ataxia is the loss of balance and coordination. Victims usually die within ten to fifteen years of onset.[22]

While she was working with graduate students on SCA1 research in her Baylor laboratory, Dr. Zoghbi learned that Dr. Harry Orr was studying the same problem with a group in his laboratory at the University of Minnesota. "We called, we talked, and we decided that instead of competing we would share information and exchange it and collaborate to enhance our productivity and move the work forward," she explained. Some collaborations are very limited, Dr. Zoghbi pointed out, but "ours is a very broad, very intense and complementary col-laboration that has been going on for seven years or so—thank God!"[23]

A Japanese discovery in 1974 had narrowed the search for the defec-tive gene to chromosome 6. A search for one gene among the great numbers on one chromosome without other clues was an impossible task. The Zoghbi and Orr groups divided the work and began "walk-ing" the chromosome, finding markers that indicated they were near-ing the mutated gene. On the same weekend, the two groups found the gene—just at the point where their research territories overlapped. After that, it took "two feverish weeks" with plenty of overtime to confirm that the gene is responsible for SCA1. "Nobody wanted to go home," Dr. Zoghbi remembered, and they soon produced the paper whose publication gave the two teams credit as the first to identify the aberrant gene.[24]

Once the scientists knew where the gene was, they cloned it, trying to discover what change within that gene led to neuronal loss in the patient. Their current objective is to "dissect" exactly the way this gene works and to try to find a pathway to normal function. Although there is no treatment for SCA1, locating the ataxia gene has led to a diag-nostic test: if the gene is suspected, a patient does not need endless MRIs, scans, and lots of blood work. There is a specific DNA test that will facilitate the diagnosis. While accurate diagnoses and genetic coun-seling are two immediate benefits of the ataxia gene identification, the ultimate goal is therapy for genes. For Dr. Zoghbi, being able to call the families "who trusted us" and gave time and blood samples and to tell them about these findings was a career high.

Chromosomes can be "seen" with today's instruments; genes can-not. However, the DNA double helix can be studied and the positions of genes on its strand can be calculated. Dr. Zoghbi designs experi-ments that her graduate students carry out. Then "we take the results and make an interpretation . . . and move on to the next step." How does she decide what experiments to propose? Through a combina-tion of knowledge of the brain, of neurology, of genetics, and of the literature. She explained, "Imagine the gene as a chapter in a book and the DNA sequences being all the letters that make up the story in that chapter. . . . Of course, if you're standing at a distance, you can see the whole book and imagine the book's being the whole body. . . . If you open to the table of contents, you can see the various chapters, but you don't really know what they are saying until you come to read each chapter."

For the study of the effects of cloned mutated genes, mice are the laboratory animals of choice. Their cerebellar structure is similar to that of humans, and one can expect effects similar to those that occur in humans. According to Dr. Zoghbi, the day will come when we can replace defective genes—not in the whole body, but in tissue. For example, in hemophilia, scientists believe it is possible to successfully put the gene that causes the clotting factor to work back into the bone marrow. But, she cautioned, this kind of work takes a lot of time, and people have high expectations. Now that genes are being discovered, "We have to fix everything!" Just as it took a long time to master by-pass surgery and to achieve bone-marrow transplantation, it will take many years to get there with gene therapy.

Dr. Zoghbi's group works on other disorders besides ataxia. Her current research projects include the cloning of two abnormal genes, the Aicardi and Golz-syndrome genes, and studying the molecular genetics of Rett syndrome. Rett syndrome is thought to be a genetic disorder because it affects only girls. It is a developmental disorder: a baby seems perfectly normal up to some time between six and eighteen months. Then she begins to lose developmental skills, lose communication, wring her hands, and show some autistic symptoms. These patients can grow to adulthood, but it is "a really tough" disease. They become isolated, develop seizures, and have balance problems. No breakthroughs on this problem have yet been made.

Currently, Dr. Zoghbi explained, most genetically caused diseases are untreatable. "If we can come to understand exactly how these mutations affect brain cell function, maybe we could then think of a good therapy. That's the stage where we are at present." Dr. Zoghbi hopes that in her lifetime "we can understand the neurologic bases for all diseases that are genetically determined and mediated by the genes . . . maybe in the next twenty or thirty years . . . and hopefully, conquer a few of them." She mentioned cancer as a genetically determined disease that is influenced by environmental factors: for example, smoking can damage cells, especially the predisposed cells. The sun, too, can injure DNA and, thereby, the genes.

Although Dr. Zoghbi is the only physician in her family, all four of her siblings have advanced degrees, and all are now in this country.

Their parents are still in Lebanon, now retired from their business. The Zoghbis try to return for a visit annually.

Dr. Zoghbi's first publication appeared in 1982, and her list of journal articles numbers seventy-four. She is the first author of seventeen articles and is also the lead author of nine of the twelve book chapters or reviews ascribed to her.

Virtually from the beginning, Huda Zoghbi has placed a great emphasis on identification of metabolic disorders in various neurologic diseases as well as on many genetic factors in these conditions. These factors include identification of genes as well as their loci on the chromosomes.

Dr. Zoghbi is responsible for clarification of the several basic metabolic and genetic factors in Rett syndrome and in one specific form of spinocerebellar ataxia. In addition, her clinical experience with these diseases and with many other forms of ataxia have established her as a recognized expert regarding these heritable conditions. Through October, 1994, the paper announcing discovery of the ataxia gene had been cited in 114 publications.[25]

Hospice Care

MARION POHLEN PRIMOMO, M.D. (1920–)

Her birth in Stolberg, Germany, in 1920 was almost a nonevent. Marion Pohlen learned afterward that she was scarcely breathing and was put aside in a corner so the doctor could concentrate on trying to keep her mother alive. Somehow, tiny Marion survived. Her father, William Pohlen, who had fought on the German side in World War I, became convinced that Germany held no future for his family, so in 1926 the Pohlens emigrated to Wisconsin, where Mr. Pohlen's brother was living.[26]

After a few years in Wisconsin and Minnesota, Mr. Pohlen, who had begun by doing odd-job repairs, established himself in the business world. He and his brother sent relief supplies to old friends in Stolberg during World War II, and later the two of them arranged for the building of a ninety-bed nursing-care facility in Stolberg—still an outstanding facility.[27]

Young Marion was dissatisfied with the school system in Brownsville, Texas, where the family had settled during her adolescence. When they sent her to boarding school at Our Lady of the Lake College in San Antonio, a whole new world opened for her. After graduating from high school at sixteen, she happily accepted a scholarship and attended Our Lady of the Lake College, graduating summa cum laude at twenty with a bachelor of arts in English.[28]

Because she had enjoyed her science courses, Marion became a lab technician and received a medical technologist degree for work in San Antonio at Fort Sam Houston Army Base at the station hospital. She worked full-time as a technician while she took prerequisite courses and applied to medical schools. In spite of her top grades, rejections kept coming: few slots for women were available, medicine was a man's field, a woman would displace a "more deserving" male applicant, women were apt to marry and not finish the courses. Her uncle, a priest, finally interested a woman physician on the Loyola School of Medicine staff in Chicago in his niece's case. Marion was admitted to medical school in January, 1944, and earned her medical degree at Loyola cum laude in 1947.[29]

Before they began their internships in Chicago, Dr. Marion Pohlen and a Loyola classmate, Dr. John S. Primomo, married. An Italian, he and his family had emigrated after the war. Her assignment paid one hundred dollars a month with room, board, and laundry. His paid thirteen dollars per month with room and board. They rented a furnished apartment for fifty dollars a month, and once in a while the young couple got to spend a few days together there.[30]

From 1949 to 1969, the Primomos practiced in their own Wintergarden medical facility in Dilley, Texas, near San Antonio. This hospital became a sixty-four-bed building and included a twenty-five-bed nursing care unit. It was just two blocks from their home, where they reared three girls and a boy. Two of the girls became nurses: Adele an R.N. and a lawyer, Janine head nurse of the pediatric and oncology section of the Children's Hospital of Santa Rosa Medical Center in San Antonio. Another girl, Michelle, is a Plano housewife. John William Primomo studied law and became a United States magistrate in July of 1988.[31]

The Primomos had been developing different special interests in their work, and in 1971 they decided to go their separate ways. Marion spent more time "mothering," but as the children left the nest, she found a burdensome amount of free time on her hands. She began to focus more on cancer and its consequences when she became physician co-ordinator of the Texas Cancer Information Service, a computerized cancer registry for Bexar County. In 1973 she began teaching in the University of Texas Health Science Center at San Antonio in its Department of Family Practice, where she is still a professor. Her elective course, "Dying Patients and Their Caregivers," is so popular that it usually fills within the first hour after it is announced.[32]

Ten of Dr. Primomo's summers, mostly in the 1970s, were spent in further medical studies at the Allgemeines Krankenhaus in Vienna, Austria. In 1976 she went to visit Saint Christopher's Hospice in London, a world-famous model of terminal care established by Dame Cicely Saunders, a nurse, social worker, and physician. This visit convinced Dr. Primomo that pain was not being handled properly in many cases of terminal illness in America. She saw the need to confront the conspiracy of silence that too often prevents free communication between the patient and family members. In 1979, Dr. Primomo became the first medical director of San Antonio's pioneer hospice program at Saint Benedict's Hospital.[33]

Concentrating on keeping a patient alert, pain-free, and mentally active until he or she dies is a psychological giant step away from a physician's usual top priority—keeping the patient alive. Dr. Primomo realized that the major concepts of hospice care needed to be skillfully articulated and presented to students and medical professionals as well as to the general public, any of whom could someday be in need of terminal care for themselves or their loved ones. Her "three C's" of hospice care are comfort, communication, and completion.[34]

Comfort, for the dying, is above all freedom from pain. Dr. Primomo emphasizes the need to use painkilling methods that will not addict the patient and that maintain his or her mental alertness. She teaches that with the use of radiotherapy, chemotherapy, surgery, and neurological methods, it is almost always possible to eliminate pain.[35]

Dying is a family affair, according to Dr. Primomo. It is important for the patients and their families to be able to speak openly of their fears, guilt, and anxieties. The doctor's attitude can set the tone for all discussions: he or she must be open and honest so that everyone involved is free from pretense about what is happening.[36]

Dr. Primomo explained the concept of completion for the dying by quoting Dr. Ira R. Byock: "What value is life if it is spent in outward pursuits, personal achievements,or even social contributions, but does not ultimately culminate with an inner sense of completion, fullness and meaning?" Dr. Primomo wants a patient to be able to withdraw gently from worldly spheres and make the connection to some larger framework. She added, "A person can die on good terms with himself, with his fellow man, and with his God. For a physician to assist in this process is a great privilege."[37]

To define "hospice" as it exists today in San Antonio and other American cities is to realize that the word does not necessarily mean a specific place. There are specific hospice buildings dedicated to caring for terminally ill patients, but the home can be a center for hospice care for many such people. In fact, Dr. Primomo believes that nobody should have to die alone. Her own practice includes frequent house calls to patients. Nurses and clergy on the hospice team also go to the homes on a regular basis.[38]

Dr. Primomo's readiness to discuss death and dying is in sharp contrast to American folkways generally and to the habits of medical practitioners as well. In a 1982 survey of 3,371 Texas doctors conducted by the University of Texas Medical Branch in Galveston, a deep discomfort was revealed concerning the idea of death. Almost half the physicians said they preferred to avoid telling the patients they were dying, over half believed that many doctors referred patients to others instead of dealing with their deaths, and more than a fourth of them admitted to avoiding dying patients. Although younger doctors were more likely to have had a course in the care of dying patients, the survey conclusion was that both age groups lacked the skills necessary to deal with the personal and interpersonal aspects of death and dying.[39]

Dr. Primomo displays a thorough understanding of her colleagues' difficulties in accepting death for their patients. "We were taught to cure," she said. "Much of the neglect of dying patients has to do with the physician's fear of death." However, she continued, "Our dying patients teach us . . . to come to grips with our own mortality by revealing to us their essence. . . . Sometimes you can be surprised at the growth that can occur in the last few moments before people die. It can stay with you a lifetime."[40]

In our death-denying society, death is not accepted as a natural part of life. The reason Dr. Primomo and other hospice caregivers work so hard for open communication is that "people at the end of life should have the opportunity to find some sense of meaning and purpose, or else life is worthless. Our objective is to help dying people find that sense of purpose. Some people don't find meaning and purpose until the very end. Sometimes the only thing they can do is express their love. . . . We make that atmosphere possible."[41]

Complex legal, ethical, and physiological questions are raised by the different focus that hospice care applies to a dying patient's needs. Dr. Primomo advocates the making (while the patient is mentally competent) of living wills—documents directing that all measures to support life be ended if the signer should be dying of incurable conditions—of durable powers of attorney, which will remain in force after the maker has died. When the individual becomes terminally ill without having made such provisions, legal difficulties more often arise. Dr. Primomo relies on guidelines published by the American Medical Association's Judicial Council in 1986, by those of a presidential commission published in 1983, and on the Texas Catholic authorities' guidelines of 1990, where ethical choices must be made concerning patient care. The latter statement describes situations where the medical means of prolonging life may be so burdensome as to become morally objectionable.[42]

According to Dr. Primomo, dehydration can result in a dying patient's becoming more rather than less comfortable because the accompanying lethargy and drowsiness can make the symptoms less bothersome. She added that advanced stages of malnutrition and dehydration result in the production of endorphins, which diminish pain. Decision making in matters of life and death should not be left to the courts, she concluded. Instead, decisions should be made case by case in a setting where patient, family, physicians, and others can communicate their feelings and values openly and honestly.[43]

Dr. Primomo's efforts to educate her colleagues, her patients, and the public in general include a barrage of speeches, interviews on radio and television, articles, and newspaper stories. She also contributed a chapter titled "Hospice Care" to a medical reference book, *Clinical Oncology*.[44] It is difficult to imagine how she finds time for all the speaking engagements and interviews in her round of hospice duties, her private practice, teaching her popular elective, and her family life. This "busy-ness" has grown right along with the rapid spread of hospice care in the San Antonio area.

Honors have marked Marion Primomo's progress. For service to her profession, she received the Outstanding Alumna Award at Our Lady of the Lake University in 1987. At a surprise luncheon in May, 1991, an announcement was made of the Texas Hospice Organization's award to her as "the 1991 Most Outstanding Hospice Physician in Texas." The newspaper article on this added that she is known locally as "the Mother of Hospice." The San Antonio Catholic Physicians' Guild presented her with its 1993 "Saint Luke Patron Saint of Physicians Award." Also in 1993, Dr. Primomo was elected vice-president-president-elect of the national Academy of Hospice Physicians.[45] This honor she later regretfully declined, unable to fit its responsibilities into her busy life.

Four times Dr. Primomo has been the first medical director of hospice programs in the San Antonio area: at Saint Benedict's in 1978, Hospice San Antonio in 1983, Santa Rosa Hospice in 1983, and, in 1992, she joined the newly organized Family Hospice of San Antonio.[46] She sometimes uses a cane nowadays because of arthritis, but a staff member recently remarked, "She can work rings around me!"

Part of Dr. Primomo's special aura is her respect for the wisdom of others. In particular, the words of Viktor Frankl, an Austrian psychiatrist who discovered meaning in his life in a concentration camp, resound in her memory: "It is the one who is ill who helps the one who is well in the struggle to find meaning. . . . One can rise above oneself. One can grow beyond oneself. Literally, up to one's last breath."[47] Dr. Primomo concluded, "Hospice work is definitely the culmination of my medical and professional activities. I have a sense that I am at the place that God wants me."

EPILOGUE

For medical women in Texas, there remain many opportunities to become pioneers. In November, 1995, for example, the American Medical Association elected Dr. Nancy Wilson Dickey, a specialist in family practice, chair of its board of trustees. She is the first woman to hold this office. Dr. Dickey has worked with various AMA groups since 1979 and was elected to its board in 1989.

She was graduated from Stephen F. Austin State University and from the University of Texas Medical School at Houston, from which she received the Distinguished Alumni Award. She has been a reviewer and editorial adviser for several professional journals. Dr. Dickey has also developed a national voice for medical women through her appearances on network television programs and in other media as a spokeswoman for the AMA.

There are many women pioneers in other medical specialties and allied sciences not covered in this work. We regret that space limitations would not allow us to mention all of them, as well as women in support groups such as the Whatsoever Chapter of the International Order of the King's Daughters and Sons, who established King's Daughters Hospital in Temple.

It has been an enriching experience for us to read and write about the medical women who are included here and especially to be able to talk with the more recent pioneers. We hope our readers will also experience the thrill of breaking down coventional barriers and will ask themselves, as Dr. Hsu and Dr. Owen did, questions nobody had considered before. Some may come up with answers that will advance medical knowledge and perhaps even save lives.

Many of the women profiled demonstrated such a degree of personal modesty that it was often difficult to find out the magnitude of their achievements. Although some of them had suffered from antagonism to women doctors shown by male peers and teachers, in most cases these women possessed such determination and willingness to work hard—often under very difficult circumstances—and such patience and tenacity of purpose as to make that antagonism ineffectual.

In every case, our women practitioners showed an eagerness to learn and a lively and useful curiosity that helped them find ways to keep up to date in their fields. These strengths were augmented by their independent habits of thought. While they were open to learning and using new therapies and techniques, they were also inclined to question established ideas.

We found these remarkable women in every kind of work setting and in communities of every structure, from tiny hamlets to large cities. They differed vastly in backgrounds, in ancestries, in religions, and in degrees of prosperity; yet in every case, we could recognize in one form or another the same intense personal motivation: a passion for healing.

We have enjoyed reminiscing about the past, but as Sister Teresa Martin remarked on the occasion of the centennial celebration of the hospital her fellow nuns had founded in Fort Worth, we know that we must "go with the times" and "live for the present and look to the future." We therefore expect and believe that women will continue to play an ever more important role in all branches of medicine.

It seems logical to expect the increasing presence in medicine of women as well as men concerning diseases that affect both. Today one hears often of new studies of groups of women patients in such areas as heart disease and cancer. For diseases specific to women, perhaps there will be kinder, more sympathetic approaches instead of the heroic treatments that originated with some male practitioners. These doctors used to think, for example, of hysteria as a women's ailment and that only women were inclined to hypochondria.

Because our exemplars uniformly demonstrated great willingness to listen to and spend time with patients, perhaps there will be an end to the patients' image of the "omniscient doctor" that has been common even with some of the most caring male doctors. Perhaps it may be replaced by the more kindly role of a wise friend in whom one is free to confide and of whom one may ask questions. It seems probable that female physicians will be prompted to step off their medical pedestals to seek what therapies are best for their patients. In a letter to Lady Byron (August 5, 1852), Elizabeth Blackwell wrote, "I would want also in my Hospital to cure my patients spiritually as well as physically, and what innumerable aids that would necessitate! I must have the church, the school, the workshop . . . to cure my patients—a whole society, in fact."

In another letter (to Barbara Bodichon, M.D.), Elizabeth Blackwell said, "I do not look on a good medical training as having power to make men of women, but as a most valuable educator of their own natures, making their benevolence, intelligence, and their activity to the purpose."

As Dr. B. J. McConnell pointed out, strength and compassion are not mutually exclusive.

NOTES

Introduction

1. Kate Campbell Hurd-Mead, M.D., *A History of Women in Medicine*, p. 7.
2. Geoffrey Marks and William K. Beatty, *Women in White*, p. 43.
3. *Encyclopaedia Britannica*, 15th ed., s.v. "Fabiola, Saint."
4. Marks and Beatty, *Women in White*, pp. 44–46.
5. Ibid., pp. 52, 62.
6. Hurd-Mead, *Women in Medicine*, p. 478; Ludwig W. Eichna, *The Pharos* 54 (winter, 1994): 14–17; *Encyclopaedia Britannica*, 15th ed., s.v. "foxglove."
7. Marks and Beatty, *Women in White*, p. 78.
8. Quoted in Esther Pohl Lovejoy, M.D., *Women Doctors of the World*, p. 48.
9. Ibid., pp. 12–17.
10. Ibid., pp. 26–27.
11. Ibid., p. 34.
12. Christine Chiew, *Mayo Alumni*, spring, 1995, p. 18.
13. Regina Markell Morantz-Sanchez, *Sympathy and Science: Women Physicians in American Medicine*, pp. 194–95.
14. Leslie Waggener, "Women's Rights," in *Alcalde*, February, 1916, p. 314.
15. "Minutes of the Board of Regents," University of Texas, May 15, 1897.
16. Lovejoy, *Women Doctors*, p. 34.

Chapter 1. Early Healers

1. Philip R. Overton and Sam V. Stone, Jr., "Medical-Legal History of Texas," *Texas Medicine* 63 (March, 1967): 117.
2. Ibid., p. 117.
3. Ibid., p. 118.
4. "Dr. Mary Jane Whittet Was First President of Atascosa County Medical Association," *Pleasanton Express*, October 4, 1956.
5. Ibid.
6. Overton and Stone, "Medical-Legal History," p. 118.
7. "Dr. Mary B. Ray," *Beaumont Enterprise*, April 27, 1901.
8. Overton and Stone, "Medical-Legal History," p. 118.
9. Virgil J. Vogel, *American Indian Medicine*, pp. 22–23.
10. W. W. Newcomb, Jr., *The Indians of Texas*, pp. 271–72.
11. Pat Ellis Taylor, *Border Healing Woman*, pp. 31–35.
12. Ibid., pp. 9–13.
13. Ibid., pp. 57–59.

14. Ibid., pp. 70–74.

15. Ibid., p. 60.

16. Ibid., pp. 21–30.

17. Ibid., p. 101.

18. Marc Lifsher, "Border Healer," *Dallas Times Herald,* December 5, 1982.

19. Taylor, *Border Healing Woman,* pp. 104–22.

20. William A. Owens, "Seer of Corsicana," in *And Horns on the Toads,* p. 24.

21. Ibid., p. 22.

22. Ibid., pp. 18–20.

23. Ibid., p. 25.

24. Ibid., p. 30.

25. Donna Bearden and Jamie Frucht, "Works in Progress," in *The Texas Sampler.*

26. Ruthe Winegarten, "Survey Questionnaire Telephone Follow-Up," typescript, September 18, 1979, Texas Woman's University Library, Denton.

27. Bearden and Frucht, "Works in Progress," p. 83.

28. Ibid., p. 85.

29. Ibid.

30. "Anne Wheeler, Crosby County Pioneer Museum," typescript, p. 2.

31. Leslie Gene Hunter and Cecilia Aros Hunter, "'Mother Lane' and the 'New Mooners': An Expression of *Curanderismo,*" *Southwestern Historical Quarterly* 99, no. 3 (January, 1996):291–325.

32. Agnes G. Grimm, "Pedro Jaramillo," in *New Handbook of Texas,* vol. 3, p. 911. Austin: Texas State Historical Assoc., 1996; Brownie McNeil, "Curanderos of South Texas," in *And Horns on the Toads,* p. 35.

33. Malinda Machato, "Curanderismo Practitioners Battle Ills with Herbs, Tradition, Spiritual Beliefs," *The Daily Texan,* Austin, June 2, 1982.

34. McNeil, "Curanderos," p. 36.

35. Ibid., p. 41.

36. Ibid.

37. Ibid.

38. Except as otherwise noted, the information on Mother Lane may be found in Hunter and Hunter, "Mother Lane."

39. McNeil, "Curanderos," pp. 33–34.

40. Pam Wilkinson, "Folk Medicine," *Southwest Airlines Magazine,* January, 1976, p. 15.

41. George Carmack, "Unraveling the Healing World of Curanderos," *San Antonio Express-News,* February 11, 1989, p. 4.

42. "Introduction," in *In Her Own Words,* ed. Regina Markell Morantz-Sanchez et al., pp. 3–35.

43. Rev. D. L. Saunders, M.D., *Woman's Own Book.*

44. Ibid., p. 27.

45. "The Negroes," in *Folklore of Texan Cultures,* pp. 126–27.

46. Florence Fenley, "Aunt Pal," in *The Cattleman* (Fort Worth, Tex.: November, 1943).

47. Ibid.

48. Ruthe Winegarten, *Texas Women, a Pictorial History: From Indians to Astronauts,* p. 76.

49. Annie Mae Hunt, "I Am Annie Mae," oral history, subject files, sec. 31, "Midwifery" (Texas Woman's University Library).

50. "The Poles," in *Folklore of Texan Cultures,* p. 207.

51. "1855—The Poles Arrive," in *The Dude Wrangler,* ed. Billie Crowell, p. 3.

52. Ibid., p. 26.

53. The information on Belle Starrett comes from "A Bicentennial History of Crosby County," typescript, n.d.

54. The information on Maggie Smith comes from Pat Ellis Taylor, typed letter, June, 1979.

55. The information on Mexican-American midwives comes from Agapito R. Sanchez, Jr., "An Exploratory Study of Mexican-American Midwives' Attitudes, Practices, and Beliefs Regarding Children Born with Congenital Defects," typescript, pp. 5-12.

56. "Texas Department of Public Health Survey," typescript.

57. Ibid., p. 2.

58. Ruth Schaffer, "Study of Midwifery in Six Counties in 1979," typescript, p. 16.

59. Nedra Bloom, "Age-Old Practice Draws Fire from Lawmakers, Physicians," *Dallas Morning News,* January 19, 1983.

60. Ibid.

61. Ibid.

62. Associated Press, "House Okays Midwife Registration Bill," *Austin American-Statesman,* May 8, 1979.

63. Laraine Benedikt, "Midwifery in Texas," typescript, n.d.

64. Ibid., p. 4.

65. Ibid.

66. Ruthe Winegarten, "Midwifery in Texas," typescript, pp. 1-2.

67. Belva Alexander, telephone interview with Geneva M. Fulgham, April 15, 1996.

Chapter 2. Nurses and Nursing

1. P. Woodbury Smith, M.D., telephone conversation with Geneva M. Fulgham, November 17, 1993.

2. Kathryn Stuart, *A Brief Biography of the Indian Princess Sarah Ridge,* pp. 4, 11-12.

3. Petition 2-1/124, OFB 64-251, Texas State Archives.

4. H. P. N. Grammel, *The Laws of Texas, 1822–1897,* vol. 3, 1847-54, p. 1042.

5. "Early Day Families," *The Dude Wrangler,* pp. 9-12.

6. Natalie Ornish, *Pioneer Jewish Texans,* pp. 246-47; *New Handbook of Texas,* vol. 4, p. 1180.

7. *The University of Texas Medical Branch at Galveston: A Seventy-five-Year History by the Faculty and Staff,* pp. 88-91.

8. Ibid., pp. 93–94; "Circular Prospectus: John Sealy Hospital Training School for Nurses, 1904."

9. "Scott and White Marks Ninety Years of Nursing," *Scott & White Options for Health* (October, 1994): 7; "Throughout Years Nurses' Mission Remains Same," *Temple Daily Telegram*, October 30, 1994.

10. Eleanor L. M. Crowder, "A. Louise Dietrich," typescript.

11. Jennie Cottle Beaty, *The History of the Graduate Nurses' Association of Texas*, p. 8.

12. Mary S. Cunningham, *The Woman's Club of El Paso*, pp. 140–41.

13. Crowder typescript.

14. Texas State Legislature, H.S.R. #195.

15. *Dallas Dispatch*, February 1, 1938.

16. "May Smith and the Dallas Baby Camp," *Heritage News*, summer, 1985, pp. 1–2.

17. Ibid., p. 2.

18. Ibid., p. 4.

19. *Dallas Dispatch*, February 1, 1938.

20. Susie Moncla, library director, Moore Memorial Public Library, to Ruthe Winegarten, May 6, 1980.

21. *Texas City Daily Sun*, August 22, 1974.

22. *Texas City Daily Sun*, September 23, 1968; *Galveston Daily News*, September 23, 1968; *New Handbook of Texas*, vol. 4, pp. 819–20.

23. *New Handbook of Texas*, vol. 6, p. 752.

24. Eleanor L. M. Crowder, *Nursing in Texas: A Pictorial History*, p. 3.

25. *New Handbook of Texas*, vol. 6, pp. 753–54.

26. Crowder, *Nursing in Texas*, p. 108.

27. "New Hospital Will Be Named for Nurse," *Galveston Daily News*, clipping, n.d.

28. In 1944, after fighting for equal status for twenty-five years, nurses were finally awarded military instead of relative rank and began receiving equal pay.

29. Patricia Kay Benoit, "Duty's Call Took 'Tex' to History," *Temple Daily Telegram*, February 14, 1994.

30. *New Handbook of Texas*, vol. 6, p. 681.

31. Ibid., vol. 5, pp. 1066–67.

32. Ibid., pp. 1065–66.

33. Ibid., p. 1067.

34. "History of Saint Paul Hospital, Dallas, Texas, 1896–1963," typescript, Texas Woman's University Library, Denton.

35. Sister Mary Loyola Hegarty, *Serving with Gladness*, p. 200.

36. Ibid, pp. 323–33; Herbert Molloy Mason, Jr., *Death from the Sea*, pp. 148–55; *New Handbook of Texas*, vol. 5, p. 765.

37. Sister Martha Ann Kirk, "Program Notes."

38. *Houston Post*, March 26, 1891.

39. Houston City Council resolution, March 25, 1892; Hegarty, *Serving with Gladness*, p. 299.

40. Hegarty, *Serving with Gladness*, pp. 305–10.

41. *Houston Post*, March 21, 1896.

42. Father James F. Vanderholt, *The Diocese of Beaumont: The Catholic Story of Southeast Texas*, p. 153.
43. Patricia Kay Benoit, *Men of Steel, Women of Spirit: History of the Santa Fe Hospital, 1891–1991*, pp. 4, 29.
44. *Saint Joseph Hospital: Over a Century of Commitment to Caring*, brochure (Fort Worth, Tex.: Saint Joseph Hospital, 1989).
45. Ibid.
46. "Dedication of a Texas State Historical Marker," program, April 29, 1967.

Chapter 3. Dentistry and Pharmacy

1. Carrie Pauley Stevenson, "The Early Amarillo Dentists," typescript, 1979.
2. Except as otherwise noted, the information on Mary Lou Shelman and other women dentists comes from Wanda Kellar Sivells, "Dr. Mary, An Early Texas Dentist," typescript, n.d.
3. Wanda Kellar Sivells, "'Dr. Mary' Shelman, Pioneer Texas Dentist," *Texas Dental Journal* (July, 1980): 8.
4. Sivells, "Pioneer Texas Dentist," p. 9.
5. "'Dr. Mary,' 89, Rites Held at Wharton," *Houston Post*, April 28, 1955.
6. The information on Henrietta Manlove Cunningham may be found in Sarah H. Emmott, "Hettie Cunningham—the First Woman Pharmacist in Texas—and Her Husband, James," typescript, n.d.
7. Bartee Haile, "Minnie Fish: Leader of the Suffragist Charge," *In Between*, p. 7.
8. Patricia Ellen Cunningham, "Cunningham, Minnie Fisher," *New Handbook of Texas*, vol 2 (Austin: Texas State Historical Association, 1996), p. 450.
9. Haile, "Minnie Fish."
10. Ibid.
11. Ibid.
12. Ibid.
13. Ibid.
14. Ibid.
15. "Honor Given Local Woman," *Galveston Tribune*, p. 24, col. 1, February 21, 1930.
16. Ibid.
17. "Minnie Fisher Cunningham, 1882–1946," typescript, n.d.

Chapter 4. Medical Practice, Research, Teaching

1. "Feminine Physicians," *Daniel's Texas Medical Journal* 3 (1888): 111.
2. "Extracts of articles," *Texas Courier-Record of Medicine*, typescript, 1979.
3. George Plunkett Red, "Dr. Margaret Ellen Holland," in *The Medicine Man in Texas*, p. 107.
4. Mary Jane Schier, "Health Director Nominee Craven Has Vision for New Job," *Houston Post*, September 27, 1980.

5. Gay E. McFarland, "Shirley Marks-Brown Worked Each Step of Way to the Top," *Houston Chronicle,* February 5, 1978.

6. Sandra M. Petrovich, "Dr. Sofie Herzog, Surgeon: A Woman Overcomes a Man's World," typescript, May 5, 1992.

7. Bobbie Saunders, "Brazoria's Woman for All Seasons," typescript, March, 1983.

8. Adele Perry Caldwell, "Character Sketch of Dr. Sofie Herzog, Brazoria, Texas," typescript, n.d.

9. Marie Beth Jones, "The Doctor Was a Lady," typescript, n.d.

10. Flora Humphries, "Brazoria's Woman Doctor Was One of South Texas' Most Noted Characters," *Houston Chronicle,* December 6, 1936.

11. Marie Beth Jones, "Brazoria's Lady Doctor—4," *Brazosport Facts,* February 3, 1961.

12. Ibid.

13. Petrovich, "Dr. Sofie Herzog," pp. 10-12.

14. "Memorial to Brazoria Woman Doctor Would Be Tribute to Picturesque, Self-Sacrificing, and Useful Career," typescript, July, 1925.

15. Petrovich, "Dr. Sofie Herzog," p. 9.

16. Marie Beth Jones, "Brazoria's Lady Doctor—5," *Brazosport Facts,* February 15, 1961.

17. "Daisy Emery Allen, M.D.," brochure, 1995.

18. "Excerpts from Diary of Dr. Frances Emery Allen, 1900," typescript, n.d.

19. Frances Marion Allen, telephone interview with Elizabeth Silverthorne, January 21, 1993; Frances Marion Allen to Elizabeth Silverthorne, April 3, 1993.

20. "Dr. Emery Allen," typescript, 1960.

21. "Daisy Emery Allen, M.D.," brochure.

22. Allen to Silverthorne.

23. Hallie Earle Journals, 1920–21, Graves-Earle Family Papers, the Texas Collection, Baylor University, Waco, Texas.

24. During the Civil War the mill was purchased in England, dismantled and run through a Union blockade into Mexico, and from there taken to east Waco, where it was reassembled to become a forerunner of Waco's textile industry (*The Handbook of Waco and McLennan County, Texas,* p. 93).

25. The Earle-Harrison House, originally located in the 800 block between South Fourth and South Fifth Streets, has been restored, renovated, and relocated at its present location in the 1900 block of North Fifth Street. It was dedicated and opened to the public in January, 1971.

26. Ellender S. Chase, "Memories of Hallie Earle, M.D.," in Jessie Lee Janes, ed., *A Woman for All Ages,* p. 13.

27. Graves-Earle Family Papers, academic records.

28. Patricia Ward Wallace, *A Spirit So Rare: A History of the Women of Waco,* p. 191.

29. Graves-Earle Family Papers, academic records.

30. Wallace, *A Spirit So Rare,* p. 193.

31. Larry Wygant, M.D., interview, typescript, p. 1.
32. Ibid., p. 2.
33. Ibid.
34. Ibid., p. 6.
35. Ibid., p. 5.
36. Ibid.
37. Edith M. Bonnet, M.D., Diary and Papers, MS no. 16.2.
38. "Hospital Board Accepts Women Interns Subject to Certain Restrictions," *Galveston Tribune*, p. 1, January 26, 1926.
39. Wygant interview, p. 7.
40. Letter, Bonnet Papers, MS no. 16.1.
41. Wygant interview, pp. 9, 10.
42. Ibid., p. 12.
43. Ibid., pp. 14, 15.
44. Ibid., p. 16.
45. Ibid., p. 15.
46. Daniel Edwards Jenkins, interview with Geneva M. Fulgham, February 11, 1994.
47. Merrill D. Wright to Rev. Albert P. Shirkey, July 20, 1950.
48. "E. A. Wright," obituary, *Texas State Journal of Medicine*, September, 1950.
49. Jenkins interview.
50. Ibid.
51. Ibid.
52. Ibid.
53. Wright obituary.
54. Ibid.
55. Jenkins interview.
56. Ibid.
57. Ibid.
58. Wright to Shirkey.
59. Elva Anis Wright, M.D., "An Analysis of Eighty-three Cases of Diarrhoea in Infants," *South Texas Medical Record*, 1916.
60. Jenkins interview.
61. Wright to Shirkey.
62. Ibid.
63. Ibid.
64. "Negro Woman Doctor Serves Migrants," *Texas State Journal of Medicine* 60 (1964): 774–75.
65. Vashti R. Curlin, M.D., "Women in Medicine: Early History of the Black Woman Physician in the United States," *KCMS Bulletin* 70 (July–August, 1991): 130–31.
66. Lisa E. Thompson, M.D., "Two Strikes: The Role of Black Women in Medicine before 1920," *The Pharos* 58 (winter, 1995).
67. Ibid., p. 130.

68. Ibid., p. 131.
69. "Negro Woman Doctor Serves Migrants," p. 775.
70. "Lady Doctor to Migrant Workers," *Ebony*, February, 1962, pp. 59–68.
71. "Negro Woman Doctor Serves Migrants," p. 775.
72. "Lady Doctor to Migrant Workers," p. 63.
73. "Negro Woman Doctor Serves Migrants," p. 774; Phil Duncan, "People-Loving Dr. Edwards Plans Again for Her Hospital," *Hereford Brand*, March 5, 1964.
74. "Medal Given Dr. Edwards," *Hereford Brand*, July 5, 1964.
75. Selden Hale, "Hereford Woman Doctor Acclaimed by Johnson," *Amarillo News Globe*, July 5, 1964.
76. Russell Shaw, "Hereford Doctor Fights Own Battle for the Poor," *West Texas Register*, October 2, 1964, Amarillo.
77. Ibid.
78. Ibid.
79. Kay Powers, "Doctoring and Earning Respect," *Austin American-Statesman*, March 2, 1986; Claude Reed, Jr., "The Yerwood Sisters: Medical Trailblazers," *National Scene*, 1983, p. 14.
80. Reed, "The Yerwood Sisters," p. 14.
81. Ibid., p. 17.
82. "Dr. Yerwood 'Made It,'" *Austin American-Statesman*, January 5, 1975.
83. Powers, "Doctoring and Earning Respect."
84. "Re: Connie R. Yerwood, M.D.: Honors Received," typescript, n.d., Texas Woman's University Library, Denton.
85. "Connie R. Yerwood, M.D., Biographical Information," typescript, n.d.
86. Jenkins interview.
87. Except as otherwise noted, the information on Francine Jensen may be found in Dr. Francine Jensen, interview with Geneva M. Fulgham, February 1, 1994.
88. Telephone verification, Harris County Public Health Department, Houston, Texas, October 20, 1994.
89. Claudia Potter, "Memoirs," typescript, 1948, p. 1.
90. C. A. Bridges, *History of Denton, Texas*, pp. 186–87.
91. Florice Green, "Veteran of Denton's Public Health Service, D. F. E. Piner, Recalls Wars against Disease," *Denton Record-Chronicle*, June 28, 1941.
92. Ibid.
93. Chester R. Burns, "The University of Texas Medical Branch at Galveston," *Journal of the American Medical Association* (September 11, 1991): 1400–1402; University of Texas Medical Branch at Galveston catalogs for 1900, 1903, 1904.
94. UTMB catalogs, 1903, 1904.
95. "Eminent Woman Doctor Served Forty-one Years—All on Probation," *Temple Daily Telegram*, December 6, 1963.
96. Charles R. Allen, *Historical Notes on the Origin and Development of The Texas Society of Anesthesiologists*, pp. 8–9.

97. Charles H. Gillespie, speech, September 20, 1991; Gillespie, interviews with Elizabeth Silverthorne: August 16 and 20, 1988; August 8, 1991; and September 16, 1991.
98. "Eminent Woman Doctor," *Temple Daily Telegram.*
99. Potter, "Memoirs," pp. 12–13.
100. G. V. Brindley, Jr., interview with Elizabeth Silverthorne, August 20, 1988.
101. Potter, "Memoirs," pp. 21–25.
102. Allen, *Historical Notes,* pp. 4–5.
103. A. Compton Broders, "Memoirs," typescript, January 14, 1981.
104. A. C. Scott, Jr., speech, typescript, November 14, 1946.
105. Allen, *Historical Notes,* p. 5.
106. Ted Stafford, *May Owen, M.D.,* p. vi. The material in this section is largely based on information found in this authorized biography of May Owen.
107. Ibid., p. 25.
108. Ibid., p. 38.
109. Lasher, Patricia, *Texas Women: Interviews and Images,* p. 141.
110. Stafford, *May Owen, M.D.,* p. 89.
111. Jean Gilliland, *May Owen, M.D.: Heritage of Achievement,* p. 4.
112. John H. Smith, "President's Paragraph," *Tarrant County Physician,* April, 1988, p. 10.
113. Lasher, *Texas Women,* p. 142.
114. Stafford, *May Owen, M.D.,* p. 105.
115. Melissa Fletcher Stoeltje, "Another Dr. Ruth Delivers," *Houston Chronicle,* October 17, 1993.
116. Ibid.
117. Randy J. Sparks, "Dr. Ruth Hartgraves," *New Titles and News,* pp. 14–15.
118. Dr. Ruth Hartgraves, interview with Larry Wygant, typescript, Blocker History of Medicine Collections, Moody Medical Library, UTMB, Galveston.
119. Dr. Edith Bonnet, interview with Larry Wygant, typescript.
120. Stoeltje, "Another Dr. Ruth."
121. Dr. Hallie Hartgraves, interview with Larry Wygant, typescript.
122. Ruth Hartgraves, M.D., "Biographical Sketch," typescript, n.d.
123. Stoeltje, "Another Dr. Ruth."
124. Ibid.
125. Ibid.
126. Ibid.
127. Sparks, "Dr. Ruth Hartgraves," p. 15.
128. Stoeltje, "Another Dr. Ruth."
129. Ibid.
130. Mary Powledge, "Prominent Houstonian Continues to Pioneer at Ninety-two," *UTMB Alumni News,* vol. 7, July–August, 1993.
131. Ibid.
132. Sparks, "Dr. Ruth Hartgraves," p. 16.

133. Stoeltje, "Another Dr. Ruth."
134. George Plunkett Red, *The Medicine Man in Texas,* p. 105.
135. Ibid., p. 109.
136. *Texas State Journal of Medicine* (February, 1910): 373.
137. Red, *The Medicine Man,* p. 109.
138. Ibid.
139. *Texas State Journal of Medicine* 8 (June, 1912): 48.
140. Obituary, *Houston Chronicle,* February 9, 1912.
141. Ray Karchmer, "The Trials of the Immigrants," *San José Daily Mercury,* December 27, 1908.
142. Dr. Louis Daily, interview with Geneva M. Fulgham, January 26, 1994.
143. Ibid.
144. Ibid.
145. Natalie Ornish, *Pioneer Jewish Texans,* p. 249.
146. Louis Daily interview.
147. Ibid.
148. Ibid.; "Credits Ballot with Influence," *Houston Post-Dispatch,* 1928.
149. "Doctors Honor Four Houstonians," *Houston Press,* November 1, 1925.
150. "Move to Bar Wives from Work Scored," *Houston Chronicle,* 1932.
151. Mildred Whiteaker, "Two Proposals Face Board of Education," *Houston Press,* February 2, 1948.
152. "School Relief Tax Backed by Dr. Daily," *Houston Post,* April 27, 1933.
153. Alvin DuVall, "School Board Member Favors Stronger Voice for U.H. President," *Houston Post,* February, 1945.
154. Ornish, *Pioneer Jewish Texans,* p. 250.
155. Ibid.
156. Louis Daily interview.
157. Ibid.
158. Ibid.
159. Ibid.
160. Ibid.
161. Joseph W. Samuels, "Dr. Ray K. Daily, a Woman of Valor," *The Jewish Herald-Voice,* December 3, 1975.
162. Except as otherwise noted, the information on Goldie Ham may be found in Elizabeth Hanson Duerr, interview with Geneva M. Fulgham, November 16, 1993.
163. Barbara McIntosh, "Doctors for Life," *Houston Post,* November, 1978.
164. Benjy F. Brooks, M.D., "Album of Women in Medicine: Goldie Suttle Ham, M.D.," *Journal of the American Medical Women's Association* 16 (January, 1961): 67.
165. Brooks, "Album of Women in Medicine."
166. "G. S. Ham Hanson," obituary, *Texas Medical Journal* 76 (January, 1980): 81.
167. Ibid.; McIntosh, "Doctors for Life."
168. Sammye Munson, "Clotilde García, Doctor of the Barrio," in *Our Tejano Heroes: Outstanding Mexican Americans in Texas,* pp. 40–44.

169. Ibid.
170. Ibid.
171. Veronica Salazar, "Dedication Rewarded: Prominent Mexican Americans," p. 39.
172. Munson, "Clotilde García," p. 42.
173. Ibid.
174. Paul Sweeney, "Wit, Stamina Keys to Dr. Clotilde García's Achievements," newspaper clipping, n.d.
175. Munson, "Clotilde García," p. 43.
176. "Résumé of Dr. Clotilde P. García," typescript, 1980.
177. Gilberto Jasso and María Padron, "Spain's Royal American Order of Isabella the Catholic Awarded by His Majesty King Juan Carlos I to Clotilde P. García, MD."
178. Brooks Peterson, "Dr. García Will Serve, Is 'Willing and Able,'" newspaper clipping, 1973.
179. Sweeney, "Wit, Stamina Keys."
180. Ibid.
181. Munson, "Clotilde García," p. 40.
182. "Women Named to Hall of Fame," Associated Press, 1984, Austin, Texas.
183. Jasso and Padron, "Spain's Royal American Order."
184. George Plunkett Red, "Petticoat Medicine," in *The Medicine Man in Texas*, p. 108.
185. "Early Physician Teaches," in "Distaff and the Caduceus," *Texas State Journal of Medicine* (November, 1960): 885–86.
186. Red, *The Medicine Man.*
187. William B. Sharp, M.D., "Microbiology at the Medical College," in *The University of Texas Medical Branch at Galveston, Seventy-five-Year History*, p. 87.
188. Ibid.
189. The information on Dr. Schaefer's speech comes from Marie Charlotte Schaefer, M.D., "Opening Address, Session of 1912–13, the Medical Department of the University of Texas," *The University Medical* 17 (October 15, 1912).
190. Red, *The Medicine Man.*
191. Jack Pruitt, M.D., to Public Relations Department, Hermann Hospital, January 11, 1982.
192. Faculty and Staff, UTMB, "William Keiller," in *The University of Texas Medical Branch at Galveston*, p. 36.
193. Ibid., p. 282.
194. Ibid. p. 39.
195. Violet Keiller, M.D., "A Contribution to the Anatomy of Spina Bifida," *Brain: A Journal of Neurology*, June, 1922.
196. Pruitt, to Public Relations Department.
197. Ibid.
198. Ibid.

199. Ibid.

200. "Dr. Violet H. Keiller," obituary, *Texas State Journal of Medicine* (November, 1958): 825.

201. Ibid.

202. Mary Jane Schier, "Hospital Will Honor Early Woman Doctor," *Houston Post,* February 15, 1982.

203. Award presentation speech, the Texas Genetics Society, typescript, March 22, 1985.

204. Natalie Ornish, "Rose G. Schneider," in *Pioneer Jewish Texans*, p. 256.

205. Rose G. Schneider, "How I Became a Harvard Person," newspaper clipping, n.d.

206. Ornish, *Pioneer Jewish Texans,* p. 256.

207. Ibid.

208. Award speech, Texas Genetics Society.

209. Mildred Robertson, telephone interview with Geneva M. Fulgham, September 9, 1994.

210. Ornish, *Pioneer Jewish Texans,* p. 257.

211. "Two File in Galveston College Regents Election," *Galveston Daily News,* n.d.

212. "Doctor Globe-Trots to Present Paper," *Galveston Daily News,* August 1, 1968; "Isle Doctor Invited to Present Paper," *Galveston Daily News,* August 27, 1971.

213. "Sickle Cell Education Plan Set," *Galveston Daily News,* August 25, 1972.

214. Mary Jane Schier, "Blood Variants Put Galveston on the Map," *Houston Post,* April 18, 1970; Ornish, *Pioneer Jewish Texans,* p. 257.

215. "Abnormal Cells Being Named for Texas Cities," *Valley Morning Star,* December 12, 1970.

216. "UTMB Scientist to Speak Here on Women's Lib," *La Marque Times,* February 4, 1971.

217. "Best Towns Those That Do It Easy—Vandergriff," *Galveston Daily News,* 1973.

218. Ornish. *Pioneer Jewish Texans,* p. 257.

219. Ibid.

220. Award speech, Texas Genetics Society.

221. June Dove Leong, "God's Ambassador, Dr. Katharine H. K. Hsu," *U.S. Asia News,* Houston, November 11, 18, 1988.

222. Ibid.

223. Ibid.

224. Ibid.

225. Ibid.

226. Ibid.

227. Ibid.

228. Ibid.

229. Ibid.

230. Ibid.

231. Dr. Katharine H. K. Hsu, interview with Geneva M. Fulgham, February 28, 1994.

232. Leong, "God's Ambassador."

233. Ibid.

234. Hsu interview, February 28, 1994.

235. Ibid.

236. Ibid.

237. Ibid.

238. Ibid.

239. Ibid.

240. Ibid.

241. Ibid.

242. Ibid.

243. Dr. Katharine H. K. Hsu, interview with Geneva M. Fulgham, March 7, 1994.

244. Ibid.

245. Dr. Katharine Hsu, "Curriculum Vitae," typescript, 1995.

246. Hsu interview, February 28, 1994.

247. Sherry Scull, "Erasing the Threat of Childhood TB," *Inside Baylor Medicine* (January–February, 1974); Dr. Katharine Hsu, "Thirty Years after Isoniazid," *Journal of the American Medical Association* (March 9, 1984); Mary Jane Schier, "Tuberculosis Cases Down for First Time," *Houston Post,* March 9, 1984; B. J. Almond, "Thirty Years Bring Landmark Achievement," *Inside Baylor Medicine* (April–May, 1984): 6.

248. F. W. Wittich, M.D., "Asthma," *World Book Encyclopedia,* vol. 1 (Chicago: Field Enterprises Educational Corp. 1959), p. 492; "Asthma," *Reader's Digest Family Health Guide and Medical Encyclopedia* (Pleasantville, N.Y.: Reader's Digest Assoc., 1970), p. 493.

249. Hsu interview, March 7, 1994.

250. Ibid.

251. Ibid.

252. "Making Asthma Attacks a Little More the Exception," *Inside Baylor Medicine* (December, 1976–January, 1977).

253. American Thoracic Society to Dr. Katharine H. K. Hsu, typescript, February 10, 1994.

254. Hsu interview, February 28, 1994.

255. Hilde Bruch, M.D., and Dorothy Cato, M.D., "Mabel G. Wilkin, M.D., 1896–1980," *Upstream,* vol. 2, no. 1, n.d.

256. Marian Fleming, interview with Geneva M. Fulgham, June 16, 1995.

257. Ibid.

258. Ibid.

259. Ibid.

260. Mabel Giddings Wilkin, articles, *Houston Post-Dispatch,* n.d.

261. Mabel Giddings Wilkin, M.D., "Curriculum Vitae," typescript, n.d.

262. Marian Fleming, videotaped interview with Susanne Gallo, n.d.

263. Mabel G. Wilkin, M.D., "Notes on a Residency Training Program," typescript, n.d.; Mabel G. Wilkin, M.D., "Further Notes on the Training of the Psychiatric Resident," typescript, n.d.

264. Elmer Grape, to Geneva M. Fulgham, October 26, 1995.

265. Susanne Gallo, "Short Biographies of Mabel Giddings Wilkin, M.D., and Hilde Bruch, M.D., Women Pioneers in Psychiatry," typescript, n.d., Fleming personal files.

266. Ibid.

267. Ibid.

268. Gallo, "Short Biographies," typescript.

269. Ibid.

270. Susanne Gallo, "Short Biographies of Mabel Giddings Wilkin, M.D., and Hilde Bruch, M.D., Women Pioneers in Psychiatry," *Texas Medicine* 90 (October, 1994): 60–67.

271. Ibid., p. 64.

272. Ibid., p. 65.

273. Ibid., p. 65.

274. Gallo, "Short Biographies," typescript.

275. Gallo, "Short Biographies," *Texas Medicine,* p. 66.

276. Gallo, "Short Biographies," typescript.

277. Theodore Lidz, M.D., "Introduction," in "Guide to the Writings of Hilde Bruch, M.D.," typescript, n.d.

278. Theodore Lidz, M.D., "Biography," in "Guide to the Writings of Hilde Bruch, M.D.," typescript, n.d.

279. Gallo, "Short Biographies," typescript.

280. Except as otherwise noted, the information on Dorothy Cato comes from Dorothy Annette Cato, M.D., interview with Geneva M. Fulgham, March 8, 1995.

281. Dorothy Annette Cato, M.D., videotaped interview, n.d.

282. Cato videotape.

Chapter 5. New Frontiers

1. Joseph L. Melnick, telephone conversation with Geneva M. Fulgham, October 23, 1995.

2. "Profile of Bettylee Hampil," typescript, n.d.

3. Melnick conversation.

4. Susan Stahl, "Female Radiologist Proves Family and Career Can Mix," *The Fourcast,* December 19, 1974.

5. Betty Jane McConnell, interview with Elizabeth Silverthorne, November 18, 1995.

6. Raymond Walters to Lowell E. Golter, June 25, 1941.

7. "Junior Advisors," *Cincinnati Alumnus,* n.d.

8. Betty Jane McConnell, interview with Elizabeth Silverthorne, November 30, 1995.

9. Ibid.

10. "Nuclear Angiocardiography," *Medical Staff Newsletter,* January, 1979.

11. B. J. McConnell, "Curriculum Vitae," 1996.

12. Robert W. McConnell, interview with Elizabeth Silverthorne, November 30, 1995.

13. J. Rudy Kasel, Ph.D., "Résumé and Recommendation," typescript, October, 1995.

14. Except as otherwise noted, the information on Janet Butel may be found in Janet S. Butel, Ph.D., interview with Geneva M. Fulgham, October 20, 1995.

15. Janet S. Butel, Ph.D., "Curriculum Vitae," 1995.

16. Joseph L. Melnick, Ph.D., interview with Geneva M. Fulgham, January 5, 1996.

17. Ernest Jawetz et al., *Jawetz, Melnick, and Adelberg's Medical Microbiology.*

18. Except as otherwise noted, the information on Huda Zoghbi may be found in Huda Y. Zoghbi, M.D., interview with Geneva M. Fulgham, October 16, 1995.

19. Ruth SoRelle, "Tracking a Killer Gene," *Houston Chronicle,* August 22, 1993, pp. 1A, 18A.

20. Huda Y. Zoghbi, M.D., "Curriculum Vitae," 1995.

21. Zoghbi, "Curriculum Vitae."

22. Untitled article, *Baylor College of Medicine Five-Year Report, 1989–1994,* p. 33.

23. Ibid.

24. SoRelle, "Tracking a Killer Gene."

25. Zoghbi, "Curriculum Vitae"; "Medical Genetics," *The Scientist* 8, no. 24 (December 12, 1994).

26. Marion Pohlen Primomo, M.D., "Biography," typescript, n.d., Primomo personal files.

27. Ibid.

28. Ibid.

29. Ibid.

30. Marion Pohlen Primomo, M.D., telephone conversation with Geneva M. Fulgham, January 17, 1995.

31. Mary Kent Norton and Catherine Norton Scherer, "When Your Mother Outranks You, Do You Salute?" *San Antonio Light,* May 8, 1983, p. 5J; Jacque Crouse, "New U.S. Magistrate Set Legal Sights Early," *San Antonio Express-News,* June 6, 1988.

32. Primomo, "Biography"; Veronica Salazar, "Celebrating Life in the Midst of Death," *West Side Sun* (San Antonio), January 29, 1987, p. 16.

33. Primomo, "Biography."

34. Marion P. Primomo, M.D., "Hospice Update," *Santa Rosa Medical Staff Newsletter,* March, 1987, p. 4.

35. Ibid.

36. Ibid.

37. Ibid.

38. "Dr. Marion P. Primomo," *San Antonio Monthly,* vol. 7, no. 11, August, 1987, p. M16.

39. Don Finley, "Health Professionals Endure Daily Life-and-Death Struggle," *San Antonio Express-News* October 30, 1988, pp. 1, 6M.
40. Ibid.
41. Marion Pohlen Primomo, M.D., untitled article in *1988 Report of the President.*
42. Marion P. Primomo, M.D., "Nutrition and Hydration: Legal, Ethical, and Physiological Aspects," *San Antonio Medicine* 43, no. 8 (August, 1990): 11.
43. Ibid.
44. Marion P. Primomo, "Hospice Care," *Clinical Oncology,* pp. 59–67.
45. Kitty Prevost, "Local Doctor Honored," *San Antonio Express-News,* May 8, 1991, p. 7B; "Dr. Marion Primomo Honored with 1993 'Saint Luke Patron Saint of Physicians Award,'" *Today's Catholic,* November 12, 1993, p. 18; "Primomo Named President-Elect of Academy of Hospice Physicians," *San Antonio Medical Gazette,* August 11–17, 1993, p. 26.
46. Primomo, "Biography."
47. Salazar, "Celebrating Life."

BIBLIOGRAPHY

"Abnormal Cells Being Named for Texas Cities." *Valley Morning Star,* Harlingen, Texas, December 12, 1970.

Alexander, Belva. Telephone interview with Geneva M. Fulgham, Austin–Houston, April 15, 1996.

Allen, Charles R., M.D. *Historical Notes on the Origin and Development of the Texas Society of Anesthesiologists.* Galveston: University of Texas Medical Branch, Department of Anesthesiology, 1989.

Allen, Frances Marion. Telephone interview with Elizabeth Silverthorne, January 21, 1993.

———. Letter to Elizabeth Silverthorne, April 3, 1993.

Almond, B. J. "Thirty Years Bring Landmark Achievements." *Inside Baylor Medicine* (April–May, 1984).

Amarillo News Globe, July 5, 1964.

American Thoracic Society. Letter to Dr. Katharine H. K. Hsu, February 10, 1994. Hsu personal files.

Anderson, Hal, M.D. Interview with Elizabeth Silverthorne, Temple, Texas, September 15, 1988.

"Anne Wheeler, Crosby City Pioneer Museum." Typescript, n.d. Texas Woman's University Library, Denton.

"Asthma." *Reader's Digest Family Health Guide and Medical Encyclopedia.* Pleasantville, N.Y.: Reader's Digest Assoc. 1970.

Austin American-Statesman, January 5, 1975; May 8, 1979; March 2, 1986.

Award presentation speech. The Texas Genetics Society, March 22, 1985. Blocker History of Medicine Collections, Moody Medical Library, University of Texas Medical Branch, Galveston.

Baylor College of Medicine Five-Year Report, 1989–1994. Booklet, Office of Public Affairs. Houston: Baylor College of Medicine, 1994.

Bearden, Donna, and Jamie Frucht. "Works in Progress," in "The Texas Sampler." Texas Woman's University Library, Denton, n.d.

Beaty, Jennie Cottle. *The History of the Graduate Nurses' Association of Texas.* El Paso: Hughes-Buie, n.d.

Beaumont Enterprise, April 27, 1901.

Benedikt, Laraine. "Midwifery in Texas." Typescript, n.d. Texas Woman's University Library, Denton.

Benoit, Patricia Kay. *Men of Steel, Women of Spirit: History of the Santa Fe Hospital, 1891–1991.* Temple, Tex. Scott and White Memorial Hospital and Scott, Sherwood, and Brindley Foundation, 1991.

"Best Towns Those That Do It Easy—Vandergriff." *Galveston Daily News,* 1973.

"Bicentennial History of Crosby County." Typescript, n.d. Texas Woman's University Library, Denton.

Bloom, Nedra. "Age-Old Practice Draws Fire from Lawmakers, Physicians." *Dallas Morning News,* January 19, 1983.

Bonnet, Edith M. Diary and papers. MSS no. 16.1, 16.2. History of Medicine and Archives Department. Moody Medical Library, University of Texas Medical Branch at Galveston.

Branda, Eldon Stephen, ed. *Handbook of Texas.* Vols. 1, 2 (1952): 3 (1976). Austin: Texas State Historical Association.

Brazosport Facts. 6-part series: January, 1961–February, 1961.

Bridges, C. A. *History of Denton, Texas.* Waco: Texian Press, 1978.

Brindley, G. V., Jr., M.D. Interview with Elizabeth Silverthorne, Temple, Texas, August 20, 1988.

Broders, A. Compton, M.D. "Memoirs." Typescript, January 14, 1981. Scott and White Archives, Temple, Texas.

Brooks, Benjy F., M.D. "Album of Women in Medicine: Goldie Suttle Ham, M.D." *Journal of American Medical Women's Association* 16 (January, 1961): 67.

Bruch, Hilde, M.D., and Dorothy Cato, M.D. "Mabel G. Wilkin, M.D., 1896–1980." *Upstream.* Newsletter of the Houston Psychiatric Society. Vol. 2, no. 1, n.d.

Burns, Chester, R., M.D. "The Development of Hospitals in Galveston during the Nineteenth Century." *Southwestern Historical Quarterly* 97 (October, 1993): 238–63.

———. "The University of Texas Medical Branch at Galveston." *Journal of the American Medical Association* (September 11, 1991): 1400–1403.

Butel, Janet S., Ph.D. "Curriculum Vitae," 1995.

———. Interview with Geneva M. Fulgham, Houston, October 20, 1995.

Caldwell, Adele Perry. "Character Sketch of Dr. Sofie Herzog, Brazoria, Texas." Typescript, n.d. Brazoria City Library.

Carmack, George. "Unraveling the Healing World of Curanderos." *San Antonio Express-News,* February 11, 1989.

Cato, Dorothy Annette, M.D. Interview with Geneva M. Fulgham, Houston, March 8, 1995.

———. Videotaped interview, n.d. Psychiatric Library, Medical Center, Houston.

Chiew, Christine. *Mayo Alumni,* spring, 1995.

"Circular Prospectus: John Sealy Hospital Training School for Nurses, 1904." History of Medicine Collection. University of Texas Medical Branch at Galveston.

"Connie R. Yerwood, M.D., Biographical Information." Typescript, n.d. Texas Woman's University Library, Denton.

"Connie R. Yerwood, M.D., Honors Received." Typescript, n.d. Texas Woman's University Library, Denton.

"Credits Ballot with Influence." *Houston Post-Dispatch,* 1928.

Crehan, Col. James A. USAF (Ret.). Telephone interview with Geneva M. Fulgham, October 23, 1995.

Creighton, James A. *A Narrative History of Brazoria County*. Angleton, Tex.: Brazoria County Historical Commission, 1975.

Crowder, Eleanor L. M. "A. Louise Dietrich." Typescript, n.d. Texas Woman's University Library, Denton.

———. *Nursing in Texas: A Pictorial History*. Waco: Texian Press, 1980.

Cunningham, Mary S. *The Woman's Club of El Paso*. El Paso: Texas Western Press, 1978.

Curlin, Vashti R., M.D. "Women in Medicine: Early History of the Black Woman Physician in the United States." *Kings County Medical Society Bulletin* 70 (July–August, 1991).

Daily, Louis, M.D. Interview with Geneva M. Fulgham, Houston, January 26, 1994.

Daily Texan (Austin), June 2, 1982.

Daisy Emery Allen, M.D. Brochure. Galveston: University of Texas Medical Branch, 1995.

Dallas Dispatch, February 1, 1938.

Dallas Morning News, January 19, 1983.

Dallas Times Herald, December 5, 1982.

"Dedication of a Texas State Historical Marker." Program. Amarillo, April 29, 1967.

Denton Record-Chronicle, June 28, 1941.

"Dr. Emery Allen." Typescript prepared for *National Cyclopedia of American Biography,* 1960. Texas Woman's University Library, Denton.

"Doctor Globe-Trots to Present Paper." *Galveston Daily News,* August 1, 1968.

"Dr. Marion Primomo Honored with 1993 'Saint Luke Patron Saint of Physicians Award.'" *Today's Catholic,* November 12, 1993.

"Dr. Marion P. Primomo." *San Antonio Monthly,* vol. 7, no. 11, August, 1987.

"Dr. Mary B. Ray." *Beaumont Enterprise,* April 27, 1901.

"Dr. Mary Jane Whittet was First President of Atascosa County Medical Association." *Pleasanton Express,* October 4, 1956.

"Dr. Violet H. Keiller." Obituary. *Texas State Journal of Medicine* (November, 1958).

Duerr, Elizabeth Hanson. Interview with Geneva M. Fulgham, Houston, November, 1993.

Duncan, Phil. "People-Loving Dr. Edwards Plans Again for Her Hospital." *Hereford Brand,* March 5, 1964.

DuVall, Alvin. "School Board Member Favors Stronger Voice for U.H. President." *Houston Post,* February, 1945.

"E. A. Wright." Obituary. *Texas State Journal of Medicine* (September, 1950).

"Early Day Families." *The Dude Wrangler,* November, 1953, Bandera, Texas.

"Early Physician Teaches." *Texas State Journal of Medicine* (November, 1960): 885–86.

Eichna, Ludwig W. "Mother Hutton." *The Pharos* 54 (Winter, 1994): 14–17.

"1855—The Poles Arrive." Ed. Billie Cravell. *The Dude Wrangler,* November, 1953, Bandera, Texas.

Emmott, Sarah H. "Hettie Cunningham—the First Woman Pharmacist in Texas—and Her Husband, James." Typescript, n.d. Houston Academy of Medicine–the Medical Center Library.

"Excerpts from Diary of Dr. Frances Emery Allen, 1900." Typescript, n.d. Texas Woman's University Library, Denton.

"Extracts of Articles." *Texas Courier-Record of Medicine.* Typescript, 1979. University of Texas Southwestern Medical School Library.

"Feminine Physicians." *Daniel's Texas Medical Journal* 3 (1888): 111.

Fleming, Marian. Interview with Geneva M. Fulgham, Houston, June 16, 1995.

———. Videotaped interview with Susanne Gallo, n.d. Psychiatric Library Medical Center, Houston.

Folklore of Texan Cultures. Booklet, n.d. Texas Woman's University, Denton.

Gallo, Susanne. "Short Biographies of Mabel Giddings Wilkin, M.D., and Hilde Bruch, M.D., Women Pioneers in Psychiatry." *Texas Medicine* 90 (October, 1994).

Galveston Daily News, August 1, 1968; August 27, 1971; August 25, 1972.

Galveston Tribune, January 26, 1926.

Gillespie, Charles A., M.D. Interviews with Elizabeth Silverthorne, Temple, Texas, August 8, 1991 and September 16, 1991.

———. Speech. Santa Fe Memorial Hospital Centennial Banquet. Temple, Texas, September 20, 1991.

Gilliland, Jean. *May Owen, M.D.: Heritage of Achievement.* Fort Worth: Women's Auxiliary to the Tarrant County Medical Society, 1968.

Grammel, H. P. N. *The Laws of Texas, 1822–1897* 3 (1897): 1042.

Grape, Elmer. Letter to Geneva M. Fulgham, October 26, 1995.

Graves-Earle Family Papers, 1848–1963. The Texas Collection, Baylor University, Waco.

"G. S. Ham Hanson." Obituary. *Texas Medical Journal* 76 (January, 1980): 81.

Haile, Bartee. "Minnie Fish: Leader of the Suffragist Charge." *In Between,* no. 258 (May, 1987): 7. Rosenberg Library, Galveston.

Hale, Selden. "Hereford Woman Doctor Acclaimed by Johnson." *Amarillo News Globe,* July 5, 1964.

Hartgraves, Ruth, M.D. "Biographical Sketch." Typescript, n.d. Houston Academy of Medicine–the Medical Center Library.

Hegarty, Sister Mary Loyola. *Serving with Gladness.* Houston: Bruce Publishing Co., 1967.

Hereford Brand, March 5, 1964; July 5, 1964.

"Honor Given Local Woman." *Galveston Tribune,* February 21, 1930.

"House Okays Midwife Registration Bill." *Austin American-Statesman,* May 8, 1979.

Houston Chronicle, February 9, 1912; December 6, 1936; February 5, 1978; August 22, 1993; October 17, 1993.

Houston City Council resolution. March 25, 1892.

Houston Post, March 26, 1891; March 21, 1896; April 27, 1933; April 28, 1955; April 18, 1970; September 27, 1980; February 15, 1982; March 9, 1984.

Houston Press, November 1, 1925; February 2, 1948.

Hsu, Katharine H. K., M.D. "Curriculum Vitae." Typescript, 1995.

———. Interview with Geneva M. Fulgham, Houston, February 28 and March 7, 1994.

————. "Thirty Years after Isoniazid." *Journal of the American Medical Association* (March 9, 1984): 1283–85.

Hunter, Leslie Gene, and Hunter, Cecilia Aros. "'Mother Lane' and the 'New Mooners': An Expression of *Curanderismo.*" *Southwestern Historical Quarterly* 99, no. 3 (January, 1996): 291–325.

Hurd-Mead, Kate Campbell, M.D. *A History of Women in Medicine.* Haddam, Conn.: Haddam Press, 1938.

"Introduction." *In Her Own Words.* Ed. Regina Markell Morantz, Cynthia Stodola Pomerleau, and Carol Hansen Fenichel. Westport, Conn.: Greenwood Press, 1982.

"Isle Doctor Invited to Present Paper." *Galveston Daily News,* August 27, 1971.

Janes, Jessie Lee, ed. "A Woman for All Ages: Dr. Hallie Earle, 1880–1963." Typescript, n.d. The Texas Collection, Baylor University, Waco.

Jasso, Gilberto G., and María Jacinta Padron. *Spain's Royal American Order of Isabella the Catholic Awarded by His Majesty King Juan Carlos I to Clotilde P. García, M.D.* Brochure. Corpus Christi: Spanish-American Genealogical Assoc. May 16, 1990.

Jawetz, Ernest, Joseph L. Melnick, Edward A. Adelberg, George F. Brooks, Janet S. Butel, and L. Nicholas Ornston. *Jawetz, Melnick, and Adelberg's Medical Microbiology,* 20th ed. Norwalk, Conn.: Appleton & Lange, 1995.

Jenkins, Daniel Edwards, M.D. Interview with Geneva M. Fulgham, Houston, February 11, 1994.

Jensen, Francine, M.D. Interview with Geneva M. Fulgham, Houston, February 1, 1994.

Jones, Marie Beth. "The Doctor Was a Lady." Typescript, n.d. Brazoria County Historical Museum, Angleton, Texas.

Karchmer, Ray. "The Trials of the Immigrants." *San José Daily Mercury,* December 27, 1908.

Kasel, J. Rudy, Jr., Ph.D. "Resume and Recommendation." Typescript, October, 1995. Baylor College of Medicine, Houston.

Keiller, Violet, M.D. "A Contribution to the Anatomy of Spina Bifida." *Brain: A Journal of Neurology,* London (June, 1922).

Kelley, Dayton, ed. *The Handbook of Waco and McLennan County, Texas.* Waco: Texian Press, 1972.

Kirk, Sister Martha Ann. "Program Notes," n.d. Incarnate Word College, San Antonio.

"Lady Doctor to Migrant Workers." *Ebony,* February, 1962, pp 59–68.

Lasher, Patricia. *Texas Woman: Interviews and Images.* Austin: Shoal Creek Pub., 1980.

Leong, June Dove. "God's Ambassador, Dr. Katharine H. K. Hsu." *U.S. Asia News,* Houston, November 11, 18, 1988.

Lidz, Theodore, M.D. "Introduction," in "Guide to the Writing of Hilde Bruch, M.D." Typescript, n.d. Houston Academy of Medicine–the Medical Center Library.

Lovejoy, Esther Pohl. *Women Doctors of the World.* New York: Macmillan Co., 1957.

McConnell, Betty Jane. Interviews with Elizabeth Silverthorne, Salado, Texas, November 18, November 30, and December 16, 1995.

McConnell, Robert W. Interview with Elizabeth Silverthorne, Salado, Texas, November 30, 1995.

McFarland, Gay E. "Shirley Marks-Brown Worked Each Step of Way to the Top." *Houston Chronicle,* February 5, 1978.

Machato, Malinda. "Curanderismo Practitioners Battle Ills with Herbs, Tradition, Spiritual Beliefs." *Daily Texan,* Austin, June 2, 1982.

McNeil, Brownie. "Curanderos of South Texas," in *And Horns on the Toads.* Mody C. Boatright, ed. Texas Folklore Society. Dallas: Southern Methodist University Press, 1959.

"Madison, Mary, Petitioner." Memorial no. 251. Texas State Archives, file box no. 64.

"Making Asthma Attacks a Little More the Exception." *Inside Baylor Medicine,* Houston (December, 1976–January, 1977): 2.

Marks, Geoffrey, and William K. Beatty. *Women in White.* New York: Charles Scribner's Sons, 1972.

Mason, Herbert Molloy, Jr. *Death from the Sea.* New York: Dial Press, 1972.

"Medal Given Dr. Edwards." *Hereford Brand,* July 5, 1964.

"Medical Genetics." *The Scientist* 8, no. 24 (December 12, 1994).

Melnick, Joseph L., Ph.D. Telephone conversation with Geneva M. Fulgham, October 23, 1995. Interview with Geneva M. Fulgham, Houston, January 5, 1996.

"Memorial to Brazoria Woman Doctor Would Be Tribute to Picturesque, Self-Sacrificing, and Useful Career." Typescript, July, 1925. Brazoria County Historical Museum, Angleton, Texas.

"Minnie Fisher Cunningham, 1882–1946." Typescript, n.d. Texas Woman's University Library, Denton.

"Minutes of the Board of Regents," May 15, 1897. University of Texas Medical Branch Archives, Galveston.

Moncla, Susie. Letter to Ruthe Winegarten, May 6, 1980. Moore Memorial Public Library, Texas City.

Morantz-Sanchez, Regina Markell. *Sympathy and Science: Women Physicians in American Medicine.* New York: Oxford University Press, 1985.

"Move to Bar Wives from Work Scored." *Houston Chronicle,* 1932.

Munson, Sammye. *Our Tejano Heroes: Outstanding Mexican Americans in Texas.* Austin: Panda Books, 1989.

"Negro Woman Doctor Serves Migrants." *Texas State Journal of Medicine* 60 (1964): 774–75.

"Negroes, The." *Folklore of Texan Cultures.* Booklet, n.d. Texas Woman's University Library, Denton.

Newcomb, W. W., Jr. *The Indians of Texas.* Austin: University of Texas Press, 1961.

New Handbook of Texas, The. Edited by Ron Tyler. 6 volumes. Austin: Texas State Historical Association, 1996.

Nixon, Pat Ireland. *The Medical Story of Early Texas, 1528–1853.* Lancaster, Penn.: Lupe Memorial Fund, 1946.

"Nuclear Angiocardiography." *Medical Staff Newsletter.* Hermann Hospital–University of Texas Medical School at Houston, January, 1979.

Ornish, Natalie. *Pioneer Jewish Texans.* Dallas: Heritage Press, 1989, pp. 249–50, 256–57.

Overton, Philip R., and Sam V. Stone, Jr. "Medical-Legal History of Texas." *Texas Medicine* 63 (March, 1967): 117–22.

Owens, William A. "Seer of Corsicana," in *And Horns on the Toads*. Mody C. Boatright, ed. Texas Folklore Society. Dallas: Southern Methodist University Press, 1959.

Peterson, Brooks. "Dr. García Will Serve, Is Willing and Able." Newspaper clipping, 1973. Texas Woman's University Library, Denton.

Petrovich, Sandra M. "Dr. Sofie Herzog, Surgeon: A Woman Overcomes a Man's World." Typescript, May 5, 1992. Brazoria County Historical Museum, Angleton, Texas.

Pleasanton Express, October 4, 1956.

Potter, Claudia. "Memoirs." Typescript, 1948. Scott and White Archives, Temple, Texas.

Powledge, Mary. "Prominent Houstonian Continues to Pioneer at Ninety-two." *University of Texas Medical Branch Alumni News*, vol. 7, July–August, 1993.

Primomo, Marion Pohlen, M.D. "Curriculum Vitae," 1995.

———. "Hospice Care," in *Clinical Oncology*. Ed. G. R. Weiss. Norwalk, Conn.: Appleton & Lange, 1993.

———. "Hospice Update." *Santa Rosa Medical Staff Newsletter*, San Antonio, March, 1987.

———. "Nutrition and Hydration: Legal, Ethical, and Physiological Aspects." *San Antonio Medicine* 43, no. 8 (August, 1990): 11.

———. Telephone conversation with Geneva M. Fulgham, January 17, 1995.

———. Untitled article in *1988 Report of the President*. San Antonio: Our Lady of the Lake University, 1988.

"Primomo Named President-Elect of Academy of Hospice Physicians." *San Antonio Medical Gazette*, (August 11–17, 1993): 26.

"Profile of Bettylee Hampil." Typescript, n.d. Department of Molecular Virology files, Baylor College of Medicine, Houston.

Pruitt, Jack, M.D. Letter to Public Relations Department of Hermann Hospital, Houston, January 11, 1982. Houston Academy of Medicine–the Medical Center Library.

Red, George Plunkett (Mrs. S. C. Red). "Dr. Margaret Ellen Holland," in *The Medicine Man in Texas*. Houston: Standard Printing, 1930.

Reed, Claude, Jr. "The Yerwood Sisters: Medical Trailblazers." *National Scene*, 1983, pp. 14–23.

"Résumé of Dr. Clotilde P. García." Typescript, 1980. Texas Woman's University Library, Denton.

Salazar, Veronica. "Celebrating Life in the Midst of Death." *West Side Sun* (San Antonio), January 29, 1987.

———. "Dedication Rewarded: Prominent Mexican Americans." Brochure, n.d. Latin American Collection, Mexican-American Culture Center, San Antonio.

Samuels, Joseph W. "Dr. Ray K. Daily, a Woman of Valor." *The Jewish Herald-Voice*, December 3, 1975.

San Antonio Daily Herald, July 26, 1959.

San Antonio Express-News, June 6, 1988; October 30, 1988; February 11, 1989; May 8, 1991.

San Antonio Light, May 8, 1983.

Sanchez, Agapito R., Jr. "An Exploratory Study of Mexican-American Midwives' Attitudes, Practices, and Beliefs Regarding Children Born with Congenital Defects." Typescript, August, 1971. Barker Texas History Center, University of Texas, Austin.

Saunders, Bobbie. "Brazoria's Woman for All Seasons." Typescript, March, 1983. Brazoria County Historical Museum, Angleton, Texas.

Saunders, Rev. D. L., M.D. *Woman's Own Book.* Little Rock, Ark.: James D. Butler, 1858.

Schaefer, Marie Charlotte, M.D. "Opening Address, Session of 1912–13, the Medical Department of the University of Texas." *The University Medical* 17 (October 15, 1912).

Schaffer, Ruth C. "Study of Midwifery in Six Counties in 1979." Typescript, n.d. Texas Woman's University Library, Denton.

Schier, Mary Jane. "Blood Variants Put Galveston on the Map." *Houston Post,* April 18, 1970.

———. "Health Director Nominee Craven Has Vision for New Job." *Houston Post,* September 27, 1980.

———. "Tuberculosis Cases Down for First Time." *Houston Post,* March 9, 1984.

Schneider, Rose G. "How I Became a Harvard Person." Newspaper clipping, n.d. Blocker History of Medicine Collection, University of Texas Medical Branch, Galveston.

"School Relief Tax Backed by Dr. Daily." *Houston Post,* April 27, 1933.

Scott, A. C., Jr., M.D. Speech, November 14, 1946. Typescript. Scott and White Archives, Temple, Texas.

"Scott and White Marks Ninety Years of Nursing." *Scott and White Options for Health.* Pamphlet. October, 1994.

Scull, Sherry. "Erasing the Threat of Childhood TB." *Inside Baylor Medicine* (January–February, 1974).

Sharp, William B., M.D. "Microbiology at the Medical College," in *The University of Texas Medical Branch at Galveston: A Seventy-Five-Year History by the Faculty and Staff.* Austin: University of Texas Press, 1967.

Shaw, Russell. "Hereford Doctor Fights Own Battle for the Poor." *West Texas Register* (Amarillo), October 2, 1964.

"Sickle Cell Education Plan Set." *Galveston Daily News,* August 25, 1972.

Sivells, Wanda Kellar. "Dr. Mary, an Early Texas Dentist." Typescript, n.d. Texas Woman's University Library, Denton.

———. " 'Dr. Mary' Shelman, Pioneer Texas Dentist." *Texas Dental Journal* (July, 1980): 6–9.

Smith, John H. "May Owen, M.D." *Tarrant County Physician* (May, 1988).

Smith, P. Woodbury, M.D. Telephone conversation with Geneva M. Fulgham, November 17, 1993.

SoRelle, Ruth. "Tracking a Killer Gene." *Houston Chronicle,* August 22, 1993.

Sparks, Randy J. "Dr. Ruth Hartgraves," in *New Titles and News.* Houston: Houston Academy of Medicine–the Medical Center Library, 1991.

Stafford, Ted. *May Owen, M.D.* Austin, Eakin Press, 1990.

Stahl, Susan. "Female Radiologist Proves Family and Career Can Mix." *The Fourcast,* December 19, 1974. Hockaday High School, Dallas.

Stevenson, Carrie Pauley. "The Early Amarillo Dentists." Typescript, 1979. Texas Woman's University Library, Denton.

Stuart, Kathryn Agnes Paschal McNeir. *A Brief Biography of the Indian Princess Sarah Ridge.* Anahuac, Tex.: Chambers County Historical Commission, n.d.

Sweeney, Paul. "Wit, Stamina Keys to Dr. Clotilde García's Achievements." Newspaper clipping, n.d. Texas Woman's University Library, Denton.

Taylor, Pat Ellis. *Border Healing Woman.* Austin: University of Texas Press, 1981.

———. Typed letter, June, 1979. Texas Woman's University Library, Denton.

Temple Daily Telegram, December 6, 1963; February 14, 1994; October 30, 1994.

Texas City Daily Sun, September 23, 1968; August 22, 1974.

"Texas Department of Public Health Survey." Typescript, 1924. Texas Woman's University Library, Denton.

Texas State Legislature, H.S.R. 195. Adopted January 29, 1962.

Thompson, Lisa E., "Two Strikes: The Role of Black Women in Medicine Before 1920." *The Pharos* 58 (winter, 1995). Menlo Park, Calif.

"Three Generations Look at Their Profession." *Texas Medicine* 71 (January–December, 1975).

"Two File in Galveston College Regents Election." *Galveston Daily News,* n.d.

University of Texas Medical Branch at Galveston: A Seventy-five-Year History by the Faculty and Staff. Austin: University of Texas Press, 1967.

"UTMB Scientist to Speak Here on Women's Lib." *La Marque Times,* February 4, 1971.

Vanderholt, James F. *The Diocese of Beaumont: The Story of Southeast Texas.* Beaumont: Catholic Diocese of Beaumont, 1991.

Vogel, Virgil J. *American Indian Medicine.* Norman: University of Oklahoma Press, 1970.

Waggener, Leslie. "Women's Rights," in *Alcalde.* Austin: University of Texas, 1916.

Wallace, Patricia Ward. *A Spirit So Rare: A History of the Women of Waco.* Austin: Nortex Press, 1984.

Walters, Raymond. Letter to Lowell E. Golter, June 25, 1941. B. J. McConnell personal files, Salado, Texas.

White, Elizabeth Borst. "Patterns of Development in Texas Hospitals, 1836–1945: Preliminary Survey." *Texas Medicine* 82 (December, 1986): 55–60.

Whiteaker, Mildred. "Two Proposals Face Board of Education." *Houston Press,* February 2, 1948.

Wilkin, Mabel Giddings, M.D. "Curriculum Vitae," 1995.

———. "Further Notes on the Training of the Psychiatric Resident." Typescript, n.d. Marian Fleming personal files, Houston.

———. "Notes on a Residency Training Program." Typescript, n.d. Marian Fleming personal files, Houston.

Wilkinson, Pam. "Folk Medicine." *Southwest Airlines Magazine,* January, 1976.

Williams, Lorece. Vignette in *Growing Up in Texas.* Ed. Bertha McKee Dobie. Austin: Encino Press, 1972.

Winegarten, Ruthe. Finders guide to *Texas Women: A Celebration of History Exhibit* archives. Texas Woman's University Library, Denton.

———. "Midwifery in Texas." Typescript, 1979. Texas Woman's University Library, Denton.

———. *Texas Women, a Pictorial History: From Indians to Astronauts.* Austin: Eakin Press, 1986.

Wolf, Brooksie Nell. Interview with Elizabeth Silverthorne, Temple, Texas, August 15, 1988.

Wright, Elva Anis, M.D. "An Analysis of Eighty-three Cases of Diarrhoea in Infants." *South Texas Medical Record* (November, 1916).

Wright, Merrill C. Letter to Reverend Albert P. Shirkey, D.D., July 20, 1950. Houston Academy of Medicine–the Medical Center Library, Houston.

Wygant, Larry. Interviews with University of Texas Medical Branch women graduates. Bound typescripts, n.d. Moody Medical Library, Galveston.

———. "Medicine and Public Health in Galveston, Texas: The First Century." Ph.D. diss., University of Texas Medical Branch at Galveston, 1992.

Zoghbi, Huda Y., M.D. "Curriculum Vitae," 1995.

———. Interview with Geneva M. Fulgham, Houston, October 16, 1995.

INDEX

Baylor College of Medicine *(contd.)*
Service, 161. *See also* Baylor medical
school (Dallas)
Baylor medical school (Dallas), 85, 86.
See also Baylor College of Medicine
(Houston)
Baylor Medicine, 162
Baylor University (Waco), 85
Beaudet, Arthur, 190
Bell County Medical Society, 116
Bellevue Hospital (NYC), 86, 122
Benedikt, Laraine, 26–27
Blackwell, Elizabeth, xx–xxii, 85–86,
200–201
Blackwell, Emily, xxi–xxii
Blattner, Russell J., 158
Blin, Saint Arsene, 49
Bloomer, Amelia, 79
Bonnet, Edith M., 89–92, 129
Bradford, Tom L., 43
Bradford Memorial Hospital for Babies
(Dallas), 43, 44
Brazoria, Tex., 74
Brazoria County Historical Museum
(Angleton, Tex.), 76
Brindley, George Valter, 113
Brown, Annie Elizabeth, 33
Bruch, Hilde, xiii, 164, 167–71, 173
Bryn Mawr (Penn.), 149
Buchanan, Annie, 9–10
Burns Hospital (Cuero, Tex.), 49
Butel, Janet S., 174, 183–88

Canales, Jose Antonio, 143, 145
cancer, 106, 122, 186
Carmelite Day Nursery (Corpus Christi),
145
Castle, Jessie Estelle, 60–61
Castro, Sarah, 27
cataract removal, 139
Cato, Dorothy Annette, 164, 170, 171–73
Chaney, Doña María, 13–14
Charity Hospital of Louisiana, 141

Chest Physicians' Congress, 161
Chiang Kai-shek, 156–57
Chicago Post-Graduate Dental College,
61
childbirth, 97. *See also* midwifery
Children's Medical Center (Dallas), 44
Children's Memorial Hospital (Chi-
cago), 90–91
Children's TB Hospital and Clinic (Hou-
ston), 161
Chinese Medical Association, 157
cholera epidemic, 1869 (San Antonio),
52–53
Chollett, Mother Madeleine, 52
Chronic Illness Control Program (CICP),
106
Chung Chen Medical College (Kiangsi,
China), 155, 156, 157
Cincinnati Children's Hospital, 157
Cincinnati General Hospital, 178
Citizens Advisory Center to the Juvenile
Board of Travis County, 102
City Federation of Women's Clubs (Dal-
las), 42
Civil Rights Act (1964), 101
Clayton, Nicholas, Jr., 52
Cleopatra, xvii
Cleveland, Grover, 68
Cleveland Homeopathic Hospital Col-
lege, 5
Cleveland Medical College, xxi
Clinical Oncology, 197
Cloudcroft Baby Sanatorium (New Mex-
ico), 41
Cohen, Rabbi (Galveston), 134–35
College and Professional Women's Or-
ganization (Houston), 136
College of American Pathologists, 124
Collins, Florence E., 71
colonial medicine in America, xx
Commission on the Status of Women, 132
Content, Tex., 80–82
Cornell Medical School (NYC), 152

Cottle, Jennie, 39
Country Doctor, A (Jewett), XXIV
Craven, Judith, 72
Cunningham, Henrietta Manlove, 60, 64–66
Cunningham, James Louis, 64–66
Cunningham, May, 66
Cunningham, Minnie Fisher, 45, 60, 66–69
Cunningham's Drug Store (Houston), 66
curanderas, 3, 11–18. *See also* individual curanderas
curanderismo: autohypnosis in, 14–15; common remedies in, 11, 12, 13, 18; extent of, 3, 11–18; fortune-telling in, 15; history of, 11; psychology of, 13
curanderos, 11

Daily, Louis, 135, 139
Daily, Louis, Jr., 133, 139
Daily, Ray Karchmer, 130, 133–39
Daily Eye Clinic (Houston), 139
Dallas Baby Camp and Hospital, 41–44
Dallas County Medical Association, 71
Danforth, Grace, 70, 71
Daniel's Texas Medical Journal, 71
Daughters of Charity of Saint Vincent de Paul, 49–50
Daughters of the American Revolution, 136
Del Mar College (Corpus Christi), 146
dentistry, 59–63
Denton County, 108
Department of Health (Houston), 72
diabetes, 106, 122, 167
"Diabetic Coma in Feed Lot Sheep" (Owen), 122
Dickey, Nancy Wilson, 199
Dickinson, Susanna, 46
Dietrich, A. Louise, 38–39, 41
Dietzel, Marie Delalondre, XXVI
digitalis, XIX–XX
diphtheria, 103, 108, 140

Doctor Breen's Practice (Howell), XXIV
Doctor Zay (Phelp), XXIV
Dolly Vinsant Memorial Hospital (San Benito, Tex.), 48
Dublin Medical Center (Fort Worth), 127
Duerr, Elizabeth Hanson, 142, 143

Earle, Adaline Graves, 83, 85
Earle, Harriet (Hallie), 83–88
Earle, Isham Harrison, 83–84, 85, 87, 88
eclecticism, medical, XXI, XXII
Edwards, Lena, XII, 71, 95–99
Edwards, Thomas W., 96
Ellersly Plantation, 78
Elliott, Ada, 10
Elva A. Wright Auxiliary, 94
Elva Wright Memorial Fund, 95
Emery, Elizabeth, 79, 80
Emery, James Wallace, 79
ergot, 20
espiritista, 11, 16
Eugenie, Empress (of France), 51

Fabiola, Saint, XVIII
Farquahar, LaVerne, 48
Female Medical College of Pennsylvania, XXII–XXIII
Ferguson, Miriam, 90
Fick, Dorthea, 35
Fiddler on the Roof, 133
Flake's *Semi-Weekly Bulletin* (Galveston), 51
Fleming, Marian, 165, 166
Fletcher, Emily Smith, XI, XIII
flu, 50, 120, 140
Foley, W. L., 54
folk and faith healers, 3, 5–11. *See also* individual names
Foote, "Aunt Frankie," 164, 165
Fort Sam Houston (San Antonio), 194
Fort Worth Academy of Medicine, 82
Fort Worth Medical College, 78–79, 83

Shanghai Children's Hospital, 156
Sharp, William B., 148
Shelman, Catherine, 60
Shelman, Mary Lou, 59, 60–63
sickle cell anemia, 152, 153
Sickle Cell Anemia Foundation, 154
Sisters of Charity, 48
Sisters of Charity of the Incarnate Word, 50–58
Sisters of Divine Providence, 49
Sisters of Mercy, 48, 49
Sisters of Saint Vincent, 48
Sisters of the Incarnate Word and Blessed Sacrament, 49
smallpox epidemic, 54, 55
Smith, Elizabeth Boyle, 10–11
Smith, Maggie, 22–23
Smith, May Forster, 41–44
Smith, R. E. ("Bob"), 158
sobadora, 11, 16
Society of Nuclear Medicine, 181
Southern Association of Anesthetists, 115
Southern Hotel (Brazoria, Tex.), 77
Southern Medical Association, 116, 125
Southwestern Medical Center (Dallas), 50
Southwestern Medical School (Dallas), 180
Southwestern University (Georgetown, Tex.), 132
Spanish–American Genealogical Association (SAGA), 146
Spanish–American War, 46, 50
specialization, 70, 71–72
spina bifida, 150
spinocerebellar ataxia type I (SCA1), 190, 191
Stamford Community Center (Conn.), 100
Starrett, Mary Isabella, 22
State Board of Dental Examiners, 61
State Constitutional Revision Committee (Texas), 146
State Medical Association of Texas, 111

Stephen F. Austin State University (Nacogdoches, Tex.), 199
streptomycin, 94, 159
Sullivan, Harry Stack, 166, 170
superstition, 10; and childbirth, 19, 24; and *curanderismo*, 12–13; and folk healing, 5–6; in Middle Ages, xix
sustos, 15

Tarrant County Junior College (TCJC), 126
Tarrant County Medical Society, 124, 125, 126
Tarrant Medical Laboratory (Fort Worth), 126
Taylor, Pat Ellis, 8, 9
Temple Sanitarium, 107, 115
Terrell, Truman, 119, 121, 122, 126
Terrell Laboratories (Fort Worth), 119, 120, 121, 124, 126
Texas A&M University Medical School, 182
Texas Association of Physicians in Nuclear Medicine, 181
Texas Cancer Information Service (Bexar County), 195
Texas Christian University (TCU) (Fort Worth), 119, 123, 126
Texas City disaster, 172
Texas City Red Cross Branch, 45
Texas Equal Suffrage Association, 68
Texas Genetics Society, 154
Texas Graduate Nurses Association, 38–39, 41, 42
Texas League of Women Voters, 41, 45
Texas Medical Association, 116, 123, 125, 126, 143, 151, 181
Texas Medical Practice Act, 5
Texas Midwifery Act, 28–29
Texas Society of Anesthesiologists, 116
Texas Society of Pathologists, 123, 124, 127
Texas State Department of Health, 101–102
Texas State Journal of Medicine, 122, 123

Texas State Medical Society, 132
Texas State Pharmaceutical Association, 65–66
Texas Tuberculosis Association, 101
Texas Woman Suffrage Association, 68–69
"Thirty Years After Isoniazid" (Hsu), 162
Thompson, James E., 149
Torbett's Sanatorium (Marlin, Tex.), 86
Travis County Medical Association, 71
Trotula, xviii–xix
tuberculosis, 92–95, 102–104, 155, 157–62; bone, of the, 161; lung, of the, 159; miliary, 159. *See also* American Lung Association; Anti–Tuberculosis League
Tulane University (New Orleans), 140

United States Army Sanitary Commission, 48
United States Naval Hospital (New York), 74
United States Public Health Service grants, 161
University of Chicago, 147, 152
University of Cincinnati, 176, 178
University of Edinburgh, 149
University of Freiburg, 168
University of Gratz (Vienna), 74
University of Houston, 137
University of Leipzig, 168
University of Maryland Medical School (Baltimore), 165
University of Michigan (Detroit), 101
University of Minnesota (Minneapolis), 190
University of Pennsylvania (Philadelphia), 157
University of Texas (Austin), 103, 108, 129, 144, 171, 174
University of Texas at Houston Medical School, 130, 151, 181, 199
University of Texas Health Science Center (San Antonio), 195

University of Texas Medical Branch (UTMB) (Galveston), 103, 109–11, 129, 135, 145, 147–49, 152–53, 165, 171–72; admission policies, xxv–xxvi; doctors, study of, 196
University of Vienna, 138
Uribe, Hector, 26, 27
Ursuline nuns, 49

Vanzant, Frances, 90
Veterans Administration Hospital (Dallas), 180
Villanueva, Andrea Castanon, 46
Villegas de Magnon, Leonor, 46
Vincent de Paul, Saint, 48
Vinsant, Wilma, 46–48
Virginia Military Institute (Lexington), 176
viruses, 184, 185, 186

Waggener, Leslie, xxv–xxvi
Wann, Murle, 46
Wesley Community Center (Fort Worth), 82
Wheeler, Paul, 150
White, Raleigh, 107, 111, 112, 114
Whitmire, Kathy, 130, 162
Whittet, Mary Jane, 4
Whittle, Reba, 46
Wilkin, Lillian, 164, 165
Wilkin, Mabel Giddings, 164–67, 170, 173
Wilkin, Marion, 164, 165
Wilkin, Minnie, 164
Wilkin, Robert, 164
Wilson, Palestine (Aunt Pal), 20
Winegarten, Ruthe, 27
"wise women," xix
witches, xix
Withering, William, xx
"woman question, the," xxiii–xxiv
Woman's Hospital in Philadelphia, 135
Woman's Medical College of Pennsylvania, 125, 132